PATTERNS OF
LANGUAGE

PATTERNS OF LANGUAGE

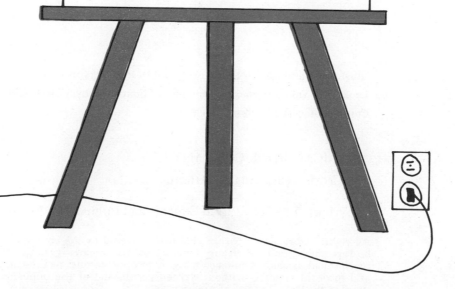

H. Thompson Fillmer

Ann Lefcourt

Nell C. Thompson

George E. Coon

Barbara B. Cramer

AMERICAN BOOK COMPANY

H. Thompson Fillmer

Professor of Reading and Language Arts, University
of Florida, Gainesville, Florida

Ann Lefcourt

Formerly Assistant Professor of Education,
Lehman and Hunter Colleges, City University
of New York. Previously of Ball State University,
Muncie, Indiana

Nell C. Thompson

Professor of English and Education, Western
Washington State College, Bellingham, Washington

George E. Coon

Professor of Education, Director of Graduate Studies,
School of Education, Oakland University,
Rochester, Michigan

Barbara B. Cramer

Formerly Elementary Teacher, Newark, Delaware,
and Binghamton, New York

Illustration and Design by International Design Organization

Looking at Your Language: Design and Illustration by Allan Philiba

Cover Photograph by Benn Mitchell

AMERICAN BOOK COMPANY

New York   Cincinnati   Atlanta   Dallas   Millbrae

Copyright © 1974 by Litton Educational Publishing, Inc.

5   7   9   11   13   14   12   10   8   6   4

CONTENTS

UNIT 1 Listening

Looking at Your Language

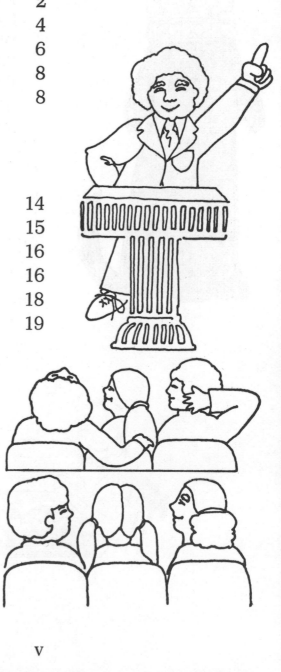

UNIT 2 The Language of Humor

Looking at Your Language

The Basic Sentence

UNIT 3 Speaking

Looking at Your Language

The Basic Sentence

UNIT 4 The Language of Feelings

UNIT 5 Resources

UNIT 6 Reading

UNIT 7 The Language of Symbolism

UNIT 8 You Can Write

Looking at Your Language

Transformations

UNIT 9 The Language of Work

Looking at Your Language

Photo courtesy of U.S. Navy.

LISTENING

ODD JOBS

What is unusual in the pictures? Why don't you usually think of women as tradespeople or athletes in contact sports?

DISCUSS IT. Discuss answers to the following questions:

1. What jobs do you usually associate with women?
2. What would you think about a man working in one of those jobs?
3. What men do you know who work in those jobs?
4. What do you think of those men?
5. What jobs do you usually associate with men?
6. What women do you know who work in those jobs?
7. What do you think of those women?
8. What other changes in the roles of men and women are taking place?
9. Why do you think the changes are taking place?
10. What do you think the effects of the changes will be?

IMPRESSIONS

Listen carefully right now. Is everything completely quiet; or do you hear pages turning, chalk scraping, or feet shuffling? What sounds do you hear coming from the hallway? from the street? from the playground?

What are some of the other sounds that are part of your world? What sounds do you hear that someone from a jungle tribe has probably never heard? What sounds that your great-grandparents never heard are part of your life? What do these sounds reveal about your life and the ways it is different from your great-grandparents' life or a jungle person's life?

American Airlines Photo

LOOK AT THE LADIES!

Listen carefully as someone reads articles about women who do jobs usually associated with men.

FOLLOW THROUGH. Tell whether each of the statements below is true or false according to the selections:

1. The tacklers on the opposing team were gentle with the lady football player.
2. Lady Carpenter Enterprises employs men as well as women.
3. The fans were interested in seeing Karen play in the game.
4. The lady football player dropped the ball every time it was passed to her.
5. The lady carpenter encountered only praise for being a carpenter.

DISCUSS IT. Explain why some persons might resent the women described in the items. Why might some persons admire them? How do you feel about the change in men's and women's roles? Why?

TELL IT. Explain how the story below demonstrates that our listening skills are affected by our interests:

An ornithologist (a scientist who studies birds) and a friend were walking along a busy street in a large city. "Listen," said the ornithologist, "I hear a mourning dove."

"How can you hear a bird in all this noise?" asked the friend.

"We hear those things that interest us," answered the ornithologist.

Just then someone dropped a coin. Everyone near them on the busy sidewalk paused and looked to the ground.

6

Persons in certain occupations become aware of particular types of sounds. For instance, a speech therapist is more aware than most persons of the voice quality of a speaker.

Match each occupation below with the sound that is most closely associated with that occupation:

Occupation	Sound
1. sailor	a. sewing machine
2. hunter	b. wood splitting
3. tailor	c. foghorn
4. lumberjack	d. engine knock
5. mechanic	e. barking dog

At the beginning of the selections, you heard these words:

Florida

Panthers

Windham College

New York City

Lady Carpenter Enterprises

Why does each of the words begin with a capital letter?

FOLLOW THROUGH. Rewrite the sentences below, using capital letters where they are needed:

1. The jets beat the colts yesterday.
2. Mother is a member of the american federation of labor.
3. My sister is learning to speak spanish.
4. Have you read about eskimo homes?
5. The battleship was sailing on the black sea.
6. I learned an african folk song.
7. The ohio river flows into the mississippi river.
8. We visited the smithsonian institution today.
9. About half the cheese made in this country is produced in wisconsin.
10. We stayed in a cabin in the rocky mountains.

Use capital letters to begin names of organizations, institutions, and geographical names. Use capital letters also to begin names of languages, people of a country, or special groups of people.

Using Your Language

Notice the words that stand out in the following sentences:

1. Some women *have chosen* to be football players.
2. A few men feel that women *have stolen* their jobs.
3. My sister *was torn* between becoming a doctor or a nurse.
4. The line between women's and men's roles *is* already *broken*.

FOLLOW THROUGH. Write these sentences as careful writers would:

1. The wind has broke all records.
2. Doors were tore off their hinges.
3. Were any windows broke?
4. Brenda has chose to stay in bed.
5. She will have stole a few more winks.
6. Who will be chose to clean up the yard?
7. The wind has broke some branches off our tree.
8. Some flowerpots have broke.
9. Has a piece of the roof been tore off?
10. Brenda's mother had stole out during the night to see that things were all right.

TYPES OF LISTENING

You have already learned that there are many different sounds in the world. You have learned also that different persons pay attention to different sounds. It is true, too, that there are different types of listening.

Attentive Listening

Answer the questions below the picture.

1. Why would inattentive listening not be appropriate in the situation shown in the picture?
2. What is attentive listening?
3. Why is attentive listening appropriate?
4. How does attentive listening differ from inattentive listening?
5. What are some other situations in which attentive listening is appropriate?

Listening carefully so that you can remember what is said is called *attentive listening*.

9

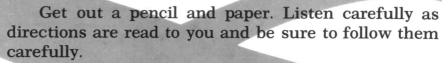

Get out a pencil and paper. Listen carefully as directions are read to you and be sure to follow them carefully.

Listen carefully as you hear a report on voodoo. Then answer the questions you will be asked about the report.

Many persons are able to listen more efficiently when they listen for specific purposes. Another report will be read to you. Listen for information to answer these questions:

1. What diseases are more common in smokers?
2. How do we know that cigarettes can be deadly?
3. Why did some persons question the results of the research with mice?
4. What did the research with dogs indicate?
5. How does a smoker's lung differ from a normal lung?

WRITE IT. Write a paragraph in which you tell which listening situation caused you to listen more efficiently. Explain why you believe that you listened more efficiently in this situation.

EDIT IT. Read your paragraph to be sure that you have done what you were asked to do. Are your ideas stated clearly? Have you checked the spelling of your words? Have you checked your paragraph also for the points listed at the left? Remember to edit all your writing that is to be read by other persons.

In what situation would you hear the announcement that will be read to you now?

DISCUSS IT. Talk about the answers to the following questions:

1. Why wouldn't the description be considered a complete description?
2. What five other characteristics would be useful in describing a person?

1. Use a capital letter:
   a. to begin each sentence.
   b. for the word *I.*
   c. to begin names of persons, languages, people of a country or special groups, and geographical names.
2. Use a period at the end of a statement.
3. Use a question mark at the end of a question.

10

3. What are five common situations in which it would be useful to pay careful attention to a person's description?
4. How are observing and listening alike?
5. What are some other characteristics of a good observer?

Divide into groups of three. Each group should select one member of the class to be the "wanted person." The group should prepare a complete description of the wanted person, and the group recorder should write the description. Each sentence should give an additional bit of information.

Group members should proofread the description and add any information that has been omitted. Then a member of the group should read the description to the class one sentence at a time. The class member who identifies the wanted person earns a point for his group. Practice good attentive listening as the descriptions are read.

Marginal Listening

Is the girl in the cartoon listening to her friend?

Morrie Turner—King Features Syndicate 1972

Do you daydream while others talk? Do you know what they are talking about? What happens when your name is mentioned? How can you hear your name when you are not really listening to a conversation?

Listening in such a way that you hear only those things that interest you is called *marginal listening*.

11

DISCUSS IT. Form groups of five or six pupils. Appoint a group secretary to record the opinions of the group as you discuss the items below. Report the findings of the group to the class.

1. Why is marginal listening sometimes desirable?
2. Describe a situation in which marginal listening is used.
3. Explain why we cannot pay full attention to everything we hear. What sounds do we learn to tune out?
4. List some advantages of marginal listening.
5. List some disadvantages of marginal listening.

Listening Analytically

Listen carefully as someone reads a set of directions.

Now answer the following questions about the information:

1. How many blocks do you go to reach Center Boulevard?
2. Which way do you turn on Center Boulevard?
3. How far do you walk on Center Boulevard?
4. What kind of building is the City Hall?
5. On what corner is the City Hall?

Was the information necessary to answer the questions given in the directions? What type of listening did you do to find information to answer these questions?

What important bit of information was not given in the directions? What kind of listening did you do to notice information not given?

Listening to hear whether information is complete and accurate is called *analytic listening.*

DISCUSS IT. Form groups of three or four. Talk about situations in which you would use analytic listening. Try to think of five situations and have the group recorder list them.

If you are to determine whether important information is given in a presentation, you must listen

12

analytically. Listen analytically as you hear part of a political speech.

Which question below seeks information not provided in the speech?

1. What is the name of the political candidate?
2. For what office is the candidate running?
3. How does he plan to reduce crime?
4. For what does the candidate stand?
5. What does the candidate oppose?

DISCUSS IT. What are the qualifications for office? As a class, discuss and list those qualifications. Then listen analytically as someone reads parts of political speeches. Identify the questions below that seek information not provided in the speeches:

1. a. How often does the speaker see Fred?
   b. In what sport does Fred participate?
   c. How does playing basketball qualify Fred to be on the student council?
   d. Why does the speaker think the listeners should vote for Fred?
   e. What qualifications must a good student council member have?
2. a. For what position is Mr. Highflier running?
   b. Does friendship with astronauts mean that a person supports space exploration?
   c. What influence does a city mayor have on space exploration?
   d. What qualities does a good mayor have?
   e. Does Harry L. Highflier have any of these?
3. a. What is the name of the candidate?
   b. What are the qualifications for a good treasurer?
   c. What qualifications does the speaker think are important?
   d. Are these qualifications related to the office of treasurer?
   e. What kind of appearance does Mary present?

13

Listening Appreciatively

Study the listening situations in the pictures below:

Listening that encourages you to establish a certain mood or form mental images is called *appreciative listening.*

Answer the following questions:

1. What do the listeners in the pictures have in common?
2. Why is it not important for the listeners to remember what they hear?
3. What is this type of listening called?
4. What are some situations in which a person would listen to music attentively?

IMAGERY IN POETRY

Do all poems tell stories? What other kinds of poems are there? Listen as someone reads three poems that create images of cities.

DISCUSS IT. Talk about answers to these questions:

1. Of what does his apartment house remind Gerald Raftery? How would you describe an apartment house?

14

2. Of what does Robert Dana think as he drives along an expressway? Of what do you think as you travel along an expressway?
3. Of what is the fabric in Dana's poem composed?
4. How does Mildred Weston help you to picture knights on horseback riding at each other?
5. How else could traffic be described?

WRITE IT. If you have a different image of any of the topics described in the three poems, describe your image.

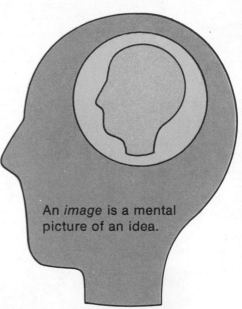

An *image* is a mental picture of an idea.

EDIT IT. After you write your image, read it carefully. Be sure that you have used fresh and unusual descriptions. Cross out any unnecessary words. State your images as clearly as possible.

Read your composition to the class. Notice how people react differently to the same topic.

ENJOYING POETRY WITH STRONG RHYTHM

Listen to the poem "The Voyage of Jimmy Poo" by James A. Emanuel.

DISCUSS IT. As you hear "The Voyage of Jimmy Poo" again, tap your fingers to the rhythm. How many beats are in each line? How does a poet create rhythm in a poem?

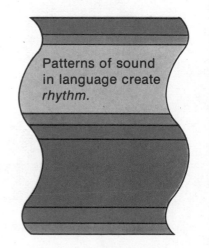

Patterns of sound in language create *rhythm.*

What other poems with strong rhythm do you know? Select a favorite poem with strong rhythm and read it to the class. Explain how the poet created the strong rhythm.

TELL IT. Work in groups of three or four, and compose a poem that uses sound patterns to create a strong rhythm. Appoint a group member as a recorder, and have the recorder copy the lines of the poem.

EDIT IT. Read the poem and make any changes that would strengthen the rhythm or make the meaning of the poem clearer. Read the poem aloud to the class.

Poems That Tell Stories

What poem do you know that tells a story? What do we call a poem that tells a story?

Listen to the narrative poem "The Fog" by W. H. Davies.

DISCUSS IT. Answer the following questions:

1. What story is told in the poem?
2. What image is created in the poem?
3. How many beats are in each line of "The Fog"?
4. Which lines contain the rhyming words in each verse?
5. What is one of your favorite songs whose words form a narrative poem?

A poem that tells a story is called a *narrative poem*.

The Way Your Language Changes

Compare the meanings of the following words with the meanings of the words as they are used in the sentence below:

hippy—having excess weight on the hips
fuzz—fine, light particles of fibers; fluff
rap—to give a quick, sharp blow
pad—something soft or stuffed, like a cushion

The hippies and the fuzz had a rap session at Elmo's pad.

Which meaning of each word is more recent? Why do some words in our language change meanings?

FOLLOW THROUGH. Copy the following words and write the first meaning that comes to your mind for each of them:

bread	dropout	cool	rock	split
dove	hip	fuzz	soul	unglued

Find each word in a dictionary. Does the dictionary give the meaning you used?

Many words in the English language change meanings over the years.

16

DISCUSS IT. Make up two sentences using each word on page 16. Be sure the word has a different meaning in each sentence. Discuss why some of the meanings assigned to the words are not in the dictionary. Explain why you think that some of these meanings will appear in the dictionary in the future.

Some new meanings of words eventually become widely used and appear in the dictionary.

FOLLOW THROUGH. The meanings of the expressions in bold letters in the sentences in Group 1 are established meanings that appear in the dictionary. Use each of the expressions in place of a blank in a sentence in Group 2. The meanings of the expressions in Group 2 are new meanings that may not appear in the dictionary.

Group 1

1. Have you ever seen a **cowboy** rope a steer?
2. Our cabin is **far out** in the woods.
3. Our family will take a **trip** to that block party.
4. I can draw a **straight** line.
5. This is my **bag** of groceries.
6. Did you hear the **rap** on the door?
7. We had to **drag** the log off the road.
8. You should put a heating **pad** on your sore ear.
9. The science teacher gave a **demonstration** of magnetism.
10. Did you **turn on** the radio?

Group 2

1. The boring party was really a ⬜.
2. My sister's outfit is really ⬜.
3. There will be a tenants' ⬜ at City Hall tonight.
4. That music can ⬜ teen-agers.
5. Drugs can send an addict on a bad ⬜.
6. My parents are pretty ⬜.
7. Let's sit down and ⬜ for a while.
8. My older brother has a ⬜ in the city.
9. This bus driver is a real ⬜.
10. My ⬜ is art, and I don't care for much else.

17

CHECK UP ON YOURSELF

Identifying Types of Listening (pages 8–14)

Match each picture with the type of listening it represents. The four types of listening are given below the pictures.

1.

3.

2.

4.

(a) Attentive listening   (c) Analytic listening
(b) Marginal listening   (d) Appreciative listening

Classifying Listening Activities (pages 8–14)

Below are some common listening activities. List each of these activities under one of the four major types of listening.

1. Listening to the radio while studying
2. Taking notes on a speech
3. Listening for propaganda techniques in a commercial
4. Listening to your favorite rock group
5. Listening to a homework assignment

MORE IDEAS FOR YOU

1. Form a committee to construct a bulletin-board display illustrating the four major types of listening.
2. Record on tape a puzzle similar to the one read for page 10 or any other selection that requires attentive listening. Pupils who need practice in listening can listen to the tapes.
3. Record a report on tape. Ask classmates to answer comprehensive questions, take notes, or write a summary of the report.
4. Listen appreciatively to records of music, poetry, or literary selections recorded by professional artists.
5. Make a bulletin-board display of news items showing women in occupations usually performed by men.
6. Make a bulletin-board display of news items showing men in occupations usually performed by women.
7. Prepare a report on "The Women's Liberation Movement" and present it to the class.
8. Plan a discussion that presents both sides of the question "Is a woman's place in the home?"
9. Prepare a tape of your favorite poems or literary selections to be played to the class.

SUBJECT	PREDICATE

1. Someone + speaks.

2. His ideas + reach you.

3. You + are a listener.

THE BASIC SENTENCE

Sentence Parts

Basic sentences are those from which all other English sentences can be made.

Look at the Language Strip at the left and answer these questions about the three basic sentences:

1. What is the **subject** of each sentence?
2. What is the **predicate** of each sentence?
3. What mark is used to separate the subject from the predicate?
4. What does every basic sentence have?

Every basic sentence has two parts:

SUBJECT + PREDICATE

FOLLOW THROUGH. Put a plus sign between the subject and the predicate as you write each of the following basic sentences:

1. Everybody listens.
2. Listening is a skill.
3. We can improve our listening.
4. Some listening is enjoyable.
5. All pupils listen to directions.
6. Marilyn listens attentively.
7. Critics listen analytically.
8. Archaeologists listen to folktales.
9. Some listening requires effort.
10. Our interests affect our listening.

Look at the Language Strip at the right and answer these questions:

1. What is another name for the subject of a sentence?
2. What is another name for the predicate of a sentence?
3. How many words are there in the noun phrase in sentence 1? in sentence 2? in sentence 3?
4. How many words are there in the verb phrase in sentence 1? in sentence 2? in sentence 3?

> The subject of a sentence is called the **noun phrase.** The predicate is called the **verb phrase.**
> Both the noun phrase and the verb phrase may have one or more words.

FOLLOW THROUGH. Tell whether each subject noun phrase in the "Follow Through" on page 20 is one word or more than one word.

FOLLOW THROUGH. Tell whether each verb phrase in the "Follow Through" on page 20 is one word or more than one word.

FOLLOW THROUGH. Use a plus sign to separate the noun phrase from the verb phrase as you write each sentence. Tell whether each subject noun phrase is one word or more than one word.

1. I listened to a program.
2. It described accidents.
3. Most accidents are preventable.
4. People fall.
5. Something trips them.

SUBJECT | PREDICATE

NOUN PHRASE + VERB PHRASE

1. Everybody + listens.

2. The bird + flew away.

3. We + heard that story.

There is another way of writing about what you have learned. What do the letters and symbols mean?

Thoughts + are in your mind.

If you had trouble, read the rule correctly:

S stands for "basic sentence"; 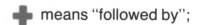 means "may be written as";

NP stands for "noun phrase"; ➕ means "followed by";

VP stands for "verb phrase."

Maria + hears
the trucks.

Look at the Language Strip at the left.

1. What word makes up the subject **NP**?
2. What is a word like *Maria* called?
3. Why is *Maria* called a **proper noun**?

Sometimes a proper noun makes up the subject **NP**.
A proper noun names a particular person or thing.

FOLLOW THROUGH. Use a proper noun as the subject **NP** in each of these sentences:

1. ☐ is my friend.
2. ☐ wrote that book.
3. ☐ is my pet.
4. ☐ starts the school year.
5. ☐ is our capital.

Look at the Language Strip at the right.

1. What word makes up the subject **NP**?
2. What is a word like *People* called?
3. Why is such a word called a **common noun**?

Sometimes a common noun alone makes up the subject **NP**.
A common noun names something that is not a particular person or thing.

FOLLOW THROUGH. List a proper noun for each of these common nouns:

1. author	3. city	5. state	7. country
2. friend	4. day	6. pet	8. language

Look at the common nouns in the box.

1. Which ones mean only one?
2. Which ones mean more than one?
3. How are most singular nouns made plural?
4. How are other nouns made plural?
5. Do all nouns change their form for the plural?

Most common nouns are made plural by adding -*s* or -*es* to the singular form. Other nouns are made plural in different ways.
Some nouns have the same form for the singular and the plural.

FOLLOW THROUGH. Tell how the plural of each noun in the box was formed.

COMMON NOUN

People + wore togas.

1. dog — dogs
2. fox — foxes
3. city — cities
4. safe — safes
5. calf — calves
6. foot — feet
7. ox — oxen
8. duo — duos
9. echo — echoes
10. deer — deer

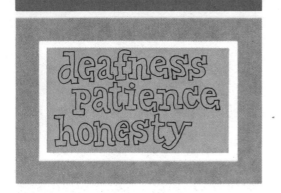

deafness
patience
honesty

NP + VP

DETERMINER + NOUN

the
YOUR
this
ANY
one

bird

1. How are the common nouns in the box different from words like *cat* and *dog?*
2. Can these common nouns be made plural?

Nouns that name something that cannot be counted usually cannot be made plural.

1. Look at the **NP** in the Language Strip. Which of the words shown there can be used with *bird* as the subject **NP** of this sentence?

☐ can fly.

2. What are the words used with *bird* called?

Determiners can be divided into five different groups:

Group 1: *the, a, an*
Group 2: *my, your, his, her, its, our, their*
Group 3: *this, that, these, those*
Group 4: *all, another, any, both, each, every, few, many, more, most, much, no, other, several, some, such*
Group 5: *one, two, ninety-nine, first, second*

Sometimes a determiner and a noun make up the subject **NP**.

FOLLOW THROUGH. Copy the subject **NP** from each sentence. Write whether it is a proper noun, a common noun, or a determiner plus a noun.

1. Archaeologists study civilizations.
2. An archaeologist must be a detective.
3. James Hall found fossils in New York.
4. Some scientists have discovered cities under the ground.
5. Earthquakes may have buried them.

1. What is the subject **NP** of each sentence in the Language Strip?
2. What is this kind of word called?

Sometimes a **personal pronoun** makes up the subject **NP**.

Look at the box.

1. What are other personal pronouns that can make up the subject **NP**?
2. Why are these words called *personal pronouns?*

The personal pronouns *I, you, he, she, it, we,* and *they* may be used as the subject **NP**.
A personal pronoun refers to a definite person or thing.

FOLLOW THROUGH. Use a personal pronoun in place of the subject **NP** in each sentence.

1. Lisa Daniel listened to a program.
2. The program was timely.
3. The streets are dirty.
4. Mr. Thomas cleaned the windows.
5. Our telephone is green.

FOLLOW THROUGH. Use a personal pronoun in place of the box in each sentence.

1. ☐ are in school now.
2. ☐ am in your class.
3. ☐ was in her class before.
4. ☐ is writing a letter.
5. ☐ were waiting for the bell.

NP + VP

PERSONAL PRONOUN

1. They + carry freight.

2. She + found a tool.

I WE it they SHE you he

NP + VP

INDEFINITE PRONOUN

Everyone + turned his head.

Something + opened
the door.

anyone	nobody
everyone	somebody
no one	anything
someone	everything
anybody	nothing
everybody	something

Look at the Language Strip.

1. What is the subject **NP** of each sentence?
2. What is this kind of word called?

Sometimes an **indefinite pronoun** makes up the subject **NP.**

Refer to the box.

1. What are other indefinite pronouns?
2. Why are these words called *indefinite pronouns*?

Indefinite pronouns do not refer to definite persons or things.

FOLLOW THROUGH. Tell whether the subject **NP** in each of these sentences is a personal pronoun or an indefinite pronoun:

1. We learned about archaeology.
2. Someone may listen to folk songs.
3. She must pick up clues easily.
4. Something buried cities beneath the ground.
5. They appear during the digging.
6. You can dig here.
7. Anyone may find something.
8. It will surprise you.

FOLLOW THROUGH. Use a personal pronoun or an indefinite pronoun as the subject **NP** in each sentence.

1. ☐ found arrowheads.
2. ☐ listened to his stories.
3. ☐ read about it.
4. ☐ had an idea.
5. ☐ lost his key.

26

CHECK UP ON YOURSELF

A. Use a plus sign to divide each of these sentences into subject noun phrase and verb phrase as you write them:

1. Ballads described the news.
2. They told a story.
3. Some ballads came to America with the first settlers.
4. Some people sing these songs today.
5. Some ballads originated in this country.
6. Mountaineers sing many of our ballads.
7. Everyone hears some of them on TV.
8. You must listen closely to ballads.
9. The stories are interesting.
10. John Lomax collected ballads.

B. List a proper noun for each of these common nouns:

1. town   3. continent   5. planet   7. mountain
2. girl   4. holiday   6. state   8. river

C. Write the plural of each of these nouns:

1. man   3. study   5. trout   7. life   9. ox
2. ax   4. thief   6. bush   8. alto   10. echo

D. Which of the following makes up the subject **NP** in each sentence in A?

a. A proper noun
b. A common noun alone
c. A determiner followed by a noun
d. A personal pronoun
e. An indefinite pronoun

THE LANGUAGE OF HUMOR

WHAT'S SO FUNNY?

"Well, you're a pretty big woman yourself."

"How is your elevator business?"

"It has its ups and downs."

© 1965 *The Saturday Review*

HI AND LOIS

King Features Syndicate 1972

You know that language is used for many different purposes. For what purpose is the language in the selections on these two pages used? Try to answer the following questions:

1. What different types of humor are represented?
2. What techniques are used to make the various examples comical?
3. In what ways does the language of humor differ from other types of language?

Many people earn their living by using the language of humor. Which of your favorite TV entertainers uses the language of humor when working?

Question: What month has 28 days in it?
Answer: They all have.

TELL IT. Think of a humorous joke or story that you have heard your favorite entertainer tell. Repeat the joke or story to the class.

Are entertainers the only persons who use the language of humor? Name some persons who are not entertainers but are well known for their humor. For what reasons do these persons use humor?

29

IMPRESSIONS

Luoma: Monkmeyer   The Press Association Ltd.

Sometimes something funny just happens all by itself, but at other times something funny happens because someone planned it. Which of these photographs show things that just happened? Which ones do you think the photographer planned? Which ones do you think are more humorous? Would these pictures be funny to someone from another country? to someone who lived a hundred years ago? to someone a hundred years from now?

Burk Uzzle

What kind of person do you think would want to take photographs of humorous happenings? What kind of person would think of planning a funny photograph? What other kinds of humorous things can you think of that can be planned?

THE HUMOR OF ABRAHAM LINCOLN

The following selections tell about a President of the United States who was famous for his humor — Abraham Lincoln. As you read the selections, find the three reasons he gave for using the language of humor.

Young Abe Lincoln read everything he could get hold of. And he seemed never to forget anything he read.

Young. Abe Lincoln listened to everything that went on around him. And he seemed never to forget anything he heard.

Lincoln's memory was like a grab-bag full of treasures. All through his life he could reach in and pull out a treasure — just the right fact or story or anecdote he needed

———to prove a point

———or help him answer a question

"You speak of Lincoln stories," President Lincoln once said. "I don't think that is . . . correct. . . ." And Lincoln explained that he almost never *invented* stories. He told stories and jokes he remembered hearing or reading.

Lincoln told a friend that he got in the habit of telling stories and jokes when he was very young. He had often found that telling a funny story was a good way to explain something serious. "I am not simply a story-teller," said Lincoln. "It is not the story itself, but its *purpose* that interests me."

Then Lincoln went on to say that, as President, he had to say *no* to many people who asked for special

Selections from *The Abraham Lincoln Joke Book*, by Beatrice Schenk de Regniers. Copyright © 1965 by Beatrice Schenk de Regniers. Reprinted by permission of Random House, Inc.

favors. And sometimes he had to tell people they were doing things they should not be doing. Or he had to tell someone to do something that was hard to do.

A joke could make a *no* or a scolding or an order easier to take.

Sometimes a visitor asked President Lincoln questions. And Lincoln could not answer, because the answer was a secret. Then Lincoln would tell a story and make the visitor forget his questions.

President Lincoln often kept a joke book or a book of humorous stories in his desk drawer. Some people asked, "Why does the President waste his time on jokes?"

But many people understood that Lincoln needed something to make him laugh. About a month after he became President, the Civil War began. President Lincoln had big problems and heavy responsibilities. Sometimes it seemed to him that he would break down under the strain. If he could smile or laugh—just for a moment—he could manage to keep going.

Lincoln himself said, "I laugh because I must not cry."

"Lincoln had the saddest face I ever tried to paint," said Francis Carpenter, an artist.

Mr. Carpenter lived in the White House while he was painting President Lincoln's portrait. And Carpenter noticed that when the President felt saddest he would try to get relief by telling a joke or reading a book of humorous stories.

Lincoln believed that jokes are good for children, too. He thought jokes and riddles were good fun and helped sharpen the wits.

Lincoln agreed with a friend who said it was as important to teach jokes and riddles in school as it was to teach reading and writing and arithmetic.

Maybe you will want to tell some of these Lincoln jokes sometimes

——to prove a point
——to answer a question
——or just for fun.

Hey! Hay!

Any good joke seemed better if it was called a Lincoln joke. Maybe that is why this joke was told as though it happened to Lincoln:

Lincoln was riding horseback on a country road, and found his way blocked by a big load of hay. The hay had fallen off a wagon. The boy driving the wagon was upset and excited.

"Now don't worry," Lincoln told the boy. "Come with me to the farmhouse and we'll find someone to help us get the hay back on the wagon."

At the farmhouse, the kindly farmer invited Lincoln and the boy to have dinner. Lincoln enjoyed his dinner, but he saw that the boy was worried and restless.

"Pa won't like this," the boy muttered. "Pa won't like this at all."

"Now don't you worry," Lincoln told the boy. "Your Pa knows that an accident can happen to anybody. No need to hurry." And Lincoln took a second helping of potatoes.

"Pa won't like my being away so long," the boy said.

"Oh come now," said Lincoln. "Your Pa will understand. He would want you to take time out to eat a good dinner. I'll go with you and explain what happened. By the way, where is your Pa?"

"He's under the load of hay!" wailed the boy.

The Longest Leg

One day a man came to Abraham Lincoln's law office. He saw Lincoln sitting with one leg stretched across the desk.

"Why Mr. Lincoln," said the man, "that's the longest leg I've ever seen!"

"Here's another just like it," said Lincoln. And he put his other leg across the desk.

34

Wolf Dog

Lincoln had a general who bragged a lot but wasn't so good at fighting. When Lincoln heard that the general had to run away from the enemy, he may have been reminded of the story about the man and his new hunting dog:

"That new dog of mine is a great fighter," the hunter bragged. "Just show him a pack of wolves and he'll go after them and eat 'em up."

And the man sent his dog into the underbrush to scare up some wolves.

Wolves and dog went racing across the fields. The hunter followed far behind. When he reached a farm yard, he asked the farmer, "Have you seen a wolf dog and a pack of wolves?"

"Yep," said the farmer.

"How were they going?"

"Pretty fast."

"What was their position when you saw them?"

"Well," said the farmer slowly, "the dog was a leetle bit ahead."

How Long Should a Man's Legs Be?

When Lincoln was a lawyer, two friends came to him and said:

"Lincoln, we want you to settle an argument for us. Tell us, exactly how long should a man's legs be?"

Now one friend had very short legs.

The other friend had very long legs.

"Hmmmmm," Lincoln said. "I never gave this matter much thought. But now that I think of it, I would say——" Lincoln stopped.

He looked at the friend with short legs.

He looked at the friend with long legs.

"Well," Lincoln went on, "I would say *a man's legs should be exactly long enough to reach from his body to the ground.*"

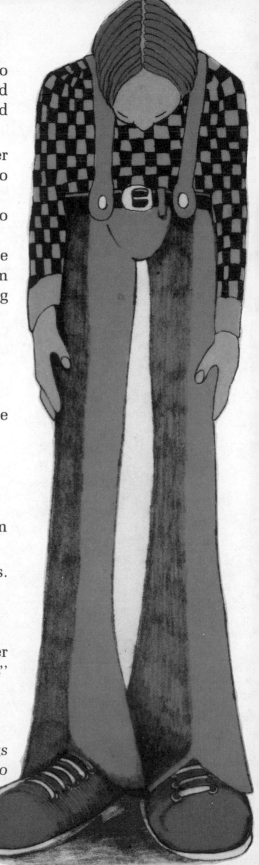

Important Business

An angry farmer came up to President Lincoln at a White House gathering. "Some soldiers helped themselves to my hay and my horse, Mr. President," said the farmer. "And I want you to see to it that I get my horse back right away."

Now President Lincoln was busy day and night. He had many important questions to think about. So he explained to the farmer as patiently as he could:

"Why, my dear sir, if I tried to take care of every person's business, I would have work enough for twenty presidents!"

After the farmer left, Lincoln turned to a friend and said, "That farmer reminds me of something that happened to Jack Chase, a riverboat captain I used to know in Illinois.

"It was quite a trick to take the boat over the rapids in the river, and Captain Jack always took the wheel himself to steer the boat through them.

"One day the rapids were especially rough and Captain Jack was working hard to get the boat through.

"Suddenly a boy came up and pulled at Jack's coattail. 'Say, Mr. Captain,' said the boy, 'stop the boat a minute! I've lost my apple overboard.'"

Lincoln Gives a Book Review

A well-known man read aloud to President Lincoln some chapters from a book he was writing.

"Tell me, Mr. Lincoln," said the man, "what do you think of my book?"

Lincoln didn't think much of it. But he didn't want to hurt the author's feelings, so he said:

"Well, for those who like that sort of thing, I think it is just about the sort of thing they would like."

The Next President

And when someone asked Lincoln who would be the next President, he is supposed to have answered:

"I cannot say for certain who will be the people's choice for President. But to the best of my belief, it will be the successful candidate."

Beatrice de Regniers

DISCUSS IT. Discuss the answers to the following questions:

1. Why did Mr. Lincoln believe that jokes and riddles should be taught at school?
2. What were the three reasons Mr. Lincoln gave for using the language of humor?
3. Where did Mr. Lincoln find the jokes and stories that he used?
4. Which two of the Lincoln stories were used to prove a point?
5. Which two of the Lincoln stories were used to help him answer a question?

LET'S think ABOUT HUMOR

Explain what happened in the pictures. Why do you think the girl laughed if she didn't understand the joke? Have you ever been in the same situation as the girl in the last picture? The language of humor appears in many different forms. Perhaps, as you learn more about these forms, you will enjoy humor more fully.

Ridicule

The form of humor used earliest by children is *ridicule*. The cartoon below is an example of ridicule:

"I'd swear that was Herman if I didn't know he was home safe in his bowl."

DISCUSS IT. Analyze the cartoon by discussing the following questions with your classmates:

1. Do you think the cartoon is funny? Why?
2. Does the cartoon make fun of someone? Who?
3. How does the cartoon make fun of the person?
4. Would most people think the cartoon is funny?
5. Does all humor make fun of someone?

We often laugh at the misfortunes of others. Two different events are shown in the pictures below:

At which of the events would you be most likely to laugh? Why? We ridicule only minor accidents or misfortunes, not serious ones.

Such ridicule is called *spontaneous ridicule* because it is not planned but just happens when someone is caught in a humorous situation. For instance, a man slipped on an icy sidewalk, took several steps trying to stay up, and then fell flat. Is this an example of ridicule? Why? The accident happened, but the man was not made an object of ridicule. Then a young boy came to help the man up and said, "Man, that was really a groovy dance step!" Is the event an example of spontaneous ridicule now? Why?

TELL IT. The mishaps below could easily be used as a basis for ridicule. Think of a humorous remark that could be used in each situation. Take turns telling your remarks to your classmates.

1. Man slips and falls into mud puddle.
2. Lady squirts water in her eye at drinking fountain.
3. Classmate misses chair when he sits down.
4. Friend spills a spoonful of soup down his shirt.
5. Baseball infielder drops a pop fly.

Another type of ridicule is called *deliberate ridicule*. Certain types of events or happenings are so common that they can be ridiculed at any time. The storyteller merely describes the accident or misfortune and makes the person involved an object of ridicule. Some common objects of ridicule are school, careless drivers, husbands, and children.

Notice who is made an object of ridicule in each of the following stories:

a. As Johnny handed a very poor report card to his father, he suggested, "Maybe I should try another line of work."
b. A man who had recently received his driver's license walked into the police station. From his pocket he produced a parking ticket and said, "Did one of your men lose this? I found it on the windshield of my car."
c. A wife pointed to her husband, who was sound asleep under a tree. She then explained to a neighbor, "Dick's hobby is letting the birds watch him."
d. A man tripped and sprawled across a baby carriage. The carriage rolled slowly down the street with the man on it.

Ridicule is a form of humor that makes someone else an object for laughter.

FOLLOW THROUGH. Number your paper from 1 through 4. After each numeral, copy the letter of the story on page 39 that is described by the statement.

1. This is not an example of ridicule.
2. A boy ridicules himself.
3. The character in the story ridicules someone else.
4. A man ridicules himself.

WRITE IT. Write a paragraph in which you explain why three of the stories are examples of ridicule and one is not.

EDIT IT. Read your paragraph to be certain that you have made your explanation clear. Check your capitalization, spelling, and punctuation. If necessary, consult a dictionary.

Is item d a ridiculous situation? Why is it not an example of ridicule? Although the man is in a ridiculous situation, he has not been made an object for laughter. To make the man an object for laughter, someone needs to make a humorous remark to him or ask him a humorous question.

TELL IT. Think of a humorous remark or question that could be asked to make item d an example of ridicule. Read your example to the class and explain why it is now an example of ridicule.

Notice the punctuation marks in the following:

1. Margaret said, "My brother is so clumsy that he can't chew gum and walk at the same time."
2. "My brother is so clumsy that he can't chew gum and walk at the same time," said Margaret.
3. "My brother is so clumsy," said Margaret, "that he can't chew gum and walk at the same time."

In the sentences above, the words *Margaret said* are called *explanatory words.* What words are the direct words of the speaker?

In what part of the first sentence are the explanatory words located? What punctuation mark follows the explanatory words? How does the second sentence differ from the first?

In the third sentence, the explanatory words are in the middle of the sentence. These words divide the direct quotation into two parts. How is the divided quotation punctuated?

How does the following example differ from the third sentence on page 40?

"My brother is so clumsy," said Margaret. "He can't chew gum and walk at the same time."

There are two sentences in this example. The third sentence at the bottom of page 40 had only one sentence. Notice the difference in punctuation.

Notice the commas in this sentence:

Head for the roundhouse, Harry, for they can't corner you there.

Who is spoken to in the sentence? How is his name separated from the rest of the sentence? Such a name is a name in *direct address*. Rewrite the sentence so that the name in direct address is at the beginning; at the end. How many commas did you need to separate the name from the rest of the sentence? Where were the commas placed in the sentences?

FOLLOW THROUGH. Separate the names in direct address in each of the sentences as you write them:

1. Her name is Mary Sam.
2. John Sue called you this morning.
3. Mother Tom said that he would be late.
4. Brother Esther is waiting to see you.
5. It was Joe Dad who told me the story.

FOLLOW THROUGH. Copy the examples of deliberate ridicule below and punctuate them correctly:

1. A driver had stalled his car and sat through several changes of the traffic light. Finally, a policeman came over to the car and looked into the window. What's the matter buddy he asked Don't we have any colors that you like

The exact words of a speaker are set off by quotation marks. They are separated from the rest of the sentence by one or two commas.

Commas are used to set off names in direct address.

2. Two fishermen were having a contest to see which one could catch more fish. One got a bite on his line and became so excited that he fell out of the boat. The other fisherman remarked If you're going into the water after them Harry the contest is off

Puns

What type of humor is referred to as a *pun*? A pun requires a special type of language referred to as a "play on words." Explain what the play on words is in this pun:

A sailor complained that the crew of his ship could not play cards because the captain stood on the deck.

On what *deck* does a ship captain really stand? On what *deck* does the pun cause the reader to think he stands? What do we call words like *deck*?

You can remember the meaning of *homograph* if you think of its two parts. *Homo* means "the same." *Graph* means "written." The use of homographs is one way a pun or play on words can be found.

Words that are spelled alike but are different in origin, meaning, or pronunciation are called *homographs*.

FOLLOW THROUGH. The words in bold letters in the sentences below are homographs. Make up a sentence using each of the words so that it has a different meaning.

1. Let the old man **lead** us through the woods.
2. John likes to **hide** in the barn.
3. This is the **second** time I have heard that story.
4. We had a **narrow** escape.
5. Ask Marcia to **iron** your shirt.

Identify ten words below that can be used as homographs. If necessary, use a dictionary.

1. wind	6. gag	11. master
2. read	7. door	12. dentist
3. rude	8. lead	13. five
4. ring	9. hut	14. mold
5. frame	10. number	15. run

42

FOLLOW THROUGH. Write two sentences for each homograph that you identified, showing two different meanings for the homograph.

The pun below demonstrates another play on words:

"Your fare, lady," demanded the bus driver.

"Thank you," replied the lady sweetly. "You're pretty good-looking yourself."

What words did the lady think the bus driver used? What words did he really use? Are the words spelled the same way? Are they pronounced the same way? Do they have the same meanings? Words like *your — you're* and *fair — fare* are called *homophones*. You have already learned that *homo* means "the same." The word *phone* means "sound."

Use one of the following words to answer each question below:

maze	break	hair	grown	pear
maize	brake	hare	groan	pair
mourning	stare	fowl	maid	fare
morning	stair	foul	made	fair

1. What grows on your head but does not live in the brier patch?
2. What is mature but not a sound of pain?
3. What represents price for transportation but no beauty?
4. What helps us to stop but not go all to pieces?
5. What can you eat that is not a confusing network?
6. What is good to eat but does not always come in twos?
7. What means "put together" but is not a female?
8. What goes up and down but does not look?
9. What is the breaking of a rule but not a bird?
10. What is the beginning of day but is not sad?

Wisecracks

Notice the unexpected reply in this conversation:

"Do you like to sunbathe?"
"I don't know; I've never bathed one."

Words that are pronounced alike but are different in meaning, origin, or spelling are called *homophones*.

A humorous remark that depends on deliberate mis-interpretation of a statement is called a *wisecrack*.

DISCUSS IT. The final statement on page 43 is a *wisecrack*. Discuss the answers to the following questions:

1. Why is the last statement funny?
2. How would you define a wisecrack?
3. How is a wisecrack different from a wise saying?

To make up a wisecrack, you must deliberately misinterpret a statement or a question. Your response is then related to the original statement or question, but not in the way the speaker intended it to be. In the example on page 43, the response related sunbathing to giving the sun a bath. The first speaker did not intend this meaning.

TELL IT. Think up a wisecrack for each of the following questions:

1. How did you find the weather on your vacation?
2. Do you like Mozart?
3. Does your roof always leak like that?
4. Did you put that paint on yourself?
5. Do airplanes like this crash very often?

Put-Ons

A form of humor that has recently become popular is the put-on. To put on a listener, you say something absurd or impossible in such a way that the listener isn't sure whether you are kidding him. The following examples of the put-on were given by the Beatles in interviews:

INTERVIEWER: How tall are you?
BEATLE: Two feet, nine inches.
INTERVIEWER: What do you think of Beethoven?
BEATLE: What group's he with?
INTERVIEWER: What do you do when you're cooped up in a hotel between shows?
BEATLE: We ice-skate.

WE ICE-SKATE.

An absurd or impossible response to a question is called a *put-on*.

44

DISCUSS IT. Discuss the answers to the following questions about the put-on:

1. How are the put-on and the wisecrack alike?
2. How are the put-on and the wisecrack different?
3. Why would anyone want to put on someone else?

TELL IT. Think up several answers that would put on the person who asked each of the following questions:

1. Is that your dog?
2. Where did you get that dollar?
3. What is your favorite activity?
4. Whom do you admire most?
5. What is your father's occupation?
6. When are you the happiest?
7. Why are you crying?
8. Where were you born?
9. Who is your favorite musician?
10. Why do your friends like you?

Take turns telling the put-ons that you gave as a response to each question above. Talk about the impossibility or absurdity of the different answers. Which answers did you like best? Why?

Put-Downs

Why are the following comments called *put-downs*?

He's as stimulating as a mouthful of sand.
He never opens his mouth unless he has nothing to say.
He lights up a room when he leaves it.
When there's nothing more to be said, he's still saying it.

How does the put-down differ from the wisecrack? How does the put-down differ from the put-on? What type of person is described in the put-downs above?

WRITE IT. Using the put-downs above as guides, make up ten put-downs to describe one of the personality types listed below:

grouch	snob	loafer
tightwad	show-off	pessimist
meanie	optimist	sissy

A cleverly worded and humorous insult is called a *put-down*.

45

EDIT IT. Read your put-downs to make certain they are fresh and original. Be sure that you have not used too many words. Check your spelling and punctuation. If necessary, consult a dictionary.

DISCUSS IT. Work in small groups as you listen to individuals in the class read their put-downs. Choose several that your group liked best. Discuss the reasons you have for liking them best.

Cartoons

Which pairs of cartoons below are alike?

1.

2.

3.

"Do you realize I'm in the twilight of my career as a Little Leaguer?"

4.

"Well, I'm glad to see that ONE day out of the year you kids can stop all that screaming and jumping around and behave like ladies and gentlemen"

Four cartoons copyright CARTOONS-OF-THE-MONTH.

1. What is humorous about each cartoon?
2. How are cartoons 1 and 2 alike?
3. How are cartoons 3 and 4 alike?
4. What is meant by a caption in a cartoon?
5. Why aren't captions necessary in cartoons 1 and 2?

In cartoons without captions, a ridiculous situation must be shown. Usually objects that are easily identified make the cartoon humorous without the use of words.

Work in small groups and think of some ideas for cartoons without captions. Have some members of your group who are good at drawing make some sketches of your ideas. Display the sketches in your room or on the school bulletin board.

The use of a caption explains what is happening in the cartoon. For that reason the same picture may have several captions. Think of different captions for cartoons 3 and 4 on page 46.

Think of several different captions for the cartoons below and write them. A class recorder can write the captions on the chalkboard as each of you reads your captions. See how many different captions you have made up.

Draw a cartoon sketch and make up a caption from any of the situations listed on page 39. Post your cartoon on the bulletin board in your classroom.

Other Graphic Humor

You have been studying humor that depends on the use of our English language. Some humor uses forms of communication other than language. Notice the techniques the artist uses to make these cartoons humorous:

Perkins by J. Miles reprinted courtesy The Register and Tribune Syndicate, Inc.

1. What happened in the first series of pictures?
2. What is humorous about these pictures?
3. What happened in the second series of pictures?
4. What is humorous about these pictures?
5. How are you able to understand the humor in the events shown above even though no language is used?

Here is a form of humor that combines both pictures and words:

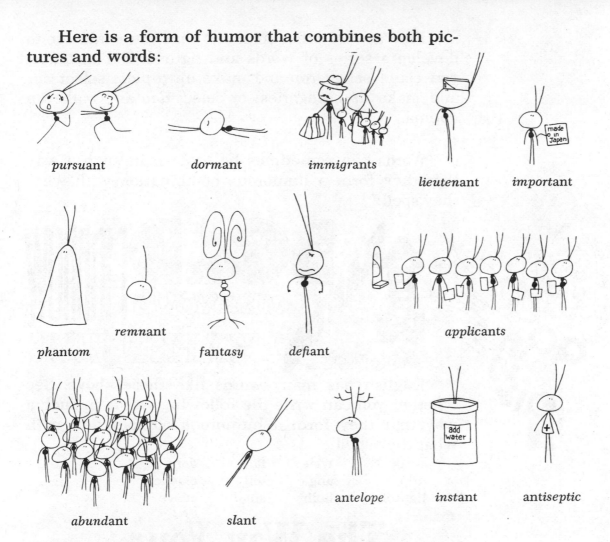

pursuant   *dormant*   *immigrants*   *lieutenant*   *important*

phantom   *remnant*   *fantasy*   *defiant*   *applicants*

abundant   *slant*   *antelope*   *instant*   *antiseptic*

Cartoons from *Antics* by Patricia Robbins and Tom Fenton. Copyright © 1969, by Patricia Robbins and Tom Fenton. Reprinted by permission of Simon & Schuster, Inc.

Define each of the fifteen words above that contains the word *ant*. Then explain how the figure and the word form a humorous combination.

Use your imagination to produce some antics of your own. The words below will give you some ideas. Draw pictures to go with at least five of the words.

1. pleasant
2. anthem
3. rant
4. plant
5. pendant
6. lantern
7. antagonize
8. propellant
9. gallant
10. panther
11. pant
12. antifreeze
13. bantam
14. deodorant
15. chant

Find a word other than *ant* that you could use to develop a series of words and figures. For instance, you could select *top* and make up *top*ics; select *cat* and make up *cat*egories; or select *dog* and make up *dog*ma.

Words can sometimes be written in such a way that they form a humorous combination with what they spell:

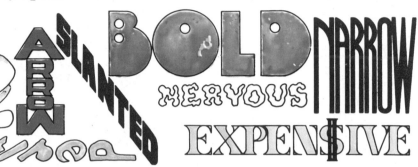

English has many words like those above. See whether you can write the following words in such a way that they form a humorous combination with what they spell:

weak	wide	flat	dent
drip	angle	tell	elastic
lightning	bulb	small	curve

The Way Your Language Changes

The English language is spoken all over the world. How can you identify a native of France, Italy, Ireland, or Cuba by the way he speaks English? Such variations within one language are called *dialects*. Even within our own country we find several dialects. Some of these dialects can be demonstrated through the language of humor.

Sometimes jokes depend on the way persons pronounce a word. The word *mouse* is pronounced the same in England and the United States. In Scotland it is pronounced as if it were spelled *moose*. The joke below depends on this word for its humor:

> An American girl was wandering through a zoo in England. An excited zookeeper rushed up to her and said, "There's a moose loose!"
>
> "Help!" cried the girl. Then she became calm enough to ask, "Are you a Scotsman or an Englishman?"

What is the point of the story? How does its humor depend on the pronunciation of a word? Jokes that use certain pronunciations of words are called *dialect jokes*.

Are you able to identify persons from other countries by the manner in which they pronounce some English words? Each joke below concerns a native of one of the following countries. See whether you can match the country with the dialect of the speaker.

Ireland   Germany   England

1. A gunman rushed into a café firing his gun in all directions. "Get out of here, all you lousy, dirty pigs," he shouted.

The crowd fled, dodging a hail of bullets, except for a mild-looking man sitting at a corner table.

"Well?" demanded the gunman.

"By Jove," remarked the customer, "there certainly were a lot of them, weren't there?"

2. A man approached the clerk in a bookstore. "Oi want to git a book to put th' photographs av all me relatives in. Oi think this wan will do."

The clerk replied, "But that isn't a family album, sir. That is a scrapbook."

"Oh, that's all right, young man; all av me relatives were scrappers."

3. A visitor from another country met a stranger while playing golf.

"See dot girl varing dos trousers," he said. "Vot's wrong mit her parents letting her look like dot?"

"That, sir, is my daughter," replied the other golfer angrily.

"Forgiff me; I didn't know you ver her fadder."

"I'm not. I'm her mother."

What words help you identify the country of the speaker in each story on page 51?

How can you tell where speakers of our language live by listening to them speak? In what sections of our country are certain words pronounced differently from the way you pronounce them?

In what sections of the country do the speakers in the following stories live?

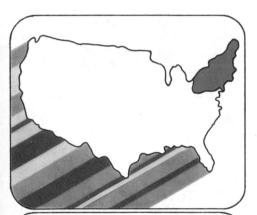

1. "Say," said one boy to another, "how do you loin a goil ter swim?"

"Oh, dat's easy," said the other boy. "You takes her gently by da hand, an' you leads her down to the water, an' you says ta her, 'Don't be afraid, I ain't goin' ter let nothin' hoit yer, an' . . .'"

"Hey," interrupted the first one, "what are you givin' me? Dis is me sister I'm talkin' about."

"Ah, shove her off da side of da pool."

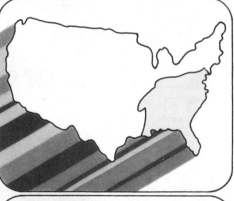

2. A pupil, writing a story in school, raised his hand and asked, "How do you spell *rat?*"

"R-A-T," answered his teacher.

"No," said the pupil, "not that kind of *rat*. I mean like *rat* now."

A person's language gives you many clues regarding background. Explain how speech gives you clues to the region in which the speakers live.

How many major dialects are spoken in the United States? In what areas of the country are these dialects spoken? The dialect spoken in New York City and the New England area east of the Connecticut River is referred to as Eastern Speech. One dialect is spoken in Virginia, the Carolinas, Tennessee, Florida, Georgia, Alabama, Mississippi, Arkansas, Louisiana, Texas, and parts of Maryland, West Virginia, Kentucky, and Oklahoma. This dialect is referred to as Southern Speech. The dialect spoken in the Midwest and Far West is referred to as General American Speech.

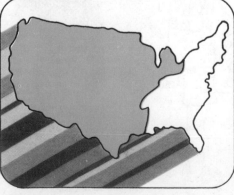

DISCUSS IT. Outline on a map of the United States the three major dialect areas. In small groups discuss the answers to the following questions:

52

1. Why do persons living in each of these dialect areas pronounce words as they do?
2. Why are there variations of pronunciation within each of these regions as well as between them?
3. Why doesn't someone decide the "correct" way to pronounce words and then teach everyone to pronounce them that way?

List five words that are pronounced differently in different areas of the country. Demonstrate the pronunciations for the class. A class member can record the words on the chalkboard to show how many different words the class can recall.

Find a short story, a poem, a movie, or a TV program in which a character speaks in a regional dialect different from yours. Describe the dialect to the class and try to tell what region it represents.

Using Your Language

You have learned that a knowledge of homophones is useful in making up puns. A knowledge of certain homophones is useful also in communicating meaning accurately. Notice the words in bold letters below:

A clever dog knows **its** master.
A clever dog knows **it's** master.

In which sentence does the dog have the upper paw? Explain.

FOLLOW THROUGH. Use *its* or *it's* in each sentence.

1. The mouse was caught by ☐ tail.
2. I don't think ☐ time for the party to start.
3. A book should not be judged by ☐ cover.
4. The bird had injured ☐ wing.
5. ☐ a long drive to my uncle's house.
6. The lion had a thorn in ☐ paw.
7. In the summer ☐ fun to swim.
8. The bird was building ☐ nest.
9. We should wear our coats because ☐ cold outside.
10. When ☐ time to go, call me.

CHECK UP ON YOURSELF

The Vocabulary of Humor (pages 37–47)

Substitute one of the following words for the term in italics in each sentence below.

a put-on	ridicule	put-down	pun
joke	wisecrack	humorist	cartoon

1. The crowd began to *mock* the unfortunate old man.
2. She laughed at the *squelching remark.*
3. The speaker used a *humorous play on words.*
4. My uncle told a *humorous short story.*
5. The artist drew a *humorous sketch* about the situation.
6. A *clever retort* often turns off a heckler.
7. The interviewer realized that he had been given *an absurd answer.*
8. My sister is quite a *wit.*

Using Punctuation (pages 40–41)

Copy the examples of deliberate ridicule below and punctuate them correctly:

1. An inexperienced driver came to an intersection and stopped his car at a yield sign. A large truck pulled up behind the car and waited for the driver to move. After several minutes had passed, the truck driver rolled down his window and shouted Buddy the sign says yield, not surrender!

2. The Little League game had been a hard-fought one. The villain of the day, in the eyes of the losing team, was the second-base umpire. Several of his decisions had been very close and had raised protests. After the game, a member of the losing team went up to the umpire. It really was a good game Mr. Umpire the young player said politely I'm sure sorry that you didn't get to see it

3. The two members of the debating team faced each other across the table. They had both prepared for weeks and were now eager to begin the debate. This is really going to be a battle of the wits remarked the first debater. Well, if you insist replied his opponent. But I think you should know that it is against my principles to fight an unarmed man

Using Homographs (page 42)

Use each word below in two sentences to show the meanings of homographs:

1. buffet
2. wound
3. gill
4. close
5. live
6. minute
7. bow
8. row
9. bass
10. tear

Using Homophones (page 43)

For each word below, write another word with the same pronunciation:

1. heir
2. beau
3. main
4. peak
5. pour
6. threw
7. bury
8. frees
9. clothes
10. heard

Identifying Dialects (pages 50–53)

Tell which of these stories is told in Irish dialect and which is told in German dialect:

1. "Vy vos dot blank piece of paper in de envelope addressed to you?"

"Ach! Dot is a letter from my vife. Ve are not shpeaking to each odder."

2. "Which would yez ruther be in, Casey, an explosion or a collision?"

"Sure, McCarthy, and it's an explosion I'd ruther be in."

"Why?"

"Well, because in a collision there yez be, but in an explosion, where are yez?"

Using Your Language (page 53)

Use *its* or *it's* appropriately in each sentence below:

1. The bull stomped ☐ hoof.
2. ☐ a beautiful day.
3. I think ☐ too bad that he must leave.
4. Did the owl wink ☐ eye at you?
5. The monkey wrapped ☐ tail around the tree limb.

55

LOOKING BACK AND CHECKING UP

Using Capital Letters (page 7)

Rewrite the sentences below, using capital letters where they are needed:

1. joe and i plan to sail across the atlantic ocean to europe.
2. the mississippi river flows into the gulf of mexico.
3. my cousin in spain studies english in her school.
4. thousands of college students spend easter vacation at daytona beach, florida.
5. the aztecs of mexico were conquered by cortes, the spanish explorer.

Identifying Types of Listening (pages 8–14)

Match each type of listening below with its definition:

Marginal listening	Analytic listening
Attentive listening	Appreciative listening

1. Listening to hear whether information is complete and accurate
2. Listening in such a way that you hear only those things that interest you
3. Listening that encourages you to establish a certain mood or form mental images
4. Listening carefully so that you can remember what has been said

The Nature of Language (pages 16–17)

Make up two sentences using each word below. Be sure that the word has a different meaning in each sentence.

bread	rock	camp	straight	bag
rap	split	pad	cool	hip

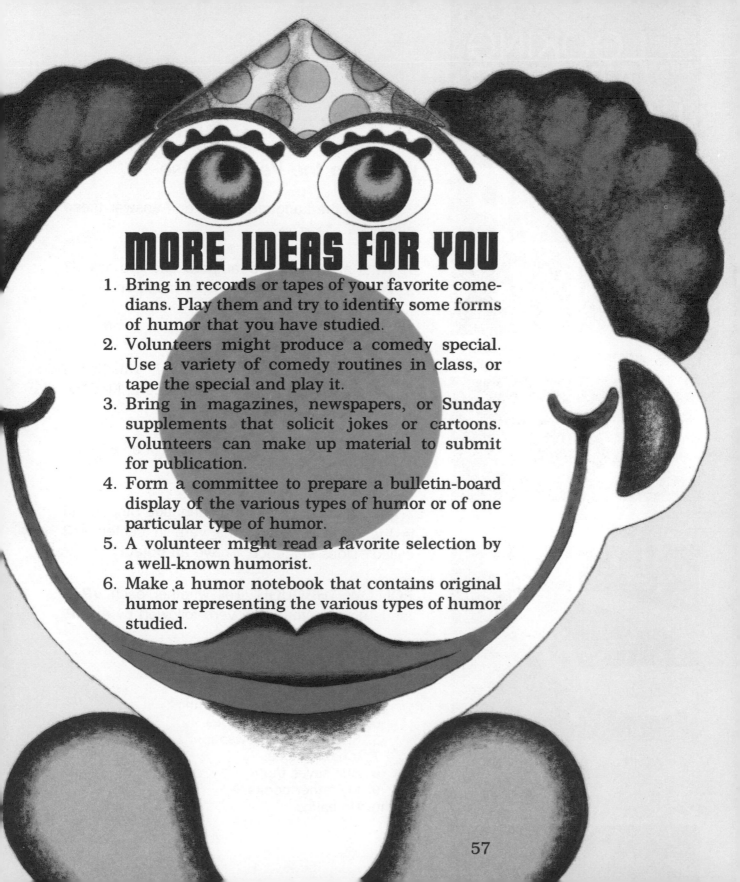

MORE IDEAS FOR YOU

1. Bring in records or tapes of your favorite comedians. Play them and try to identify some forms of humor that you have studied.

2. Volunteers might produce a comedy special. Use a variety of comedy routines in class, or tape the special and play it.

3. Bring in magazines, newspapers, or Sunday supplements that solicit jokes or cartoons. Volunteers can make up material to submit for publication.

4. Form a committee to prepare a bulletin-board display of the various types of humor or of one particular type of humor.

5. A volunteer might read a favorite selection by a well-known humorist.

6. Make a humor notebook that contains original humor representing the various types of humor studied.

1. The audience + laughed.

2. Joe Joker + told jokes.

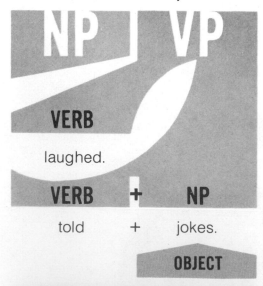

VERB

laughed.

VERB + NP

told + jokes.

OBJECT

THE BASIC SENTENCE

Words in the Verb Phrase

Look at the Language Strip and answer these questions:

1. What are words like *laughed* and *told* called?
2. What is the **VP** in sentence 1 made up of?

Sometimes the **VP** is made up of a verb.

3. In the sentence "Jokes are funny," what is the subject **NP**? Now look at sentence 2. Find the verb. What follows the verb?

Sometimes the **VP** is made up of a verb followed by an **NP**.

Look at the bottom of the Language Strip. What is the **NP** that follows the verb in sentence 2 called? Does sentence 1 have an **object**?

FOLLOW THROUGH. Tell whether each **VP** is made up of a verb or a verb followed by an **NP**.

1. I like jokes.
2. My brother collects cartoons.
3. We roar.
4. Our newspaper has comics.
5. My mother subscribes.
6. She likes our newspaper.
7. It has recipes.
8. She saves them.
9. My father cooks.
10. He bakes.

Study the **VP**'s in the Language Strip. How are the object **NP**'s like the subject **NP**'s you studied on pages 22-26?

NP's that are used as objects are made up of the same kinds of words that make up subject **NP**'s.

FOLLOW THROUGH. Tell whether the **VP** in each sentence is a verb or a verb followed by an **NP**.

1. Donna studied Ogden Nash.
2. He joined a magazine once.
3. His lines rhyme.
4. Some run on.
5. They snap suddenly.
6. He misspelled deliberately.
7. His poetry has humor.
8. His first book appeared early.
9. Readers enjoy him.
10. His poetry tickles everyone.

FOLLOW THROUGH. For each verb followed by an **NP** above, tell whether the **NP** is: (a) a common noun alone, (b) a proper noun, (c) a determiner followed by a noun, (d) a personal pronoun, or (e) an indefinite pronoun.

FOLLOW THROUGH. Copy each sentence below. Write *P* if the verb is followed by a personal pronoun and *I* if the verb is followed by an indefinite pronoun.

1. Marcia heard something.
2. Her brother heard it.
3. The noise scared them.
4. They gathered everything.
5. They saw nothing.

VERB + NP

1. People + enjoy comedians.

COMMON NOUN

2. They + watched Joe Joker.

PROPER NOUN

3. He + told many jokes.

DETERMINER + NOUN

4. We + studied him.

PERSONAL PRONOUN

5. He + pleased everyone.

INDEFINITE PRONOUN

NP + VP

VERB + NP

1. She + saw Joe.

2. Joe + saw her.

NP

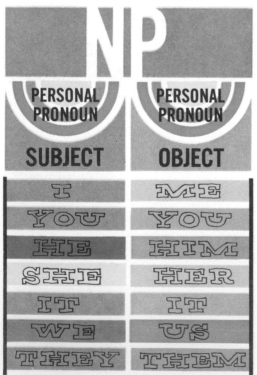

PERSONAL PRONOUN SUBJECT	PERSONAL PRONOUN OBJECT
I	ME
YOU	YOU
HE	HIM
SHE	HER
IT	IT
WE	US
THEY	THEM

FOLLOW THROUGH. Write five sentences using a verb alone in the **VP**, and five sentences using a verb followed by an **NP** in the **VP**.

Look at the basic sentences in the Language Strip.

1. Which pronoun form is used as the subject **NP** in sentence 1?
2. Which pronoun form is used as the object **NP** in sentence 2?

Now study the pronoun forms in the box in the Language Strip.

1. Which pronouns have the same form as subjects and objects?
2. Which pronouns have different forms as subjects and objects?

Most of the personal pronouns have one form when they are used as the subject and another form when they are used as the object.

FOLLOW THROUGH. Which personal pronoun should be used in each of the following sentences?

1. (He, Him) is a comedian.
2. That man tickles (I, me).
3. (We, Us) listen closely.
4. The comedian sees (she, her).
5. (They, Them) are friends.
6. He entertains (we, us).
7. The women watch (he, him).
8. He amuses (they, them).
9. (I, Me) sit still.
10. (She, Her) notices me.

Look at the Language Strip. Then answer these questions about the five basic sentences:

1. In each **VP** what is the word in italics a form of?
2. In each **VP** what is the form of *be* followed by?

   A **VP** may be made up of a form of *be* followed by an **NP**.

3. Look at the bottom of the Language Strip. What is the **NP** that follows *be* called?
4. Look at the complement **NP** in each of the basic sentences. How is the complement **NP** like the subject and object **NP**'s you studied earlier?

   NP's that are used as complements are made up of the same kinds of words that make up subject and object **NP**'s.

5. Look at sentence 4 again. What form of the personal pronoun is used after *be*?

   The subject form of a personal pronoun is used after a form of *be.*

FOLLOW THROUGH. Each of these sentences contains a form of *be* followed by an **NP**. Tell what kinds of words make up each complement **NP**.

1. Another star is Jackie Whacky.
2. I am a fan.
3. We are followers.
4. His audience was everybody.
5. His followers are we.
6. My brother is an admirer.
7. We were viewers.
8. The comic was a winner.

NP + VP

be + NP

1. His work + *was* pantomime.

2. His people + *are* Mexicans.

3. The men + *were* his friends.

4. An admirer + *am* I.

5. He + *is* somebody.

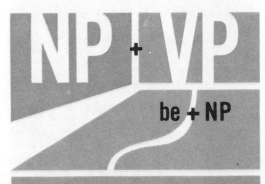

NP + VP

be + NP

was	pantomime.
are	Mexicans.
were	his friends.
am	I.
is	somebody.

COMPLEMENT

1. One man + became
   a piano player.

2. He + seemed
   a winner.

3. He + remained a star.

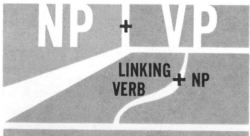

LINKING VERB	+ NP
became	a piano player.
seemed	a winner.
remained	a star.

COMPLEMENT

FOLLOW THROUGH. Write five sentences in which the **VP** is *be* followed by an **NP**.

The **VP** in a basic sentence sometimes contains another kind of word. Look at the three basic sentences in the Language Strip.

1. What kind of verbs are *became, seemed,* and *remained?*
2. What is each linking verb followed by?

   A **VP** may be made up of a **linking verb** followed by an **NP**.

3. Look at the bottom of the Language Strip. What is the **NP** that follows a linking verb called?

FOLLOW THROUGH. Write three sentences using linking verbs. Each sentence should have an **NP** as the complement in the **VP**.

FOLLOW THROUGH. Copy these sentences. Write *Be* if the **VP** contains a form of *be* and *LV* if the **VP** contains a linking verb.

1. Another entertainer was Sally Dally.
2. She became a star.
3. Many people were her admirers.
4. Her jokes are in this book.
5. Sally remains a legend.

FOLLOW THROUGH. Write these sentences. Underline each complement and tell whether it is a proper noun, a common noun alone, or a determiner followed by a noun.

1. Billy Ballyhoo became a cartoonist.
2. A syndicate was his publisher.
3. Many people were readers.
4. One follower was Jennie.
5. She remained a fan.

62

CHECK UP ON YOURSELF

A. Tell whether the **VP** in each sentence contains a verb or a verb followed by an **NP**.

1. That man worked hard.
2. He played piano.
3. He performed well.
4. He sang.
5. He ridiculed his nose.
6. People liked Nosy Parker.
7. They applauded him.
8. He responded.
9. His act cheered everyone.
10. That man entertained weekly.

B. In A, what kind of object appears in each sentence with a verb followed by an **NP**?

C. Tell whether the **VP** in each sentence below is made up of: (a) a linking verb followed by an **NP** or (b) a form of *be* followed by an **NP**.

1. Another comic is Fay Sunshine.
2. She became a contestant at 3.
3. Entertaining is everything to her.
4. Her songs are ballads usually.
5. The winner was she.

D. Describe the **NP** that is used as the complement in each sentence in C. Tell whether it is (a) a common noun alone, (b) a proper noun, (c) a determiner followed by a noun, (d) a personal pronoun, or (e) an indefinite pronoun.

SPEAKING

LISTEN TO THE SPEAKERS!

The people in the pictures above use speaking in a variety of ways and for many different purposes. They rely on speaking as a necessary part of their daily lives.

DISCUSS IT. Talk about answers to these questions:

1. Why is it important for a political candidate to speak effectively?
2. Who are some people you consider effective speakers?
3. What are some occupations that require an ability to speak effectively?
4. What are some characteristics of effective speakers?
5. Which of these characteristics do you need to improve in your own speaking ability?

IMPRESSIONS

Although all people use language to communicate, some people also choose to express their feelings and ideas in other ways. What means of expression are shown in the pictures? What materials does each of these persons use to express his or her ideas?

What kinds of messages can each of these persons express? How will each person's point of view toward people

Canadian National Film Board

and the world affect the messages he or she produces? Which
of these forms do you think would be most effective in giving
other people a new point of view on an important subject?
What other ways can you think of for people to express their
ideas and feelings without using words? Which way would
you choose to express a feeling or a belief that is important
to you? Why would you choose that one?

Quebec Government House

Preparing to Read

You will soon read a selection about Shirley Chisholm. Some words in it may not be familiar. Ten of them appear in bold letters in the sentences below. See whether you can match each word with its definition.

a. farming
b. not considered
c. take part
d. the smaller number
e. treated badly
f. become aware of
g. a phrase used to draw attention
h. order of importance
i. activities to bring about a special result
j. money given to provide for one's education

1. She was so successful that she was offered **scholarships.**
2. However, she was **rejected** for many jobs.
3. She came to **realize** that changes can be made.
4. Black members were **mistreated** by white members.
5. They weren't allowed to **participate.**
6. The money had been collected for her **campaign.**
7. Her **slogan** was "Fighting Shirley Chisholm—Unbought and Unbossed."
8. Mrs. Chisholm was assigned to an **agriculture** committee.
9. She speaks out for rights of all **minority** groups.
10. Education should be the number one **priority.**

THE STORY BEHIND THE LADY

Do you believe that people in politics will not be elected if they really say what they think? Then you should learn about Congresswoman Shirley Chisholm.

SHIRLEY CHISHOLM: THE LADY WHO SPEAKS OUT

Shirley Chisholm was born in 1924 in a section of New York City called Brooklyn. Her parents were working

68

people who had come to the United States from the West Indies. The family was very poor. For a time she lived with her grandmother on the island of Barbados because her parents could not afford to keep her with them. Her grandmother taught her that people must have the courage to speak out for the things they believe.

When Shirley returned to her parents' home in Brooklyn, they also taught Shirley to speak out for what she believed. Moreover, they encouraged her to obtain a good education.

She was so successful in school that she was offered scholarships from many colleges. She attended Brooklyn College and was graduated with high honors. However, she was rejected for many jobs. She knew that she was rejected for two reasons: she was a woman and she was black.

Mrs. Chisholm became a schoolteacher. Because she was interested in people's problems, she was asked to represent the people in many organizations. She soon came to realize that changes can be made in the system through politics. But women and blacks don't have much of a chance to be elected to political office.

Mrs. Chisholm remembered the early teachings of her grandmother. She decided to speak out for what she believed.

She joined the Democratic Club in Brooklyn. At that time, black members were mistreated by white members. They sat at the back of the room and weren't allowed to participate. Mrs. Chisholm spoke out against this practice. The club changed it. The men's club refused to give the women's club money for fund-raising activities. Mrs. Chisholm spoke out against this practice. The club changed it.

Mrs. Chisholm forced the Democratic Club leaders to change many other policies. Even so, the party leaders realized that she was a person who was trusted by the people. She became the first black woman ever elected to the New York State Assembly.

When it was time for congressional elections, Mrs.

Chisholm thought of all the changes she might make as a congresswoman. She tried to decide whether to run. One evening a man came to her door and handed her an envelope. Inside the envelope was $9.60. It had been collected for her campaign by people on welfare. She decided to run for Congress. Her slogan was "Fighting Shirley Chisholm—Unbought and Unbossed." After the votes had been counted, Fighting Shirley Chisholm became the first black woman ever to be elected to Congress.

Again Mrs. Chisholm remembered the teachings of her grandmother. She spoke out for what she believed. Congressmen who have served the longest are put on the best committees. Mrs. Chisholm was assigned to an agriculture committee. This committee had nothing to do with the problems of her people. She spoke out and was moved to a better committee. Now she is working to have people assigned to the committees they are best qualified for.

In 1972, many people in several states thought that Mrs. Chisholm would make a good president They liked her honesty, and they liked the way she openly expresses what she believes. She was nominated as one of the candidates for the Democrats to consider for the presidency You may know that George McGovern, a senator from South Dakota, won the nomination.

Shirley Chisholm is active as a congresswoman from New York. She speaks out for equal rights for women, the poor, and all minority groups. She believes that education is the most important way for people to secure equal rights. Read what Mrs. Chisholm has to say as she speaks out about education:

"Education should be the number one priority. Every black home today should be discussing with their youngsters the importance and need for education. I know there are homes where there isn't enough to eat, and the rats are running all over, and the water bugs are fighting for space with the children. Perhaps these things seem of more immediate importance than the question of education, but if the children are to escape them they must have an education.

70

"And you can escape them. The lives of many of us who have made it out of poverty prove that it is possible if you have the will. But you have got to realize that the world has no room for weaklings, and that it is only weaklings who give up in the face of obstacles."

H. T. Phillips

DISCUSS IT. See how well you read the selection by answering the following questions:

1. What lesson did Mrs. Chisholm learn as a child that was useful to her in politics?
2. Why are her sex and race considered political handicaps?
3. How did Mrs. Chisholm first become interested in politics?
4. What are some of the issues that she speaks against?
5. Why do both her friends and her foes respect her?
6. How does she believe that changes can be made in the system?
7. What incident helped her to decide to run for Congress?
8. How is Mrs. Chisholm elected when she represents mainly minority groups?
9. What is the meaning of her campaign slogan?
10. How does Mrs. Chisholm believe people can work themselves out of poverty?

How are commas used in these sentences?

1. Moreover, they encouraged her to obtain a good education.
2. However, she was rejected for many jobs.
3. You may know that George McGovern, a senator from North Dakota, won the nomination.

Which sentences contain words that lead the reader from one thought to another?

In which sentence do the words set off by commas give additional information about a person?

Words and word groups such as *moreover, however, as a result, therefore, first, second, third,* and *finally* are *transitionals.* Transitionals are usually set off from the rest of the sentence by a comma or commas.

Commas are used to set off a word or a word group that gives additional information about an item.

1. Shirley Chisholm a black woman was elected to Congress.
2. Moreover she was supported by many white voters.
3. Mrs. Chisholm who speaks out for her beliefs is changing many policies.
4. She is first of all concerned with the welfare of the poor and mistreated.
5. Therefore the people in her district support her.

using oral language

Sometimes in schools for actors, the teacher plans a situation. The actors fit themselves into the scene and begin to play their roles. Then the teacher creates an incident. The actors must produce a type of drama by basing their conversation and actions on the situation. Such acting is called *improvisation*.

The picture below might serve as a setting for improvisation. Some of the incidents that might be created are listed on the next page. Discuss ways in which actors might relate to these incidents. What other incidents might be created in this setting?

1. A lost child cries as he wanders up the aisle.
2. An elderly lady walks past the counter and faints.
3. Two customers begin to argue loudly over a piece of merchandise.

Divide into groups of five or six. Plan a setting that can be handled by as many actors. Also plan an incident that requires improvisation, but do not include the incident in the setting.

TELL IT. Exchange your setting with another group. As the second group dramatizes the roles of the characters, a member of your group should enter and create an incident. Members of the second group must react to the incident in conversation and actions.

DISCUSS IT. After each group has performed its improvisation, discuss the performance. The following questions might be considered:

1. What examples of improvisation were particularly strong?
2. Were dialogue and actions of all the actors consistent?
3. Were dialogue and actions of all the actors appropriate for the situation?
4. Did dialogue and actions appear to be natural?
5. What other reactions could the actors have made to the situations?

GROUP PLANNING

Notice the comments made by each person in the discussion below:

MIKE: Since we are the members of the food committee, it is our job to make arrangements for lunch at the picnic.

NANCY: Why did we have to get on this lousy committee?

MARGE: Well, there's nothing complicated about a picnic lunch. Just have everybody bring his own lunch.

PATTY: That's out! Mike's sack would be so heavy he couldn't carry it.

NANCY: I don't like sack lunches.

MIKE: Sack lunches are a good suggestion, Marge. We could also consider bringing some sliced lunch meat, cheese, tomatoes, lettuce, potato chips, and bread. We could split the cost.

NANCY: That's too much trouble.

PATTY: Let's have the picnic catered.

MARGE: We're just wasting time here. I've already told you that sack lunches are better.

NANCY: How do you always know what's best for everybody? I don't like sack lunches.

TOM: I think we have been given two excellent suggestions by both Marge and Mike. Does anyone else have another suggestion?

MIKE: Since there don't seem to be any other suggestions, we should discuss the two we have and vote for the one that seems better.

Match each person in the discussion with the role that you think he played in the discussion.

1. Mike	a. clown
2. Marge	b. peacemaker
3. Patty	c. dictator
4. Nancy	d. organizer
5. Tom	e. sniper

After discussing the five roles in class, write a definition of each.

TELL IT. Form a group of five and select a controversial subject. Each member of the group should select one of the five roles to play. Take turns discussing your topic with each member playing the role he chose. Class members should guess the role of each member. Some suggested topics for discussion are:

1. How can we make our room more attractive?
2. What is the appropriate dress for school?
3. What can the individual citizen do about pollution?
4. How can pupils our age earn money?
5. How should drug use be controlled?

74

Points of View

Often in a group discussion people react to statements rather than to the point of view being expressed. Only when you can identify and respond to a person's point of view can you hope to change his opinion.

Read each dialogue below. Then write the opposing points of view reflected by the statements.

1. JOHN: Nobody has a right to tell me what to wear to school.
   MARY: Some people take advantage of their freedom. They wear such weird clothes that they create a disturbance in class.
2. SUE: Citizens who don't vote in elections should be made to pay a fine.
   PAULA: Democracy gives us the right not to vote as well as the right to vote.
3. MARK: Citizens have a duty to report lawbreakers.
   BOB: Everyone should tend to his own affairs and allow others to do the same.

WRITE IT. Sometimes a point of view is dependent on the speaker's purpose. Compose a description of the place you live in for the purposes stated below. Be sure to use language appropriate for each situation.

1. You have moved to a new town. Compose a description of your new home for a friend who lived next door to you in your previous neighborhood.
2. Describe your home for a new friend from school.
3. Explain how the real-estate salesperson described the home to your father when the salesperson was trying to rent or sell it.
4. Describe your home the way you think the builder would describe it to another builder.

EDIT IT. Read your description and make sure you have remembered to use capital letters for:

1. Names of buildings and firms
2. Names of specific persons, pets, streets, cities, states, days, and months
3. Initials

Not only can you learn a person's point of view from his conversation, but also what kind of person he is. After reading the following dialogue, answer the questions below:

MR. JACOBS: Look at this report card! Another D! What have you been doing in class?

KEITH: I've done every assignment, Dad. I just can't seem to get them right.

MR. JACOBS: People don't get D's in classes where they do all the assignments. You're just lazy!

KEITH: I *have* done all the assignments, but I don't get good grades on the tests. I have trouble reading.

MR. JACOBS: Well, young man, you'd better start getting better grades on the tests and learning to read. Starting today you are not going out in the evenings except for weekends until you bring that D up to a B.

KEITH: But, Dad, report cards don't come out again for nine weeks! You can't ground me for more than two months!

MR. JACOBS: I can and I am. And what's more, if you don't have a B by then, I'll ground you for nine weeks after that.

KEITH: I don't really need punishment, Dad. I need help. I've worked hard in that class, but I just have trouble reading and writing. I think your punishment is unfair, and it won't help me to become any better in my lessons.

MR. JACOBS: Don't tell me how to handle my children! Get out those books and start studying, or you'll never have any social life.

1. From his conversation, what kind of person do you think Mr. Jacobs is?
2. What are the purposes behind his remarks?
3. What kind of person is Keith?
4. What are the purposes behind his remarks?
5. Will the purposes of either one be accomplished by their remarks? Why?

TELL IT. Choose a partner. Work together and compose a dialogue similar to the one above. Present the dialogue to the class. Ask class members to answer questions about your dramatization.

76

INTONATION

What does this cartoon tell you about communication?

"SHE ALWAYS WHISPERS. BUT DON'T HER FACE LOOK LIKE SHE'S *YELLIN'* AT YA?"

What message does the lady's facial expression communicate to the boys? Explain how our voices can say one thing and our facial expressions can say something else. What is meant by the expression "It wasn't what he said; it was the way he said it"?

Linguists tell us that the total meaning of a speaker's message can be shown by the following formula:

MESSAGE = 7% words + 38% voice + 55% face

The highness and lowness of your voice is called *pitch.*

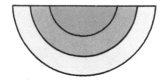

Stress on words or syllables gives meaning to what we say.

The breaks or pauses between words and word groups are called *juncture.*

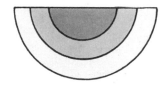

Say the words below as if the day were beautiful and sunny. Then say them as if the day were dreary and rainy.

What a day for a picnic!

In which situation did you make your voice sound high and light? In which situation did your voice sound low and draggy?

As you read each sentence below, emphasize the word in color by giving it more stress than the other words:

I didn't tear your book.
I didn't tear your book.
I didn't tear your book.
I didn't tear your book.
I didn't tear your book.

Explain how the sentences have different meanings although the words are the same.

How do these sentences differ in meaning?

1. Mr. Stone, our teacher was late.
2. Mr. Stone, our teacher, was late.

Notice where you pause as you read each sentence. What punctuation marks show you where to pause? Explain how the pauses affect the meaning of each sentence.

As you raise and lower your voice, make it go loud or soft, and pause to show meaning, you are using *intonation.* Intonation is made up of pitch, stress, and juncture. Linguists tell us that intonation is one of the strongest signaling systems to meaning in the English language. Punctuation marks in writing help you to know how the writer would have said the word if he were speaking.

Practice reading the following poem together. Use the appropriate intonation to communicate the meaning of the poem to your audience. Experiment with various voices in solo parts and small groups until you achieve the intonation that creates the effect that sounds best. Remember to read the words clearly and to keep together in the reading.

78

Daddy Fell into the Pond

Everyone grumbled. The sky was grey.
We had nothing to do and nothing to say.
We were nearing the end of a dismal day,
And there seemed to be nothing beyond,
      THEN
Daddy fell into the pond!

And everyone's face grew merry and bright,
And Timothy danced for sheer delight.
"Give me the camera, quick, oh quick!
He's crawling out of the duckweed." *Click!*

Then the gardener suddenly slapped his knee,
And doubled up, shaking silently,
And the ducks all quacked as if they were daft,
And it sounded as if the old drake laughed.

O, there wasn't a thing that didn't respond
      WHEN
Daddy fell into the pond!

Alfred Noyes

DISCUSS IT. Discuss the following questions:

1. How well did the group stay together?
2. How well did the subgroups perform their parts?
3. How could the reading have been improved?

Purposes Of Speaking

Speeches are sometimes classified according to their purpose. Some types of speeches are: giving directions, demonstrating, persuading, entertaining, and informing.

"Daddy Fell into the Pond" from *Daddy Fell into the Pond and Other Poems* by Alfred Noyes, Copyright 1952 Sheed and Ward Inc., New York.

Select a topic on which you will plan to talk for three to five minutes. Follow these steps in planning your speech:

1. Be sure that your topic is limited enough to be covered in three to five minutes.
2. Decide the purpose of your talk, and plan how you will accomplish this purpose.
3. Organize your speech, making sure that you can deliver it within the assigned time limit.
4. Decide whether an object, a diagram, or another visual aid would help you to accomplish the purpose of your speech.
5. Plan a beginning that will make the class want to listen to what you have to say. Plan an ending that leaves the audience with a good impression of your talk. Do not end by saying, "Well, I guess that's all."

Before speeches are presented, develop with your classmates a checklist to use in evaluating each speech. Perhaps the following model will give you some ideas:

Each of the items below will be rated: 1 = excellent; 2 = good; 3 = fair; 4 = poor.

a. Accomplishment of purpose
b. Organization of speech (stayed on topic, presented information in logical sequence)
c. Beginning and ending of speech
d. Delivery of speech (voice, posture, gestures, intonation)
e. Observance of time limit

TELL IT. Present your speech to the class.

DISCUSS IT. Discuss each speech in terms of the evaluation checklist. Determine which three received the highest rating for each speech.

PANTOMIME

How can you communicate a message by using your body but not your voice? Demonstrate how you could ask the class to be quiet without using your voice. How can you say good-bye to someone without using your voice?

What messages are communicated by pantomime in these pictures?

Communicating a message by using facial expressions and body movements but not your voice is called *pantomime.*

On a piece of paper, note something that one person can act out alone. Exchange papers with a classmate. Take turns acting out suggestions, and let members of the class guess what is being pantomimed.

The following topics might give you some ideas for subjects to pantomime:

1. Paddling a canoe
2. Jumping rope
3. Washing windows
4. Climbing a ladder
5. Combing hair before a mirror
6. Hanging wash on a clothesline
7. Raking leaves
8. Icing a cake
9. Cutting down a tree
10. Playing tennis

Divide into groups ranging in size from five to ten members. For your group, select a fairy tale, a story, a play, or a wise saying and dramatize it without using words. Or your group might prefer to compose an original production to dramatize. After each dramatization, your classmates will explain what the production communicated to them.

Productions may be evaluated by using the following guidelines:

1. Was the selection suitable for production?
2. Did actors portray the characters effectively?
3. Were props used to make the dramatization clear?
4. Did actors use facial expressions and other body movements as effective substitutes for words?
5. Was the overall effect of the production poor, good, or excellent?

The Way Your Language Works

One of the techniques employed by speakers to change the point of view of their audience is the use of emotional words. Read the statements below and tell which makes you feel pleasant, which makes you feel unpleasant, and which makes you feel neutral.

1. Maria is frugal.
2. Maria is thrifty.
3. Maria is stingy.

Words that make you feel pleasant or unpleasant are called *emotional words*. Words to which you have not attached emotional meanings are called *neutral words*.

82

FOLLOW THROUGH. Classify each of the words below as pleasant, unpleasant, or neutral:

ugly	acquaintance	slimy	love	winner
happy	weird	capable	slippery	beautiful

DISCUSS IT. Each pair of statements below may have been made by two speakers to describe the same event. Tell which remark reflects disapproval; approval.

1. a. Nora's hair is long.
   b. Nora's hair is stringy.
2. a. Sara is really humorous.
   b. Sara is a smart aleck.
3. a. Sam is quiet and reserved.
   b. Sam is a drag.
4. a. Tony is a skillful boxer.
   b. Tony is a bully.
5. a. Alan is large and powerful.
   b. Alan is a fat slob.

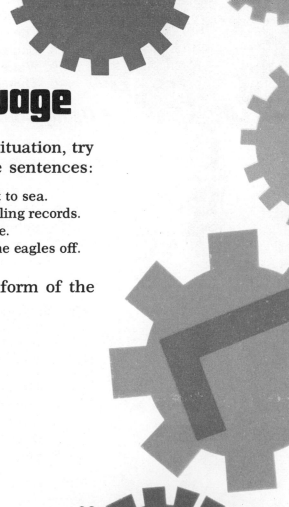

Using Your Language

In the classroom, and in any formal situation, try to speak and write carefully. Study these sentences:

1. The wind blew (not "blowed") the ship out to sea.
2. The merchants broke (not "busted") all selling records.
3. They drew (not "drawed") crowds of people.
4. The traders drove (not "driv" or "druv") the eagles off.

FOLLOW THROUGH. Use the appropriate form of the word in parentheses for each sentence.

1. Limbs (break) off trees during the storm.
2. People (drive) through lashing waters.
3. One driver (draw) up to a cattle shed.
4. The doors (blow) back and forth.
5. The wind (drive) him into the shed.
6. The driver (draw) the doors closed.
7. The gale force (break) the door hinges.
8. Again the doors (blow) open.
9. The girl (draw) in her breath.
10. Finally the storm (blow) out.

CHECK UP ON YOURSELF

Vocabulary (page 68)

Substitute one of the following words for each of the expressions in italics below:

scholarship   minority   rejected   participate   campaign
agriculture   realize   priority   mistreated   slogan

1. When did she *become aware of* what he was doing?
2. He *treated* his horse *badly*.
3. She was asked to *take part* in the contest.
4. The committee *refused to consider* his application.
5. My cousin is studying *farming*.
6. She selected a catchy campaign *phrase to attract attention*.
7. The college gave a *financial award* to the student.
8. Education was her first *order of importance*.
9. White people are in the *smaller number* world wide.
10. The candidate planned his *activities to be elected*.

Using Commas (page 71)

Copy these sentences and use commas where they are needed:

1. As a result we were late.
2. Mr. Leonard Martin conductor of the local symphony orchestra was there.
3. Moreover he enjoyed the reception.
4. Finally we all went home.
5. Mr. Sellers who went to Peru sent me this present.

Identifying Group Roles (pages 73–74)

Tell which role in the first column is described by the words in the second column.

1. Clown
2. Peacemaker
3. Dictator
4. Organizer
5. Sniper

a. Helps group to understand the problem
b. Seeks attention by trying to be funny
c. Criticizes everyone else's ideas
d. Tries to force his ideas on the group
e. Helps to maintain pleasant atmosphere

84

Points of View (page 75)

Pretend that your cat has had ten kittens. Write a description of the kittens for each of these situations:

1. You are complaining to a friend because you must take care of the kittens.
2. You are describing them to a friend who does not know much about cats or other animals.
3. You are writing an ad to find homes for the kittens.

Characterization (page 76)

List three characteristics you believe would apply to the person who said the following:

I had a lousy time at school today. But that's not unusual. The teachers always pick on me. So do the other kids. I can't wait to get out of school. Nobody will push me around then.

Drawing Inferences (pages 82–83)

The following pairs of statements describe the same event. Tell which remark reflects approval or disapproval.

1. a. Angela was the life of the party.
   b. Angela was a show-off at the party.
2. a. Tyrone is high point man on our basketball team.
   b. Tyrone hogs all the shots on our basketball team.
3. a. Cindy is outgoing and friendly.
   b. Cindy is a loudmouth.

Using Your Language (page 83)

Use the appropriate form of each word in parentheses as you write the sentences.

1. We (drive) to the lake last week.
2. The artist (draw) a picture of my boat.
3. Jack (blow) on the neck of the bottle.
4. My dog (break) my mother's vase.
5. We (draw) the number from the hat.

LOOKING BACK AND CHECKING UP

Classifying Listening Activities (pages 9–14)

List each of the listening activities below under one of these major types of listening:

a. Marginal   c. Analytical
b. Attentive   d. Appreciative

1. Listening to a guitar solo
2. Listening to an assignment
3. Listening for propaganda techniques in a speech
4. Listening to someone give you directions
5. Listening to the radio while studying

Identifying Types of Humor (pages 37–46)

Tell which of the items below describes each of the following types of humor:

    ridicule   put-down   put-on   pun   wisecrack

1. Makes someone else an object for laughter
2. A play on words
3. A remark that depends on deliberate misinterpretation of a previous statement
4. An absurd or impossible response to a question
5. A cleverly worded and humorous insult

Writing Direct Quotations (pages 40–41)

Write each sentence correctly.

1. I am going home now he said.
2. The driver said please step to the rear.
3. When you want to leave she said please let me know.
4. Please put the book on the table he directed.
5. Beverly said it's time to eat.

Using Homophones (page 43)

For each word below, write another with the same pronunciation:

1. maize	3. cede	5. gate	7. stare	9. idle
2. morning	4. hair	6. ball	8. foul	10. fair

MORE IDEAS FOR YOU

1. Prepare and demonstrate a pantomime to the class. Ask them to explain what you are dramatizing.

2. Read a book about a well-known politician. Present a report about the politician to your class.

3. Organize two teams of five members each to play charades. Each team should select five titles of books, songs, or movies and write them on slips of paper. Each player draws a slip from the opposite team. Then he acts out the words in the title for his team to guess. If the team guesses the title in two minutes or less, they score a point. If they don't, the other team gets the point. When all ten players have had a turn, the points are totaled. The team with the most points wins.

4. Collect cartoons with captions that show good examples of pitch, stress, or juncture. Use the cartoons to prepare a bulletin-board display on intonation.

5. Choose a library selection appropriate for choral reading. Organize a choral group willing to practice until the reading sounds professional. Record on a tape recorder until you get a good reading. Play the tape for your own class and other classes in the school that express an interest.

6. Select editorials, feature stories, and letters to the editor from newspapers. Try to state in one sentence the point of view of each writer.

7. Form a group and practice giving a choral reading. Present your selection to the class either as a live group or on tape.

1. The speaker + was witty.

2. People + were attentive.

3. She + is clever.

THE BASIC SENTENCE

More Words in the Verb Phrase

What kind of words make up the **VP** in the basic sentence? You have discovered that the **VP** may be made up of:

1. A verb

   Joe stood.

2. A verb followed by an **NP**

   He made a speech.

3. A form of *be* followed by an **NP**

   The speaker was Paul Brooks.

4. A linking verb followed by an **NP**

   He became a printer.

Look at this example of a form of *be* followed by an **NP**: *The speaker was Paul Brooks.* Now look at the Language Strip. In sentences 1, 2, and 3, what word follows a form of *be* in the **VP**? What kind of words are *witty, attentive,* and *clever*?

A **VP** may be made up of a form of *be* followed by an **adjective**.

FOLLOW THROUGH. Tell whether each **VP** is a form of *be* followed by an **NP** or a form of *be* followed by an adjective.

1. Mr. Jones is our neighbor.
2. I am busy.
3. They were cousins.
4. We are friendly.
5. Hank was cautious.

Look at the Language Strip. In the **VP** in each basic sentence, what kind of verb does the adjective follow?

A **VP** may be made up of a linking verb followed by an adjective.

Besides *become, seem,* and *remain,* other linking verbs are: *feel, smell, taste, appear, look, sound.*

FOLLOW THROUGH. Tell whether the **VP** is made up of a form of *be* followed by an adjective or a linking verb followed by an adjective.

1. The woman felt ill.
2. The kittens were tiny.
3. It smelled bad.
4. The rocks are huge.
5. He appeared unhappy.

On page 23 you saw how nouns change their forms to show more than one. In each set of boxed sentences, three persons or things are being compared. What happens to the adjectives?

1. What suffixes are added to the plain form of *proud* to show comparison?
2. What words are used with the plain form of *cautious* to show comparison?
3. What different words are used to show the comparison of *good*?

FOLLOW THROUGH. Write the forms of comparison of each of these adjectives:

1. hot	3. witty	5. small	7. careful
2. bad	4. much	6. many	8. patient

NP + VP

LINKING VERB + Adj

1. One man + became sleepy.

2. He + seemed ill.

3. He + remained quiet.

1
Ellen is proud.
Carol is prouder.
Roberta is proudest.

2
Jim is cautious.
Bob seems more cautious.
John seems most cautious.

3
This story is good.
That one is better.
The third one is best.

NP + VP

be + ADVERBIAL OF PLACE

1. Bella + is there.

2. Bella + is on the platform.

NP + VP

be + Adv_p

is   there.

ADVERB

is   on the platform.

PREPOSITIONAL PHRASE

PREPOSITION + NP

on   the platform.

OBJECT OF PREPOSITION

You've discovered that an **NP** or an adjective can follow a form of *be* in the **VP**. Look at the Language Strip.

1. In sentence 1 what word in the **VP** tells where Bella is?
2. In sentence 2 what words tell where she is?
3. What are *there* and *on the platform* called?
4. What kind of word does each **adverbial of place** follow?

Sometimes the **VP** is made up of a form of *be* followed by an adverbial of place. An adverbial of place tells *where.*

Look at the bottom of the Language Strip.

1. In which sentence is the adverbial of place a single word called an **adverb**?
2. In which sentence is the adverbial of place a **prepositional phrase**? In a prepositional phrase, what is the **NP** that follows the preposition called?

An adverbial of place may be an adverb or a prepositional phrase.

Here are some prepositions used in adverbials of place:

above	behind	beyond	into	over
against	below	down	near	through
along	beside	from	off	toward
at	between	in	on	under

FOLLOW THROUGH. Find each adverbial of place in the **VP**. Tell whether it is an adverb or a prepositional phrase.

1. The books are on the shelf.

90

2. They were here.
3. One is in the library.
4. It was at the back.
5. I am behind the desk.

Look at sentences 1 and 2 in the Language Strip.

1. In sentence 1a, what is the **VP** made up of?
2. In sentence 1b, what has been added to the **VP**? What does the adverbial tell?
3. In sentence 2a, what is the **VP** made up of? In sentence 2b, what has been added to the **VP**? What does the adverbial tell?

> An adverbial of place sometimes appears in the **VP** when the **VP** is a verb or a verb followed by an **NP**.

The same generalization is true of different kinds of adverbs. Find the adverbs in the **VP**'s in sentences 3, 4, and 5 in the Language Strip.

1. In sentence 3, what does the adverb *slowly* tell?
2. What do we call adverbials that tell *how* or in what manner something is done?
3. Look at this sentence: *He is slow.* To what kind of word do we add *-ly* to produce *slowly,* an adverbial of manner?
4. In sentence 4, what does the adverb *well* tell? Are all adverbials of manner made by adding *-ly* to an adjective?
5. In sentence 5, what kind of word group is the adverbial of manner?

> Adverbials that tell how are called **adverbials of manner.** An adverbial of manner may be an adverb or a prepositional phrase.

NP + VP

1. a. She + spoke.
   b. She + spoke from the platform.

2. a. He + hit the ball.
   b. He + hit the ball far.

3. He + spoke slowly.
4. He + spoke well.

5. He + chose his words with care.

ADVERBIAL OF MANNER

NP + VP

1. We + leave tomorrow.

2. He + spoke at noon.

ADVERBIAL OF TIME

1. Jill arrived early.
   Emma arrived earlier.
   Becky arrived earliest.

2. Bill spoke intelligently.
   José spoke more intelligently.
   Willie spoke most intelligently.

3. Mr. Dodd speaks well.
   Mr. White speaks better.
   Ms. Whiling speaks best.

FOLLOW THROUGH. Find the adverbial of manner in each **VP**. Is it an adverb or a prepositional phrase?

    1. The child cried bitterly.
    2. A police officer stopped her with a smile.
    3. The girl told her story well.
    4. She lost her mother somehow.
    5. The girl took the cone with pleasure.

Find the adverbials in sentences 1 and 2 in the Language Strip.

1. What does the adverbial *tomorrow* tell? What kind of word is *tomorrow*?
2. What does the adverbial *at noon* tell? What kind of word group is *at noon*?

Adverbials that tell *when* are called **adverbials of time**. An adverbial of time may be an adverb or a prepositional phrase.

FOLLOW THROUGH. Is the adverbial of time in each **VP** an adverb or a prepositional phrase?

    1. The polly squawked at noon.
    2. It wanted lunch then.
    3. Mrs. Grundy fed him late.
    4. He screeched during the afternoon.
    5. He quieted at night.

Like adjectives, adverbs can show comparison.

1. What suffixes are added to the plain form of *early* to show comparison?
2. What words are used with the plain form of *intelligently* to show comparison?
3. What different words are used to show the comparison of *well*?

92

FOLLOW THROUGH. Write the forms of comparison of each of these adverbs:

1. far
2. fast
3. high
4. sweetly
5. little
6. much
7. quickly
8. late

FOLLOW THROUGH. Copy the **VP** from each sentence. Tell whether the adverbial is an adverbial of place, manner, or time.

1. Dwight D. Eisenhower made speeches during World War II.
2. Most of the speeches came from his head.
3. He spoke extemporaneously.
4. Staff officers listened attentively.
5. He delivered one speech before Congress.

FOLLOW THROUGH. Write six sentences: two containing adverbials of place, two containing adverbials of manner, and two containing adverbials of time.

CHECK UP ON YOURSELF

A. Tell whether the **VP** in each sentence is made up of a form of *be* followed by an adjective or a linking verb followed by an adjective.

1. Pantomime is popular.
2. A Frenchman became successful.
3. His Bip remains famous.
4. Bip is white-faced.
5. His motions are silent.

B. Copy the **VP** from each sentence below. Tell whether the adverbial is an adverbial of place, manner, or time.

1. One comic appears on television.
2. He uses pantomime frequently.
3. "The Silent Spot" is in his act.
4. He uses gestures meaningfully.
5. He times his gestures well.

UNIT 4

THE LANGUAGE OF FEELINGS

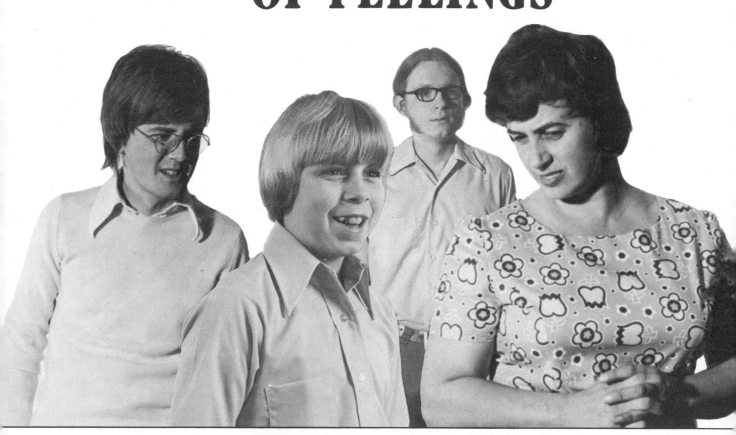

FEELINGS AND FACIAL EXPRESSIONS

What feeling does the expression of the young boy at the left of the picture show? the expression of the girl in the right foreground? the woman in the left foreground? the older woman to the right of center? the other persons in the group? What do you think they were seeing as the picture was taken? After you have made a guess, look at the bottom of the next page to see whether you guessed correctly.

All of us express strong feelings through our facial expressions. But the photograph indicates that facial expressions are not accurate clues to the type of strong feeling being expressed.

Why is it important for us to express our feelings accurately? What are some ways that we do express our emotions? All ways of expressing feelings are forms of communication. As you study this unit, you will learn how to use the language of feelings more effectively.

The persons in the picture were witnessing a murder in the street.

IMPRESSIONS

Often writers compare their feelings to things in nature because nature, like people, has many different moods. Think about the moods of the scenes below. Which moods match feelings that you have had?

Suppose you had a machine that could transport you to any mood you wanted. Which of these places would you choose if you were sad and wanted to be cheered up? If you were upset and wanted to think about how to solve a problem, where would you go? Would you choose the same place or a

different one if you were angry and wanted nature's mood to match your own? What other feelings might make you want to use your machine to visit one of these places? What things in the pictures helped you decide?

WHAT'S IN A NAME?

The following selection is about a boy your age or a little older. As you read the selection, notice the different kinds of feelings that are mentioned. Notice also what causes the feelings and how they are expressed.

HENRY 3

"All right," I told him. "I'm a hundred and fifty-four percent." By then, everything hurt. And the only way to keep him from hammering at me, at my ear, at my neck, at the side of my head, was to let him into the biggest secret there is about me.

He stopped hitting me, at least. "You're a hundred and fifty-four percent normal!" He didn't move from where he sat on the top of my chest. But his mouth, open full and pulling for air, turned into a smile. "Where'd you ever get all that I.Q.?"

I found the collar of my T-Shirt where it was ripped and wiped the blood away from under my nose. "It's just the I.Q. I happen to have, that's all, and the thing is," I whispered with what breath I had left, "you won't tell anyone, will you?"

"Why not?" He shifted to the rear and made himself comfortable on my stomach. He seemed to admire the sight of me. "You must be a natural born genius."

"I don't know about that. All I'm asking is for you not to spread it around Crestview, the percent I am."

"Why not?"

I lay there in the drive that led up to the empty school and I rolled my head in the white gravel. There was no way I could tell him, why not. Without going back, way back to the very beginning.

To begin with, I don't come from anywhere. I was born in a lower berth of the Atchison, Topeka and Santa Fe Railroad about an hour outside of Flagstaff, Arizona. Ever since, I've lived outside a half dozen other places all the way from Seattle, Washington, to Easton, Pennsylvania. That was on account of my Dad. He was forever getting a better job somewhere else, with the company he's always worked for.

Wherever we lived I was alone, mostly. That was on account of me. I'm smart. When I read a page in a book I can't forget it. Explain something to me and I catch on quick. I like school. Mostly I'm at the top of my class.

But it's no great help in making friends, moving so much and being smart. The truth is I never did have a best friend except for three weeks once, a kid by the name of Paco Gibson in Berkeley, California. That broke up when I got appointed crossing guard for the fourth grade, which was Paco's job, because I had higher marks.

I couldn't help it. There may be some who can manage how smart they are. Not me. You hear that whiz kids are getting popular and how brains are all the fad now on account of outer space. But it's never worked out for me. No one cheers the A's I get on my report card. Or rushes in to pal with an example, when that's what the teacher points me out to be. Hardly anybody wants to hang out with a guy who keeps showing him up all the time. Maybe it's my fault, the way I handle things.

This time it was going to be different. This time we were going to do something about it, about me. Because Crestview, outside of New York City, was the end of the line for us. Dad was in the Home Office of his company now with a chance to make Vice-President. And Crestview was going to be the first permanent home I ever had, for five years at least. I talked it over with Ma that maybe I'd get along better, now we'd arrived, if I laid off at least being so smart. In school, especially. Ma thought it might help, just to get me started.

That was the idea I had, that first day in Crestview. But it was nothing I could explain to the guy who was sitting on top of me.

He was kept in after class that first day for setting off a paper airplane during social studies. Miss Dokstra, the teacher of the eighth grade, set him to work in the back of the room copying some sentence a hundred and fifty times while she gave me an aptitude test.

That's what usually happens in a new place. They hand you this quiz with boxes and circles and words to fill in. Considering all the different schools I've been in, I'm used to them. I let myself go, since the score you make is private.

Once or twice, when she was marking my test, Miss Dokstra looked up at me with a surprised nod. Tired as she seemed, the way you find most teachers, she had a nice smile with a dimple. By the time she came to the end she was running a pencil through her hair like it was a one tooth comb. "From the records you brought, I expected something special. But this," she said, "this is about as good a performance as we've ever seen in Crestview."

He delivered his sentences just then, this other fellow. Miss Dokstra told him he could leave.

"I really don't think I ought to keep this from you," she turned back when we were alone. "It's against regulations. But the way it scores is one hundred and fifty-four percent." She was as pleased as if I'd been handed to her for a present.

We left the school together and Miss Dokstra promised I was going to find Crestview very enjoyable. I made the remark I certainly hoped so and watched her stoop into her Volkswagen, the only car still in the parking lot.

That's when he showed up again, the one who was in class with us. He came out from behind a corner of the school. I was certainly glad to see him, anyone who'd wait around just for the chance to meet me. But after the remark he'd heard from Miss Dokstra, about my performance, all he wanted to talk about was my I.Q. He was

100

excited to find out how much brighter I was than anyone else in Crestview. What'd I score? That's all he kept asking. I wasn't going to tell him, not when the whole idea was to keep it secret. I tried to get away. He thought I was brushing him off. That's what did it.

I've had my share of fights. My best hold is sort of a half nelson where you get a guy's arm behind his back. Once you do you can force it up to his neck and practically wreck him. I couldn't even find this one's arm to grab onto, the size of him and the speed he had and my power.

And that's how I came to be dug into the sharp white pebbles of the driveway with him on top asking me, why not?

"For the simple reason," I told him, "it'll ruin me here if anyone finds out."

"I wouldn't say that. Myself, I'm really glad to meet you." Whenever he moved, it felt as though my ribs were caving in. "I'm Fletcher Larkin." He put out his hand. I thought it was to help me up. But after a couple of shakes he sat where he was. "How about you?"

"I'd just as soon get up."

"I mean your name."

I twisted away from the rock that was wedged into my back. "Henry."

"Henry what?"

"Henry Three."

"What kind of last name is that?"

At least he was being sociable. No matter how I felt, my left shoulder, and the bruise on my right knee, and the weight in my jaw, the best thing was to get on the right side of Fletcher Larkin. Maybe he was someone who'd keep a secret. "It isn't any last name," I explained. "It's just that my grandfather was Henry. And Dad, he's Henry Lovering, Junior. I'm Henry Three."

"Henry Third, you mean."

"Not me. Henry Third's some character out of Shakespeare or he's a king with a beard. It gives you the wrong idea. I don't want to spread the notion I'm proud of my-

101

self. Three's good enough. With the American number."
I wrote it in the air. "Henry 3."

"Then all I want to tell you, Henry Three, is that I'm sorry I slugged you." He swung off me and sat on his heels in the lawn that bordered the drive. "It's only that I couldn't let you walk out on me. Not the first day you show up here. You don't know me well enough for that."

With the weight of him gone, big as he was, everything was a lot easier except to understand Fletcher Larkin. "How long does someone have to know you, I mean before they walk out on you?"

"Well, it depends," Fletcher said, "on the individual. But with your I.Q. it shouldn't be too long, you know, before you size things up. I give you a couple of days, maybe, before you never want to see me again."

"Maybe you're wrong." I sat up in the gravel and spoke to him as sincerely as I could. "As long as you're sorry about what happened, I certainly don't want to be the one to keep up any hard feelings. You're the first guy I've met in Crestview, I mean to have anything to do with. And far as I'm concerned, I came here wanting to be friendly."

I don't know why Larkin thought that was so funny, the laugh it gave him. "Not with me?"

"I wouldn't say that?"

"You don't even know me."

"Well, aside from the beating you handed out, you seem all right. Offhand, I'd say you looked fine."

"Me?" Fletcher asked. He searched around till he found a blade of grass that suited him and he chewed on it, studying me. "You know, maybe you are different, Henry Three. Maybe with you, it could work out."

"What?"

"Well, you mentioned being friendly."

"I wouldn't like anything better."

Fletcher shook his head in surprise. "You're the only one I ever had a battle with who took it that way. And when you consider this is the second year I've put in with Dokstra, in the eighth grade," he blew out the piece of grass, "it might be a good idea if, you know, I did team up with a brain. So it's fine with me, too, Henry Three."

"Well, good." The way it hurt all over, that didn't matter anymore, long as there was the chance of keeping the truth about me quiet. I crawled out of the gravel and sat where it was softer, at least, on the grass. "Is there anything I can do for you?" I asked Larkin.

"No." It startled him, the question did. "Not that I can think of."

"Well, if there's anything you ever need that I can lend you a hand with, just let me know."

"Thanks."

"Me, though, long as we're being friendly, I had in mind to ask you to keep quiet about my percent. Just not to mention it."

"Where'd be the fun of that?" Fletcher asked. "I mean that was the thought I had when I heard Dokstra talking to you. I couldn't help think of the shock you were going to hand this crowd, the kids they got running around here."

"You're not going to tell them?"

"Sure I am. First thing tomorrow morning. Wait'll you see their faces!" Larkin went pop-eyed to give me the effect.

"You can't!" I told him.

"I sure can."

"Not if we're going to be friendly."

"Just a second." Larkin came to one knee and rubbed a hand around the back of his neck. "Is that what it depends on? Me promising you that I'll shut up?"

"Well, sort of. That's what I had in mind."

"Then we're quits." Fletch came to his feet. He looked around and went to pick up his books that lay in the gravel road. "I don't know what kind of a guy you are. Right off, you seem a lot different from the rest of the bunch here in Crestview. But me, I don't shut up about anything. And I don't give promises just to make a friend. So the both of us, Henry Three, we're quits."

"Then all I'm asking you, Larkin, is to do me a favor. Do you have to tell them?"

"No." He kept from starting down the driveway. "I don't see why you're so Federal dead set against anyone hearing your percent. If it was me, with any kind of an I.Q. like that, brother! I'd put it out over Channel Five. But if that's the way you feel about it," he shrugged, "I don't have to tell them. I don't have to do anything. I'm just not making any promises."

"Look, Larkin," I stopped him for just another second. "Please."

"It was good to meet you, Henry Three." Fletcher swung one finger at me. "I'll be seeing you around."

I watched the square back of him going away, down the road that led to the street below. He turned light and then dark through the late afternoon shadows of the trees along the block. Then he turned a corner and was gone, Fletcher Larkin, some guy I never knew before, who all of a sudden my whole future depended on.

Joseph Krumgold

DISCUSS IT. Discuss the following questions about the types of feelings appearing in the selection:

1. How would you describe Henry 3's physical feelings at the beginning of the selection?
2. What unpleasant feelings did Henry 3 have about himself?
3. What caused Henry 3's unpleasant feelings about himself?
4. In which paragraph does Henry 3 explain why his classmates don't like him?
5. How can this selection be used to support the idea that happiness depends on the way you feel about yourself?

Notice the words in bold letters:

1. By then, everything **hurt**.
2. He shifted to the rear and made himself **comfortable** on my stomach.

104

What feeling is described in sentence 1? in sentence 2? What sense is involved in the feelings?

What are your five senses? What are some words used to describe feelings received through the senses? Since you receive feelings through your five senses, many of the words you use to describe your feelings are words of the senses.

FOLLOW THROUGH. Below are fifty words of the senses. Across the top of your paper, write: *Touch, Taste, Smell, Hearing,* and *Sight.* Under each heading list the sensory words that fit into each group.

aroma	spicy	slippery	quack	biting
salty	shiny	putrid	tart	silky
furry	incense	sugary	knock	echo
deodorant	chilly	sparkling	stench	twinkle
whistle	peppery	scent	drone	heavy
observe	sticky	limp	notice	tangy
fragrant	odor	moan	chime	chant
gleam	blur	bumpy	flavor	appearance
tingle	thud	image	blare	vision
fumes	gingery	perfume	warm	bitter

FOLLOW THROUGH. Think of a time when you had strong feelings. You may have been very happy, sad, angry, discouraged, frightened, or proud. List words of the senses that describe the event and your feelings.

A pupil who had observed a neighbor's house burn wrote these notes:

dark night, bright sky, bitter taste, heavy smoke, shrill sirens, shouting, excitement, quiet family, sadness

Using notes on the sensory observations of the fire, the pupil wrote the following paragraph:

One dark night there was a bright orange glow dancing in the sky behind my house. As I walked into the backyard, the bitter taste of heavy smoke formed in my nose and throat. Bright flames covered my friend's home. Sirens screamed, firemen shouted, and people milled around in an air of excitement. My friend and his family watched in silence as their house burned. I felt sad.

105

WRITE IT. Using your notes as a guide, write a paragraph describing the impressions you experienced.

EDIT IT. Read your paragraph to be sure all notes are included. Check your vocabulary to see whether you have used the sensory words that will best help the reader to understand your feelings.

Check also to see whether you have used the right punctuation mark following an introductory word:

1. Help! The house is on fire.
2. Ouch! A spark hit my arm.
3. Well, it didn't really hurt.

Words like *help, ouch,* and *well* often begin sentences. Sometimes they are used to show strong feeling. Which independent words above show strong feeling? What mark follows each?

DISCUSS IT. Read your paragraph to the class. Notice which paragraphs seem to be most descriptive. Talk about why some are more descriptive than others.

USING COLOR WORDS

Notice how colors can cause various feelings:

What Is Purple?

Time is purple
Just before night
When most people
Turn on the light——
But if you don't it's
A beautiful sight.
Asters are purple,
There's purple ink.
Purple's more popular
Than you think. . . .

"What Is Purple?" copyright © 1961 by Mary Le Duc O'Neill from the book *Hailstones and Halibut Bones.* Reprinted by permission of Doubleday & Company, Inc.

It's sort of a great
Grandmother to pink.
There are purple shadows
And purple veils,
Some ladies purple
Their fingernails.
There's purple jam
And purple jell
And a purple bruise
Next day will tell
Where you landed
When you fell.
The purple feeling
Is rather put-out
The purple look is a
Definite pout.
But the purple sound
Is the loveliest thing
It's a violet opening
In the spring.

Mary O'Neill

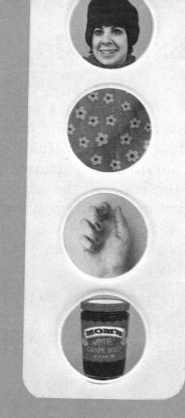

DISCUSS IT. Discuss the following questions about the poem:

1. What feelings are expressed in the poem?
2. What is the purple feeling stated in the poem?
3. What is the purple look?
4. What is the purple sound?
5. What other feelings do you associate with purple?

WRITE IT. Write a paragraph or a poem that expresses your feelings about a particular color.

EDIT IT. Read your paragraph or poem. Make sure that each feeling or sensory word is the best one to use to describe the feeling you are attempting to describe.

DISCUSS IT. Read your composition to the class. Discuss how colors are able to affect our feelings. You may find the information on pages 82 and 83 useful.

Expressing Feelings

You already know what pantomime is. Write the word for a feeling on a slip of paper. Put the papers in a container. Take turns choosing slips from the container and pantomime the feeling on the slip. Members of the class will attempt to guess what feeling is being pantomimed.

Sometimes we express our feelings with words instead of actions. Notice the feeling expressed in this poem:

REFLECTIONS

On this street
of windowed stores
see,
in the glass
shadow people meet
and pass
and glide to
secret places.

Ghostly mothers
hold
the hands of dim gray children,
scold
them silently
and melt away.

And
now and then,
before
the window mirror
of a store,
phantom faces
stop
and window shop.

Lilian Moore

108

1. What feeling is expressed in the poem?
2. What words does the poet use to express this feeling?
3. How would the poem be changed if the author stated the feeling directly?

On Christmas Eve, 17-year-old Juliane Koepcke boarded an airplane that was to take her to her parents' home in a jungle in Peru. As the airplane climbed into a thunderstorm over the towering Andes Mountains, a blinding flash of lightning encircled the plane. Juliane felt herself tumbling through the air outside the airplane. She awoke in the middle of a jungle wilderness alone. Here is the story of her courageous fight for survival as it was told in Life:

SHE LIVED!

Juliane first heard the jungle birds. A canopy of green trees screened the late afternoon sunlight from above. About three hours had passed. She was lying on the jungle floor, still in her airplane seat. The two seats next to her were empty. There seemed to be no other people around. She called, but no one answered. There was a pain in her right shoulder—her collarbone was fractured—and a cut on her upper right arm. Besides these and some bruises and scratches, she seemed otherwise unhurt. . . .

Though probably suffering from shock, she never lost her wits or the confidence that she would be found. She had spent much of her childhood in the jungle with her parents and she remembered that her father had taught her to walk downhill to find water and then to follow the water downstream. Eventually, he had said, as the stream becomes bigger, one is bound to find civilization.

Selection from *Life* Magazine, © 1972 Time Inc.

She began pushing through the thick underbrush. The rain had turned the ground into a muddy swamp and her high-heeled shoes sank in. The underbrush ripped at her dress. After a while, she lost one shoe and stumbled on for a day with one bare foot. Then she lost the other. . . .

After the first three days, rain fell continually, and she was always wet. At night, shivering under trees, she slept only intermittently. She tried unsuccessfully to start a fire with her watch crystal. Insects and leeches bit her and her bites and cuts became infested with wormy larvae laid by flies. She saw few wild animals; some small crocodiles slithered off the shore after her in curiosity. . . .

Four days after the crash, Juliane reached a small, thatched lean-to on the bank of the river. She had covered about ten air miles, but far more along her winding river course. Too weak to go any farther, she dragged herself inside and found some kerosene and salt. She tasted a little salt and, with the kerosene and a splinter of wood, began cleaning the fly larvae out of her skin. Later, she complained more of the worms than of anything else. They were not painful, but she could feel them moving around under her skin.

After five days in the lean-to——nine days after the plane crashed——three hunters came by in a canoe. Struggling to the river bank, she waved and attracted their attention. The superstitious jungle men drew back, certain that the blond girl was some sort of evil spirit, but eventually they came ashore and gave her sugar, salt, and some *fariña* meal. With gasoline, they helped her clean more worms out of her skin.

The next morning, two more hunters appeared and took Juliane in their canoe to the hut of a native woman for further help. When the woman saw the red of Juliane's bloodshot eyes, she screamed "Demon!" and tried to chase them away.

The hunters then took Juliane to the small settlement of Tournavista. There, a doctor treated her cuts and bruises and bandaged her. The following day, 11 days after the crash, an American woman pilot, Jerrie Cobb, flew into the jungle airstrip and took Juliane to a camp of American missionaries at Yarinacocha, near Pucallpa, where she was reunited with her father.

What unpleasant feelings might Juliane have experienced during her push through the jungle? What feelings might have forced her to struggle to survive? What do you learn about Juliane by reading the account of her struggle?

WRITE IT. Compose a short paragraph telling about an incident in which you experienced both pleasant and unpleasant feelings. Perhaps one of the suggestions below will help you to get started:

1. You were tired, battered, but happy after winning the game.
2. You were frightened, but your performance was excellent.
3. You were embarrassed, but your "goof" helped you to meet some new friends.
4. You were angry, but your anger drove you on to perform extremely well.
5. You were discouraged, but everything turned out well.

EDIT IT. Read your paragraph to be sure you used the best technique possible to help the reader share your feelings.

Read the statements below and notice the feeling that they express:

1. Herb was angry when his sister appeared wearing his new shirt.
2. "Why does she always have to wear my shirts?" Herb thought. "She has more clothes than I do."
3. Herb's face clouded up when he saw his sister wearing his new shirt.

Which statement tells you exactly how Herb feels? How does statement 2 make it possible for you to interpret Herb's feelings? statement 3? Explain why you should know several ways to express feelings in order to write effectively.

You can express feelings directly or give clues to feelings by statements or descriptions of behavior.

111

pride
anger
pain
joy
weakness
embarrass-
ment
fear
hate

FOLLOW THROUGH. Tell which of the following feelings are represented by the statements below:

pride   anger   pain   weakness   embarrassment

1. "I must get to a chair," she said. "My legs are so shaky."
2. When Connie discovered her mistake, her face turned scarlet.
3. "I'll get even with you for this," he screamed.
4. The stranger was doubled up on the sidewalk, moaning softly, when the ambulance arrived.
5. Her face lit up when the mayor presented the award to her father.

WRITE IT. Make up a description of behavior and a statement containing a direct quotation to describe each of the feelings below:

fear   joy   surprise   hate   sadness

Notice the clues to feelings in this poem:

Incident

Once riding in old Baltimore,
    Heart-filled, head-filled with glee,
I saw a Baltimorean
    Keep looking straight at me.

Now I was eight and very small,
    And he was no whit bigger,
And so I smiled, but he poked out
    His tongue, and called me, "Nigger."

I saw the whole of Baltimore
    From May until December;
Of all the things that happened there
    That's all that I remember.

Countee Cullen

What were the author's feelings in the first verse of the poem? How were the feelings abruptly changed in the second verse? How did the incident affect the author's feelings? How would the author's memories of his visit have been affected if the other child had returned his smile?

Think of a time that someone called you an undesirable name. What caused the person to call you the name? How did you feel before you were called the name? How did you feel afterwards?

WRITE IT. Compose a paragraph or a short poem describing the incident in which someone called you an undesirable name.

EDIT IT. Edit your composition to be sure that you have described both the incident and your feelings clearly. Remember that there are several ways that you might describe feelings.

Pretend that you are Charlie Brown in this cartoon:

© 1958 United Feature Syndicate, Inc.

How do you feel about Lucy's list? Why don't people like to be criticized? Which of the following statements would cause you to have angry feelings if it were directed toward you?

1. It hurts my ears when you yell so loud.
2. You are a loudmouth.

113

Which of the statements expresses the feelings of the speaker? Which statement criticizes you? What clues do these sentences give you for criticizing the behavior of others in a nice way?

You can criticize a person without making him angry by telling your own feelings instead of your opinion of him.

FOLLOW THROUGH. Tell which of the pairs of statements below is the more polite way of criticizing a friend's behavior:

A.
1. It makes me angry when you push my little brother around.
2. You are a big bully.

B.
1. I feel uncomfortable when you talk out loud to me during the movie.
2. You are rude because you disturb other people in the theater.

C.
1. If you think the government should control everything, you are a Communist.
2. I don't agree with you that the government should make decisions that could be made by people on a local level.

D.
1. You are clumsy because you spill everything you touch.
2. I'm sorry that you spilled milk on your lap.

E.
1. Anyone who criticizes someone else in public is an inconsiderate slob.
2. It embarrasses me when you criticize me in front of others.

FIGURES OF SPEECH

Simile

Sometimes people use comparisons to express feelings. Notice the comparisons in the sentences below:

1. She was as nervous as a long-tailed cat in a room full of rocking chairs.
2. He flew across the finish line like a man shot out of a cannon.

114

To what is the person in the first sentence compared? the second sentence? What words are used to show the comparison?

All of us dream about what we want to do or be. Often much of our energy is spent trying to make our dreams come true. How do you feel when a dream you have worked for is deferred, or put off? when a dream does not come true? Notice how the poet has used comparisons to show what happens to a dream deferred.

Harlem

What happens to a dream deferred?

Does it dry up
like a raisin in the sun?
Or fester like a sore——
And then run?
Does it stink like rotten meat?
Or crust and sugar over——
like a syrupy sweet?

Maybe it just sags
like a heavy load.

Or does it explode?

Langston Hughes

DISCUSS IT. Find five similes in the poem. Explain how the similes help you to "feel" the various ways that people react to broken dreams. Substitute another comparison for each simile.

FOLLOW THROUGH. Complete each simile below by using the first word that comes to your mind:

    1. As smooth as ☐
    2. As cold as ☐

3. As weird as ☐
4. As old as ☐
5. As sore as ☐
6. He ran like ☐.
7. The child cried like ☐.
8. Our football team played like ☐.
9. The thunder roared like ☐.
10. My broken arm ached like ☐.

Did you use expressions that you have heard many times before? What are such expressions called?

FOLLOW THROUGH. Now complete each simile above again, using fresh new comparisons.

Metaphor

Notice the comparisons in these sentences:

1. He was a bull as he charged into the opposing tackles.
2. The kitten was a soft bundle of warmth in his arms.

To what is the football player compared in sentence 1? To what is the kitten compared? Explain how the comparison is made.

This poem is made up almost entirely of a metaphor:

Window

Night from a railroad car window
Is a great, dark, soft thing
Broken across with slashes of light.

Carl Sandburg

What two things are compared in the poem? How does the poet help you to form in your mind a picture of night from a railroad car window?

"Window" from *Chicago Poems* by Carl Sandburg, copyright, 1916, by Holt, Rinehart and Winston, Inc.; copyright, 1944, by Carl Sandburg. Reprinted by permission of Harcourt Brace Jovanovich, Inc.

WRITE IT. Compose a poem similar to "Window" in which you use a metaphor. Notice that the poem consists of only one sentence. Perhaps the suggestions below will help you to start:

1. The crowd at a baseball game is . . . .
2. Traffic on the expressway is . . . .
3. The fire escapes on the side of the building are . . . .
4. Rats in the sewer are . . . .
5. Swimmers in the pool are . . . .

EDIT IT. Notice the form of "Window." What do you notice about the beginning of each line? Many poets begin each line of poetry with a capital letter. Other poets use capital letters only at the beginning of a sentence. You may use either form, but you should check to make sure you have used capital letters wherever they are required by the form that you selected.

Personification

How is the same information presented differently in each sentence below?

1. The wind blew with gale force.
2. The angry wind bent the trees almost to the ground.

In which sentence is the wind shown as a person? What word is used to give the wind human characteristics? In what other ways could the information above be presented so that the wind seems to be human?

117

A statement that treats a lifeless object or idea as if it were alive is called *personification*.

The following poem was also written by Carl Sandburg. See whether you can find examples of personification in it.

Night gathers itself into a ball of dark yarn.
Night loosens the ball and it spreads.
The lookouts from the shores of Lake Michigan
    find night follows day, and ping! ping! across
    sheet gray the boat lights put their signals.
Night lets the dark yarn unravel, Night speaks and
    the yarns change to fog and blue strands.

How does Sandburg make Night seem as if it is a live person? How does he make the boat lights seem alive?

WRITE IT. Make up sentences in which you personify each of the following objects or ideas:

1. rain	3. sky	5. stars	7. ship	9. stream
2. ocean	4. sun	6. kite	8. jet	10. ambulance

Happenings in Your Language

A question that has interested linguists for years is: How did people learn to talk? No one has found a definite answer yet. Some linguists believe that the first words were sounds imitating something heard in nature. Small children call a dog "bow-wow" and a duck "quack-quack."

We still name things from the sound made by the thing itself. In fact, there is a special word for this kind of name-making. It is called *onomatopoeia*.

Selection from "The Windy City" in *Slabs of the Sunburnt West* by Carl Sandburg, copyright, 1922, by Harcourt Brace Jovanovich, Inc.; renewed, 1950, by Carl Sandburg. Reprinted by permission of the publishers.

Notice the examples of onomatopoeia as you read the following poem:

Song of the Train

Clickety-clack,
Wheels on the track,
This is the way
They begin the attack:
Click-ety-clack,
Click-ety-clack,
Click-ety, *clack*-ety,
Click-ety
Clack.

Clickety-clack,
Over the crack,
Faster and faster
The song of the track:
Clickety-clack,
Clickety-clack,
Clickety, clackety,
Clackety
Clack.

Riding in front,
Riding in back,
Everyone hears
The song of the track:
Clickety-clack,
Clickety-clack,
Clickety, *clickety,*
Clackety
Clack.

David McCord

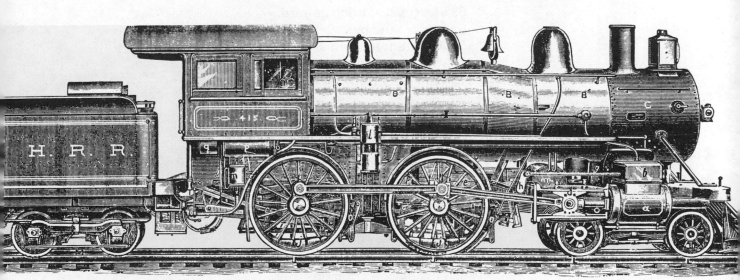

FOLLOW THROUGH. Make up sentences in which you use each of the following words:

buzz	ping	drip	crash	toot
pop	murmur	chug	rumble	rip

Using Your Language

DISCUSS IT. Why are these words grouped as they are?

I, *you, we, they,* and
plural forms of naming } *ride, collect, sit, play,* and so on
words

he, she, it, and
singular forms of } *rides, collects, sits, plays,* and so on
naming words

FOLLOW THROUGH. Use the appropriate form of each word in parentheses.

1. He (play) his guitar every morning.
2. My brothers (watch) all the football games.
3. They (yell) at the players.
4. The siren (blow) whenever there is a fire.
5. You (know) the reason.
6. It (rouse) everyone.
7. Karen (ride) her bicycle to school.
8. She (chain) it in the yard.
9. I (take) the bus.
10. We (study) together.
11. We (like) to read.
12. This story (tell) about a horse.

FOLLOW THROUGH. Use one of these words in each sentence:

am   is   are   was   were

1. Yesterday ____ Tuesday.
2. You ____ my best friend.
3. The doctor ____ in now.
4. I ____ a member of that club.
5. The firemen ____ there in two minutes.
6. This dog ____ a pug.
7. I ____ at the library yesterday.
8. Puffins ____ seabirds.
9. I ____ sure you are right.
10. The Joneses ____ here last week.
11. The dogs ____ in the kennel last week.
12. You ____ a friend of mine.

120

CHECK UP ON YOURSELF

Interpreting Feelings from Statements (pages 111–113)

Tell which of the following feelings is represented by each statement below:

hate   joy   fear   jealousy   pain

1. "What will ever happen to me?" she cried.
2. I wish Dad had given the new roller skates to me instead of you.
3. "If I never see you again, it will be too soon," he hissed.
4. He screamed and rolled around in the grass, holding his crushed wrist.
5. "This is the happiest moment of my life," she laughed as she jumped up and down and clapped her hands.

Distinguishing Between Feeling and Opinion (pages 113–114)

Tell which statements below are feelings and which are opinions:

1. That man is rude.
2. It annoys me to have smokers blow smoke in my face.
3. My sister is a very selfish person.
4. My feelings are hurt because you didn't invite me to your party.
5. I am sorry that you disagree with me.

Identifying Figures of Speech (pages 114–118)

Tell whether each figure of speech below represents simile, metaphor, or personification:

1. He was a lion in a flock of lambs.
2. Nancy was as awkward as a rhinoceros at a tea party.
3. The North Wind chilled us with his icy fingers.
4. Our team rolled across the field like a mighty army.
5. He was Santa Claus to children in his neighborhood.

121

LOOKING BACK AND CHECKING UP

100

Using Capital Letters (page 7)

Rewrite the sentences below, using capital letters where they are needed:

1. Do you know how to say any words in spanish?
2. The chinese had an advanced civilization early in history.
3. Nigeria is a country in africa.
4. We camped in the smoky mountains last summer.
5. Many boats sail up and down the mississippi river.

Writing Direct Quotations (pages 40–41)

Copy the following direct quotations and punctuate them correctly:

1. I would like to know he said where you put my books
2. She asked have you met my brother
3. I have never been to Kansas he stated
4. And this he said must be your younger brother
5. We must go home at five o'clock Nancy announced

Using Your Language (pages 8 and 83)

Use the appropriate form of the word in parentheses in place of the blank as you write each sentence.

(break)   1. Mark has ☐ his promise.
(choose) 2. May is always ☐ first for the team.
(steal)   3. Cynthia's bicycle was ☐ last night.
(tear)   4. The first page in my book has been ☐.
(steal)   5. The man who ☐ Cynthia's bicycle has been caught.
(blow)   6. The wind ☐ hard all night.
(drive)   7. Dad ☐ his new car into a ditch.
(draw)   8. The artist ☐ a picture of Ann.
(break)   9. I ☐ my new boomerang.
(tear)   10. Lester has ☐ his new shirt.
(choose) 11. I have ☐ this pen.
(steal) 12. He has ☐ a picture from her album.
(break) 13. The chain on the bicycle ☐.
(drive) 14. Mr. Sparks ☐ hastily to the bank.

122

More Ideas For You

1. Bring in pictures of audiences at athletic games, fires, accidents, and other events. Pass the pictures around the class and ask class members to identify the event the audience is witnessing in each picture.

2. Read *Henry III* by Joseph Krumgold and write a brief review to include in the class book-review file.

3. Form a committee to prepare a bulletin-board display explaining *simile, metaphor,* and *personification.*

4. Make a special effort to communicate more openly with your friends. Try to express feelings rather than opinions. Keep a record of your success.

5. Locate some poetry that contains onomatopoeia. Record the poems on tape and play them for the class.

6. Compile a class literary publication made up of the sensory writings, autobiography, feeling paragraphs, or poetry written by members of the class.

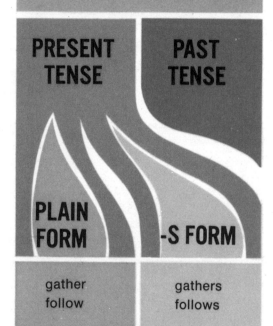

PRESENT TENSE	PAST TENSE
PLAIN FORM	**-S FORM**
gather follow	gathers follows
buzz clutch	buzzes clutches
carry try	carries tries

THE BASIC SENTENCE

Tense in the Verb Phrase

The **VP** in a sentence must show **tense**. Tense refers to changes made in a verb to show changes in time. Look at the Language Strip.

1. What are the two tenses in English?

    In English there are two tenses: **present tense** and **past tense**.

2. What are the two verb forms that show present tense?

    The two verb forms that show present tense are the **plain form** and the **-s form**.

3. How is the *-s* form of each of the verbs in the Language Strip made?

    The *-s* form of a verb is made by adding *-s* or *-es* or by changing the *y* to *i* and adding *-es*.

FOLLOW THROUGH. Write the *-s* form of each verb.

1. dance	6. push	11. rely
2. agree	7. change	12. go
3. box	8. match	13. write
4. dry	9. bay	14. do
5. love	10. pitch	15. say

124

Look at the Language Strip.

1. What is the plain form of *have?*
2. How is the *-s* form of *have* made?

The verb *have* changes its spelling for the *-s* form: *has.*

The plain form of *be* is *be.* Look at the Language Strip. What are the present forms of *be?*

The present tense forms of *be* are *am, is,* and *are.*

The Language Strip shows how the past forms of most English verbs are made. What is added to the plain form to make the past form?

The past form of most verbs is made by adding *-ed* to the plain form, by changing the *y* to *i* and adding *-ed,* or by doubling the final consonant and adding *-ed.*

FOLLOW THROUGH. Find the verb in each sentence below and tell whether it shows present tense or past tense:

1. The bees buzzed around the flowers.
2. Bees are noisy.
3. A bee carries pollen.
4. That bee carried pollen to the clover.
5. Most bees have stingers.

FOLLOW THROUGH. Write the past form of each verb.

1. care   3. cry   5. jam   7. hope   9. trip
2. rush   4. skim   6. envy   8. wait   10. spy

125

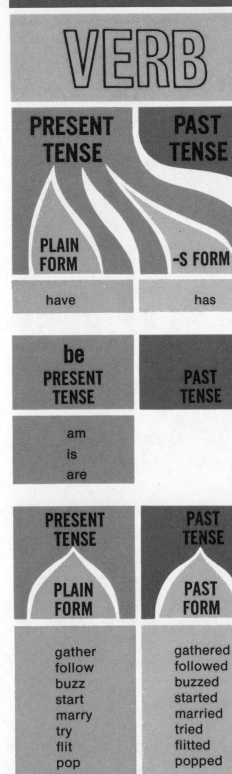

VERB

PRESENT TENSE   PAST TENSE

PLAIN FORM   -S FORM

have   has

be PRESENT TENSE   PAST TENSE

am
is
are

PRESENT TENSE   PAST TENSE

PLAIN FORM   PAST FORM

PLAIN FORM	PAST FORM
gather	gathered
follow	followed
buzz	buzzed
start	started
marry	married
try	tried
flit	flitted
pop	popped

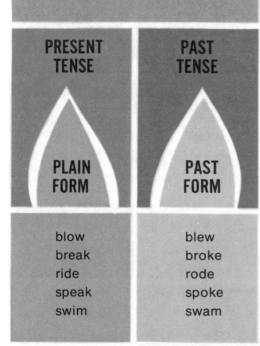

IRREGULAR VERB

PRESENT TENSE	PAST TENSE
PLAIN FORM	**PAST FORM**
blow	blew
break	broke
ride	rode
speak	spoke
swim	swam

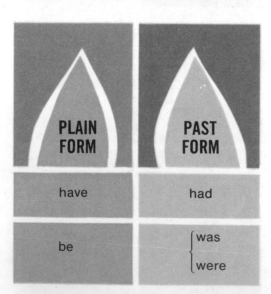

PLAIN FORM	**PAST FORM**
have	had
be	{ was were

Look at the Language Strip.

1. What are verbs like *blow, break,* and so on called?
2. Do these verbs add *-ed* to the plain form to make the past form?

Irregular verbs do not add *-ed* to the plain form to make the past form.

Other irregular verbs are given below. The past form of an irregular verb can be found in the dictionary.

Plain Form	Past Form
burst	burst
choose	chose
draw	drew
drive	drove
fall	fell
fly	flew
freeze	froze
steal	stole
tear	tore
wear	wore

Look at the Language Strip.

1. What is the past form of *have?*
2. What are the past forms of *be?*

The past form of *have* is *had.* The past forms of *be* are *was* and *were.*

FOLLOW THROUGH. Use the past form of the verb in parentheses in each sentence.

(be) 1. The wind ⬚ strong.
(blow) 2. It ⬚ through the house.
(be) 3. Papers ⬚ on the table.
(have) 4. We ⬚ weights on them.
(break) 5. The wind ⬚ a vase.

126

FOLLOW THROUGH. Find the verb in each sentence below and tell whether it shows present tense or past tense.

1. Two boys are at the door.
2. Omaha is in Nebraska.
3. Paul spoke to his teacher.
4. The twins ride to school.
5. Mrs. Semple carried a briefcase.
6. I have two pens.
7. The team swam across the pool.
8. Sue lives on Tenth Street.
9. The cat was under the table.
10. The pilot flew the plane to Chicago.

CHECK UP ON YOURSELF

A. Use the past form of the verb as you write each sentence.

(tear)   1. The child _____ a hole in his sleeve.
(cry)   2. A baby _____ in the night.
(ride)   3. Esther _____ her bike to the park.
(flit)   4. The butterfly _____ to the flowers.
(be)   5. You _____ a stranger then.

B. Find the verb in each sentence and tell whether it shows present tense or past tense.

1. That cat had four kittens.
2. Don wears a uniform to school.
3. I am in school.
4. The snow fell fast.
5. The lake froze over.

ACME

RESOURCES

types
of
resources

A usable stock or supply is called a *resource*.

What do you think of when you hear the word *resources*? Of what resources do the scenes above remind you?

128

DISCUSS IT. Talk about various types of resources that are used by people in the following occupations:

A	B
1. Automobile manufacturers	1. Writers
2. Welders	2. Teachers
3. Carpenters	3. Researchers
4. Plumbers	4. Editors
5. Electricians	5. Philosophers

What is the major difference between the resources used by workers in the first group and workers in the second group? Which occupations would probably include women? Why do you believe that the other occupations will soon include women?

Why may facts and ideas be considered resources? Where is the best place to find facts, ideas, and other resources of this type?

129

IMPRESSIONS

If you were interested in learning a hobby, how would you find out what you need to know about it? You could read one of the many books about hobbies and crafts, but how else could you investigate your interest? Which way do you think you would learn more about what the hobby is really like?

Many people have found their professions through hobbies. They found a hobby they liked and did it so well that other people were willing to pay them for doing it. What hobbies can you think of that you could engage in to earn a living? Would you still enjoy your hobby as much if you did it for a living, instead of just in your spare time? Why do you feel that way?

USING THE LIBRARY

The Card Catalog

A library is one of the best resources for finding information and ideas. In some school systems, libraries are called *instructional materials centers, media centers, learning centers, or resource centers.*

So much information is stored in a library that you need help in finding what you are seeking. The most helpful guide for locating information in a library is shown below.

The picture shows a *card catalog*. The card catalog is a file in which there are cards for every book in the library. What is the purpose of the letters on the front of each drawer? What are the letters called?

The letters on each drawer in a card catalog tell which cards are in that drawer. They are called *guide letters.*

DISCUSS IT. On the cards, find the information that answers the questions below:

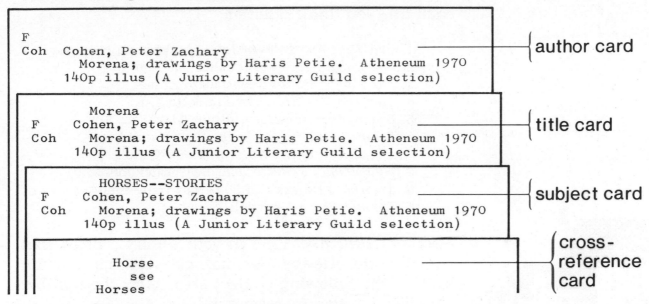

```
F
Coh   Cohen, Peter Zachary
         Morena; drawings by Haris Petie.  Atheneum 1970
      140p illus (A Junior Literary Guild selection)
```
author card

```
         Morena
F        Cohen, Peter Zachary
Coh        Morena; drawings by Haris Petie.  Atheneum 1970
        140p illus (A Junior Literary Guild selection)
```
title card

```
         HORSES--STORIES
F        Cohen, Peter Zachary
Coh        Morena; drawings by Haris Petie.  Atheneum 1970
        140p illus (A Junior Literary Guild selection)
```
subject card

```
         Horse
            see
         Horses
```
cross-reference card

1. Who is the publisher of the book?
2. What is the date of the publication?
3. What is the location symbol of the book?
4. What is the title of the book?
5. What subject appears on the subject card?
6. Under what other subject is the book listed?
7. On which card is the other subject listed?
8. How does the cross-reference card differ from the other cards?
9. How can you tell that the book is illustrated?
10. In what drawer of the card catalog would the subject card be filed? Why?

How are the location symbols of the following titles different? Why?

1. 538   Lieberg, Owen S., *Wonders of Magnets and Magnetism*
2. F   Fox, Paula, *How Many Miles to Babylon?*

Books in libraries are divided into two large classifications—fiction and nonfiction. What kinds of books are fiction? nonfiction? Which title above represents a fiction book? a nonfiction book?

The card catalog is the best single source of information in the library.

Books of fiction are grouped together in libraries. The location symbol for a book of fiction is the first letter or letters of the author's last name.

133

FOLLOW THROUGH. Copy the following titles. Put *N* before each title you think is nonfiction. Put *F* before each title you think is fiction.

1. *The Time-Ago Tales of Jahdu* by Virginia Hamilton
2. *The Ghost Boat* by Jacqueline Jackson
3. *The Pueblo Indians* by Richard Erdoes
4. *Stories of the States* by Frank Ross, Jr.
5. *Escape to Witch Mountain* by Alexander Key
6. *Football Talk for Beginners* by Howard Liss
7. *A Walk Out of the World* by Ruth Nichols
8. *What Makes a Clock Tick?* by Chester Johnson
9. *America's Horses and Ponies* by Irene Brady
10. *The Bat-Poet* by Randall Jarrell

FOLLOW THROUGH. Find in your library a chart that explains the Dewey decimal classification. Match each of the following subject areas with the number classification that represents it.

1. 000–099   a. Social Sciences
2. 100–199   b. The Arts
3. 200–299   c. Religion
4. 300–399   d. Philosophy
5. 400–499   e. Pure Science
6. 500–599   f. History
7. 600–699   g. Literature
8. 700–799   h. General Works
9. 800–899   i. Language
10. 900–999   j. Technology

FOLLOW THROUGH. Write the headings "394.2 — Festivals and Anniversaries," "594 — Shells," and "920 — Collective Biography." Arrange the following titles alphabetically by authors under the headings:

1. *Celebrations* by Robert J. Myers
2. *Sea Shells of the World* by R. Tucker Abbott
3. *Baseball's Most Colorful Managers* by Ray Robinson
4. *The Easy Way with Holidays* by Sandra Sanders
5. *Black American Leaders* by Margaret Young
6. *The Shell Collector's Handbook* by A. Hyatt Verrill
7. *Captains of Industry* by Bernard A. Weisberger with Allan Nevins

8. *Celebrate the Sun* by Betty Nickerson
9. *The Shell Book* by Julia E. Rogers
10. *Festivals for You to Celebrate* by Susan Purdy

FOLLOW THROUGH. Use a card catalog to answer the following questions:

1. Who wrote *Sounder?*
2. How many books about dogs are given?
3. What books were written by E. B. White?
4. What is the subject of *Escape to Witch Mountain?*
5. Who wrote *J. T.?*

Planning a Report

Select a topic on which you will write a report. Remember that the topic should be:

1. Of interest to you and to the persons who will read or listen to the report.
2. Specific enough that you can cover it in 500 to 1000 words.

FOLLOW THROUGH. Look in the card catalog to find books related to your topic. Review them and take notes of material that seems useful.

Notice the form of the note card below:

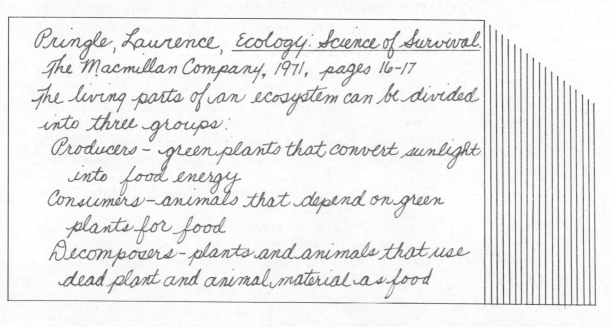

Pringle, Laurence, *Ecology: Science of Survival.*
The Macmillan Company, 1971, pages 16-17
The living parts of an ecosystem can be divided
into three groups:
  Producers - green plants that convert sunlight
    into food energy
  Consumers - animals that depend on green
    plants for food
  Decomposers - plants and animals that use
    dead plant and animal material as food

DISCUSS IT. What information is included at the top of the notes? Why is it useful to include such information at the top of the card or paper used for notes? What information should be included in your notes? Why isn't it necessary to arrange your notes in any particular form? What is the advantage of using a separate card or sheet of paper for each source of information?

Sometimes when you write a report, you want your reader to know the books from which you obtained your information. In such cases you list the titles of the books at the end of your report under the heading *Bibliography*. Entries in a bibliography are listed alphabetically by the last names of authors. Notice the information included in the bibliography entry below and the way the entry is punctuated:

> Hirsch, S. Carl, *Guardians of Tomorrow, Pioneers in Ecology*. The Viking Press, New York, 1971.

Which words in the title begin with capital letters? Which words in the title do not begin with capital letters? Why is the title printed in italics?

What line in the bibliography is indented? What punctuation marks are used in the bibliography entry?

FOLLOW THROUGH. Arrange the following entries as a bibliography. List them in alphabetical order and punctuate them properly.

> Partners, Guests, and Parasites by Hilda Simon, The Viking Press, New York, 1970
>
> Keith Reid, Doubleday and Company, New York, Nature's Network, 1970
>
> Eleanor B. Heady and Harold F. Heady, Grosset & Dunlap, High Meadow: The Ecology of a Mountain, New York, 1970
>
> This Hungry World, Elizabeth S. Helfman, Lothrop, Lee & Shepard, 1970, New York
>
> Laurence Pringle, The Macmillan Company, New York, One Earth, Many People, 1971
>
> The Sea Around Us by Rachel Carson, 1966, New York, Franklin Watts, Inc.

Periodicals

If you're trying to find the latest information on ecology, would you look for the information in books? Why? In what sources would you look for information on current topics?

The best guide to current information in magazines is *Readers' Guide to Periodical Literature.* Notice the information given in the following entry from *Readers' Guide:*

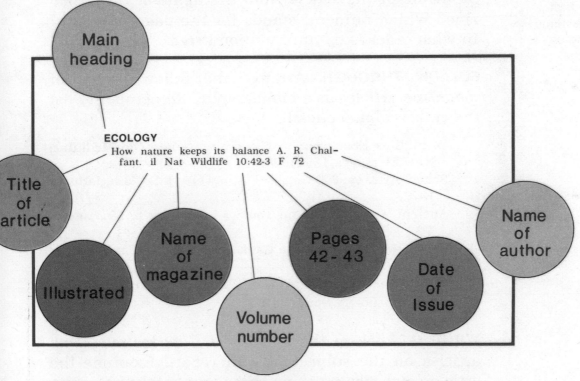

ECOLOGY
How nature keeps its balance A. R. Chalfant. il Nat Wildlife 10:42-3 F 72

Main heading

Title of article

Illustrated

Name of magazine

Volume number

Pages 42 - 43

Date of Issue

Name of author

TELL IT. Answer the following questions based on information presented in the entry:

1. How do you know that the entry is from a periodical?
2. What is the main heading of the entry?
3. Who is the author?
4. What is the title of the article?
5. What is the name of the periodical?
6. What is the date of the periodical?
7. What is the volume number of the periodical?
8. How can you tell that the article is illustrated?
9. On what pages of the magazine does the article appear?

Notice the differences in form between the bibliographical entry for the magazine and that for the book below:

Davis, D., "Portrait of Young Artists," *Newsweek*, February 7, 1972, p. 79.

Glubok, Shirley, *Art of the Old West*. The Macmillan Company, New York, 1971.

What punctuation marks separate the parts of the book entry? the magazine entry? How can you tell the name of the article from the name of the magazine? Which numeral stands for the page numbers? In what order is the information listed?

FOLLOW THROUGH. Arrange the following list of magazine articles as a bibliography. Remember to list the entries alphabetically.

D. Phillips Ebony pp. 33–6 and continuing, Old Mediums, New Messages, December '71

School Arts, pp. 8–9 Copper Foil Jewelry J. D. Kain, January 1972

Ancient Art of Macrame Today's Education p. 59 January '72

C. J. Weaver Crafting Tin Cans Design pp. 27–9 mid-Winter '72

Painting as a Pastime W. L. S. Churchill Saturday Evening Post pp. 65-7 + Spring, 1972

WRITE IT. Look in the *Readers' Guide* for magazine articles on the subject of your report. Examine the articles and take notes on those that might be of use to you in writing your report.

Other References

There is a section in every library called the *reference section*. What are some of the different types of books found in the reference section? What types of information do these books provide? Why is it important to check the publication date of reference books?

To use reference books efficiently, you must be able to use certain reference skills. Practice some of your reference skills by using your book.

TELL IT. Follow the directions and answer the questions:

1. Look at the page following the title page of this book. What is the date of publication?
2. Who wrote the book?
3. What is the name of the publisher?
4. What chapter is concerned mainly with writing, according to the table of contents?
5. Turn to the index. What pages might you read to learn about the propaganda technique called *glittering generalities?*

The Dictionary

The dictionary is one of our most useful reference books. What type of information does the dictionary provide?

TELL IT. To help you understand the great amount of information provided in a single dictionary entry, answer the following questions about this entry:

bo here l bv (ever *mind* vour mistake) (does n t *mind* the co' l) **5** : to be careful about : watch out for ⟨*mind* the brol en rule⟩ **6** : to take charge of : TEND ⟨*mind* the chil lren⟩
mind·ed \'min-d d\ *adj* **1** : l aving a sp cficd l ind of mind ⟨narrow-*minded*⟩ **2** : DISPOSED, INCLINED
mind·ful \'mīn(d)-fəl\ *adj* : bearing in mind : HEEDFUL — **mind·ful·ly** \-fə-lē\ *adv*
mind·less \'m n- lləs\ *adj* : lacking mind or consciousness; *esp* : UNINTELLIGENT — **mind·less·ly** *adv* — **mind·less·ness** *n*
¹**mine** \(')mīn\ *adj, arc ac* : MY — used befor a word beginning with a vowel or *l* ⟨*mine* host⟩ or as modif er of a preceding noun ⟨mother *mine*⟩
²**mine** \'mīn\ *pron* : my one : my ones
³**mine** \'mīn\ *n* **1** : a pit or tunnel from which mineras (as coal o l d, or diamonds) are taken **2** : a deposit of ore **3** : an underground pa sage dug bene th an enemy position **4 a** : a charge buried in the ground and set to explode when disturbed (as by an enemy soldie or vehicle) **b** : an explosive c arge placed n a case and sunk in the water to sink enemy

b : to become mingled ... **c** : to come in contact : ASSOCIATE ⟨*mingles* w th al sorts of people⟩
syn MINGLE, MIX, LEND, COMBINE can mean to put or come together in one place. MINGLE implies that the elements are still at least somewhat distinguishab e; MIX m y or may not impl loss of each element's separate ide tity; BLEND implies that the elements undergo much or complete loss in individuality; COALESCE may suggest an organic unity brought about when like things row together

¹**min·i·a·ture** \'min-ē-ə-,chùr, 'min-i-,chùr, -chər\ *n* [from Italian *miniatura* "the art of illuminating manuscripts", "a picture in an illuminated manuscript", from medieval Latin, from Latin *miniare* "to color with red lead", from *minium* "red lead"] **1** : something much smaller than the usual size; *esp* : a copy on a much reduced scale **2** : a very small portrait or painting (as on ivory or metal) **3** : the art of painting miniatures — **min·i·a·tur·ist** \-,chùrəst\ *n*
²**miniature** *adj* : very small : represented on a small scale ⟨collects *miniature* books⟩

1. Where may *miniature* be divided at the end of a line? How can you tell?
2. What are the three pronunciations of the word?
3. How many written syllables does it have?
4. How many spoken syllables does it have in the second pronunciation?
5. Which syllable receives heavy stress?
6. In what ways may the word *miniature* be used?
7. How many definitions are given for *n* (*noun*)?
8. How many definitions are given for *adj* (*adjective*)?
9. From what word was *miniature* derived?
10. From what language was *miniature* borrowed?

Dictionaries also help us to unlock the meanings of words by discovering the meanings of prefixes and suffixes.

FOLLOW THROUGH. Add one of the following prefixes to the beginning of each word below. Be able to tell the meaning of the new word. Check with your dictionary if you need help.

ad-	co-	non-	trans-	mis-
anti-	en-	sub-	dis-	pre-

1. profit   3. operate   5. honest   7. form   9. aircraft
2. cook   4. print   6. minister 8. normal 10. case

FOLLOW THROUGH. Combine a word with each suffix below. Use a dictionary if you need help.

A	B	C	D
-hood	-ize	-ative	-ly
-ist	-en	-ish	-ward
-ment	-ate	-ful	

Look for the plural forms of the words below in your dictionary:

A. weed, lunch, boy, safe, piano
B. city, half, goose, man, tomato, deer

Why does the dictionary show the plural forms of the words in Group B, but not those in Group A?

Plurals made by the addition of *-s* or *-es* are considered regular and are not usually shown in a dictionary. Irregular plurals are always shown.

140

FOLLOW THROUGH. Write the words "Regular" and "Irregular" at the top of your paper. Copy each of the words below under the proper heading and add the plural form:

1. lady	6. baby	11. mouse	16. soprano
2. alto	7. uncle	12. wife	17. kangaroo
3. witch	8. waif	13. hero	18. woman
4. thief	9. sheep	14. trio	19. moose
5. turkey	10. bug	15. child	20. burro

How is each of the following nouns made to show the possessive form?

> the boy's book
> the boys' books
> the men's books

FOLLOW THROUGH. Write the singular possessive and the plural possessive form of each of these:

1. mouse	3. thief	5. moose	7. donkey	9. alto
2. lady	4. woman	6. burro	8. cuckoo	10. witch

Singular nouns form the possessive by adding an apostrophe and s. Plural nouns ending in s form the possessive by adding an apostrophe. Plural nouns that do not end in s form the possessive by adding an apostrophe and s.

Happenings in Your Language

The language of the United States, like the country itself, has been referred to as a *melting pot*. What is meant by the term?

You can use a dictionary to help find out how individual words came into our language. If you cannot find this type of information in your dictionary, you may need to refer to an unabridged dictionary in your school library. However, many school dictionaries contain this type of information.

Words are brought into our language from many other languages.

FOLLOW THROUGH. Use your dictionary to find the historical origin of the following words. Write the word, the language from which it came, and its original meaning.

1. pen	3. farewell	5. husband	7. delicatessen	9. alarm
2. fit	4. comrade	6. gingham	8. circus	10. Sunday

Some words in our language were taken from the names of real persons.

TELL IT. Find the name of the person from whom each of the following was taken. Explain why.

1. dahlia 3. galvanism 5. derby 7. derrick   9. watt
2. boycott 4. pasteurize 6. volt   8. quisling 10. Fahrenheit

Other words came to our language from the literature of mythology.

TELL IT. Tell the name of the mythical character from which each word below was taken and why:

1. calliope   3. mercurial   5. Tuesday   7. Thursday
2. tantalize   4. nemesis   6. January   8. titanic

Using Your Language

The dictionary can be of help to you in learning the forms of verbs, which are labeled *v.* or *vb.* For which of the verbs in bold letters does the dictionary list other forms?

1. Some people **walk** many miles a day.
2. Others **ride** everywhere.

What are the other forms of *ride*? Why are other forms of *walk* not shown?

FOLLOW THROUGH. Use the appropriate form of *ride* in each sentence below:

1. She has ⬚ her new pony every day this week.
2. Have you ever ⬚ a horse?
3. I have ⬚ three different kinds of horses.
4. Where have you ⬚?
5. Carol has never ⬚ a horse.
6. My uncle ⬚ a bull in a rodeo.
7. He had ⬚ for about three seconds.
8. Uncle Joe had ⬚ against the bull's wishes.
9. My uncle had never ⬚ a bull before.
10. He wishes now that he had still never ⬚ one.

> When the past form of a verb is made by the addition of *-ed* to the entry word, it is usually not listed in a dictionary unless a spelling problem is involved.

142

FOLLOW THROUGH. Use the appropriate form of *speak* in each of the following sentences:

1. Pam ☐ at the girls' club banquet.
2. She had never ☐ to an audience before.
3. When she had ☐ for about ten minutes, she relaxed.
4. After she had ☐, everyone applauded.
5. She had ☐ like an experienced speaker.

Find the word *able* in your dictionary. Does the entry show the endings *-er* and *-est*? What is the purpose of those endings?

The endings *-er* and *-est* can be added to many words to compare persons or things.

Some dictionaries include *-er* and *-est* endings only when the spelling of a word is changed before adding the endings.

WRITE IT. Give the *-er* and *-est* forms of each word below. In each case, tell why the forms are or are not entered in the dictionary.

1. fat	3. blue	5. little	7. short	9. noble
2. dark	4. thin	6. lively	8. early	10. pretty

ENCYCLOPEDIAS

There are many different types of encyclopedias for young people. Which of these encyclopedias are available to you in your school?

The New Book of Knowledge
Britannica Junior Encyclopædia
Compton's Encyclopedia
The World Book Encyclopedia

Each of these encyclopedias may be a little different from the others. Examine several sets. Which sets have a separate volume for the index? Which sets have an index in each volume? How are the guide words used in an encyclopedia? Explain how the cross references are used.

143

Encyclopedia articles are arranged alphabetically by author. If no author is listed, the name of the article is given first.

Quotation marks are placed around the name of the article, and the name of the encyclopedia is underlined.

The volume number, the year of publication, and the page numbers of the article are shown in that order.

An almanac is a publication containing statistical and factual information. An atlas is a book of maps.

FOLLOW THROUGH. Use an encyclopedia to find the answers to the following questions:

1. In what kind of climate does the tallow tree grow?
2. What is a spelunker?
3. What is the nickname of the state of Mississippi?
4. For what purpose was Gallaudet College founded?
5. On whose experiences was *Robinson Crusoe* based?

Notice these bibliography entries:

Starkey, Marion L., "Witchcraft," *The New Book of Knowledge,* Vol. 20, 1971, pages 208–209.

"Witchcraft," *Compton's Encyclopedia,* Vol. 22, 1972, page 209.

Which entry is a signed article? How does it differ from the unsigned entry?

WRITE IT. Consult an encyclopedia to find information about your report topic. Make a correct bibliography entry on the top of your note card or paper. Copy notes that might be of use to you in writing your report.

ALMANACS AND ATLASES

What is an *almanac*? What is an *atlas*? What type of information is found in each of these references?

FOLLOW THROUGH. Use an almanac or an atlas to find answers to the following questions:

1. What country in the world has the largest population?
2. Into what body of water does the Volga River empty?
3. Japan is made up of four main islands plus many smaller islands. What is the name of the largest Japanese island?
4. The longest river in the world is found in Africa. What is the name of that river?
5. What is the capital of Australia?
6. What is the wettest spot in the world?
7. On what day of the week will Christmas come in the year 2000?
8. In what year was Ohio University founded?
9. What United States port handles the most commerce?
10. Who won the Soap Box Derby in 1970?

OTHER INDEXES

Sometimes in writing a report you will want to find a statement or a poem written by a particular person. Or you may want to find out who made a particular statement or wrote a particular poem. There are indexes of quotations and poetry. Find an example of each in your school library.

FOLLOW THROUGH. Use the appropriate index to identify the author of each poem or quotation below:

1. I write from the worm's-eye point of view.
2. His bark is worse than his bite.
3. Whose woods these are I think I know.
   His house is in the village, though;
4. Listen, my children, and you shall hear
   Of the midnight ride of Paul Revere,
5. Well, son, I'll tell you:
   Life for me ain't been no crystal stair.

HUMAN RESOURCES

In planning an interview, remember to include these items:
1. Arrange a time and a place for the interview.
2. Have your questions ready ahead of time.
3. Record the name, position, and qualifications of the person interviewed.
4. Take accurate notes of the interview.
5. Thank the person for helping you.

In addition to books and periodicals, where else might you find information for your project? Sometimes there are persons in your community who have spent many years studying the topic of your report. What help could they provide that would not be found in books? What preparation should be made in arranging for an interview?

Collect information on your report topic by using the card catalog, appropriate reference books, and local authorities. Take notes on information that you wish to include in your report.

OUTLINING

Now you are ready to organize your notes and make an outline. Your notes probably center around a few major headings with subheadings under each. Notice the form of the following outline:

CATS
I. History of cats as pets
   A. Ancient Egypt
   B. Europe
   C. United States
II. Care of the cat
   A. Grooming
   B. Feeding
   C. Training
III. Types of cats
   A. Domestic shorthair
   B. Siamese
   C. Burmese
   D. Abyssinian
   E. Russian blue
   F. Manx
   G. Rex
   H. Himalayan
IV. General facts about cats
   A. Temperament
      1. Playfulness
      2. Curiosity
      3. Independence
   B. Physical characteristics
      1. Teeth
      2. Body
      3. Fur
   C. Superstitions about cats

How are the main headings indicated? subheadings? Where are capital letters and periods used?

WRITE IT. Organize the information from your notes into an outline that will help you write your report. Keep track of all your sources of information so that you can include them in your bibliography.

146

WRITING YOUR REPORT

WRITE IT. Write your report. Remember not to copy information directly from your references. Take the information you have, think about it, and put it in your own words. Remember to add your bibliography.

EDIT IT. Carefully read your report and check it to be sure you have used:

Capital letters for:
1. Titles of books, reports, poems, songs, and stories.
2. Titles of persons.
3. Initials.
4. Names of newspapers and magazines.
5. Names of railroads, ships, and ship lines.
6. Names of documents (Mayflower Compact).

Periods:
1. After abbreviations and initials.
2. To separate parts in your bibliography.

Commas to:
1. Separate parts of an entry in a bibliography.
2. Separate parts in the source of notes.
3. Set apart a title following a name.
4. Set off a transitional word or group of words.
5. Set off a word group used to add information.

TELL IT. Form small groups. Read your report aloud to the members of your group.

DISCUSS IT. Evaluate the reports given in your group by using the following guidelines:

1. Did the report cover the topic thoroughly?
2. Was the report interesting?
3. Did the report flow smoothly from beginning to end?
4. Was the information presented in a logical sequence?
5. What were the strong points of the report?

147

The Card Catalog (pages 132–135)

Answer each of the following questions:

1. What is a card catalog?
2. In what order are catalog cards filed?
3. Why is the card catalog the best single source for finding information in a library?
4. How do author cards, title cards, subject cards, and cross-reference cards differ?

Classification of Books (pages 133–134)

Tell which of the following books would be classified as fiction and which would be classified as nonfiction:

1. *Mystery of the Fat Cat* by Frank Bonham
2. *America's Endangered Wildlife* by George Laycock
3. *Experiments with Electric Currents* by Harry Sootin
4. *Alice's Adventures in Wonderland* by Lewis Carroll
5. *Reptiles as Pets* by Paul Villiard
6. *The First Book of National Monuments* by Norman M. Lobsenz
7. *Grimbold's Other World* by Nicholas S. Gray
8. *The Night They Stole the Alphabet* by Sesyle Joslin
9. *Enchantment of Montana* by Allan Carpenter
10. *A Wizard of Earthsea* by Ursula K. Le Guin

Prefixes and Suffixes (page 140)

Combine a word with each prefix and suffix below and define it:

1. ad-	5. non-	9. mis-	13. -ment	17. -ful
2. anti-	6. sub-	10. pre-	14. -en	18. -ly
3. co-	7. trans-	11. -hood	15. -ate	19. -ward
4. en-	8. dis-	12. -ist	16. -ish	20. -ize

148

Writing a Bibliography (pages 136–138 and 144)

Write the following entries in alphabetical order and punctuate and capitalize them correctly:

freeman s h basic baseball strategy doubleday and company inc. new york 1965

sports illustrated book of baseball j b lippincott company philadelphia 1966

baseball the new book of knowledge vol 1 pp 69–81 1969

weiskopf h baseball's week sports illustrated 35:107 september 27 1971

jackson c paul how to play better baseball thomas y crowell company new york 1963

Possessive Forms (pages 140–141)

Write the singular possessive and the plural possessive form of each of the words below:

1. woman	7. hero	13. student
2. baby	8. pony	14. goat
3. child	9. thief	15. musician
4. monkey	10. wife	16. juror
5. chief	11. friend	17. dog
6. aunt	12. lamb	18. mate

Encyclopedias, Almanacs, and Atlases (pages 143–144)

Answer each of the following questions:

1. What is an almanac?
2. What is an atlas?
3. In which would you be most likely to find the information listed below——an encyclopedia, an almanac, or an atlas?
   a. A biography of Martin Luther King
   b. The name of the island country situated about 20 miles off the southeastern coast of India
   c. A list of the cash deposits in U.S. commercial banks with deposits over one billion dollars

149

LOOKING BACK AND CHECKING UP

Listening Analytically (pages 12–13)

Tell what information is not included in the following directions:

> To get to the First National Bank, walk four blocks south, turn the corner, and walk two blocks. The bank is on the southwest corner of the second block.

Types of Humor (pages 38–45)

Tell which example below represents each of the following types of humor:

ridicule   pun   wisecrack   put-down   put-on

1. He is as funny as an earthquake.
2. Baseball infielder drops a pop fly. A spectator yells, "Get him a basket."
3. Do you like Edgar Allan Poe?
   I don't know, I never met him.
4. What do you do for a hobby?
   I pop corn.
5. How do you know that is a dogwood tree?
   I can tell by its bark.

Classifying Words (pages 82–83)

Classify each word below as pleasant, unpleasant, or neutral:

ugly   acquaintance   satisfactory   victory   friendship
love   death   beautiful   acceptable   defeat

Identifying Figures of Speech (pages 114–119)

Tell whether each of the following is a simile, a metaphor, personification, or onomatopoeia:

1. The night enfolded us in her velvet arms.
2. Clickety, clackety go the wheels on the train.
3. The speaker was a giant to the audience.
4. He was as friendly as a political candidate at a rally.
5. The sea threatened us with her giant waves.

150

More Ideas For You

1. Make a bulletin-board display showing appropriate bibliography entries for a book, a magazine article, and an encyclopedia article.

2. Divide into teams of four. Each team should list five items that can be found in the library, such as famous quotations, facts, authors, or publications. Exchange lists. Teams should take turns going to the library for their treasure hunt. The team that finds the information on their list in the shortest amount of time wins the treasure hunt.

3. Select another language, such as Latin, German, or Greek. Use a dictionary that tells word origins and list ten American words that were taken from that language.

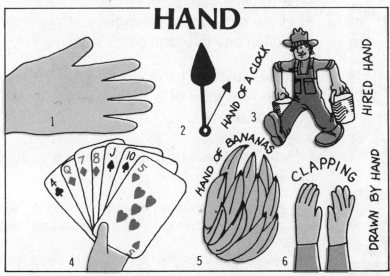

HAND

1 | 2 | HAND OF A CLOCK 3 | HIRED HAND | DRAWN BY HAND | 4 | HAND OF BANANAS 5 | CLAPPING 6

4. Make an illustrated chart of some words that have many different meanings, such as *run*, *horn*, *hand*, and *beat*.

5. Prepare a class booklet on "Interesting Word Facts." Use the reference books in the library to begin your study. You might want to begin by looking up anagrams and palindromes.

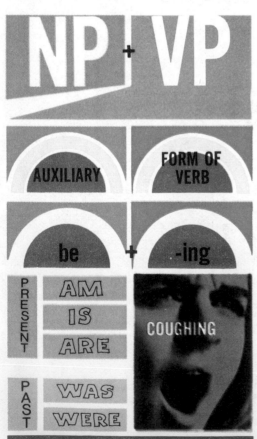

LOOKING AT YOUR LANGUAGE

NP + VP

1. My mother + works daily.
2. She + is working now.

NP + VP

AUXILIARY | FORM OF VERB

be + -ing

PRESENT
AM
IS
ARE

COUGHING

PAST
WAS
WERE

THE BASIC SENTENCE

Auxiliaries

What are the two tenses in English? If you have forgotten, go back to page 124. Then look at the Language Strip.

1. In sentence 1 the *-s* form of what verb shows present tense?
2. In sentence 2 what is the form that shows present tense?
3. When a form of *be* is used with another verb form, what is *be* called?
4. With what verb form is the auxiliary *be* used?
5. In the sentence *My mother was working,* what tense does the form of *be* show?

The auxiliary *be* is used in the **VP** with the *-ing* form of a verb to show present or past tense.

Here are the *-ing* forms of the verbs listed on page 126:

bursting   drawing   falling   freezing   tearing
choosing   driving   flying   stealing   wearing

The auxiliary *be* is sometimes used with the *-ing* form of *be* to show present or past time:

He is being noisy.
He was being noisy.

FOLLOW THROUGH. Write five sentences using *be* followed by an *-ing* form. Tell whether the form of *be* is a present or a past tense form.

Other words besides *be* can be used as auxiliaries. Look at the Language Strip.

1. In which sentence is a form of *have* a verb followed by an **NP**?
2. In which sentence is a form of *have* an auxiliary followed by a verb form?
3. In sentence 2 what tense does the auxiliary *has* show?
4. In the sentence *He had gone to the stacks,* what tense does the auxiliary *had* show?
5. Which verb form is used with forms of the auxiliary *have?*

The auxiliary *have* is used in the **VP** with the **participle form** of the verb to show present or past tense.

In the Language Strip compare the participle form of each regular verb with the past form. What can you tell about the forms?

Now compare the participle form of each irregular verb with the past form. What can you tell about the forms?

Regular verbs have a participle form that is the same as the past form. Most irregular verbs have a participle form that is different from the past form.

The participle form of most irregular verbs can be found in the dictionary.

153

NP + VP

1. The librarian + has my card.
2. The librarian + has gone
       to the stacks.

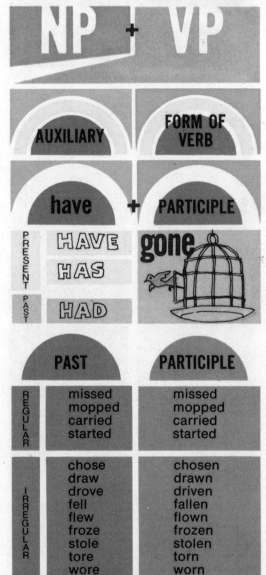

AUXILIARY	FORM OF VERB
have +	PARTICIPLE

	AUXILIARY	
PRESENT	HAVE	gone
	HAS	
PAST	HAD	

	PAST	PARTICIPLE
REGULAR	missed	missed
	mopped	mopped
	carried	carried
	started	started
IRREGULAR	chose	chosen
	draw	drawn
	drove	driven
	fell	fallen
	flew	flown
	froze	frozen
	stole	stolen
	tore	torn
	wore	worn

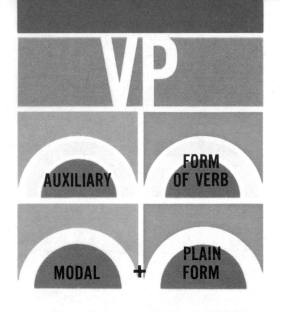

Be and *have* also have participle forms that are used with the auxiliary *have:*

> Marty + has been lucky.
> She + has had lunch.

FOLLOW THROUGH. Write five sentences using *have* followed by the participle form of the verb.

Study these sentences:

1	2
We + *shall* **try**.	I + *should* **go** there.
Carla + *will* **look**.	I + *would* **find** items.
Ann + *may* **search**.	You + *might* **find** one.
He + *can* **find** books.	It + *could* **be** useful.
	I + *must* **leave** now.

Now look at the Language Strip and answer these questions:

1. In each sentence above, what form of the verb is used with the auxiliaries in italics?
2. What are these auxiliaries called?
3. In the sentences in column 1, what tense does each modal show?
4. In the sentences in column 2, what tense does each modal show?
5. Which modal has the same form for the present and the past?
6. In the next-to-last example above, the plain form of what word is used with the modal?

Modals are used in the **VP** with the plain form of the verb or of *be* to show present or past tense.

154

Another auxiliary is *do.* The present forms of *do* are *do* and *does.* The past form is *did.* With what form of the verb is the auxiliary *do* used?

1. I + *do* **try** hard.
2. He + *does* **search** carefully.
3. We + *did* **find** the books.

The auxiliary *do* is used in the **VP** with the plain form of the verb to show present or past tense.

FOLLOW THROUGH. Write five sentences using forms of *do* as auxiliaries.

FOLLOW THROUGH. Copy the **VP** from each sentence. Show whether the auxiliary is a form of *be,* a form of *have,* a modal, or a form of *do.* Then tell which form of the verb follows the auxiliary.

1. Card catalogs will give information.
2. Arthur has found the card.
3. He was looking for a subject.
4. The boys had chosen topics.
5. *Readers' Guide* does provide help.
6. You should use it.
7. I have used it often.
8. Selma was using it earlier.
9. It does list topics.
10. They are finding some topics now.

FOLLOW THROUGH. Use an auxiliary in place of each box as you write the sentences.

1. Encyclopedias ☐ give information.
2. They ☐ include most subjects.
3. I ☐ using one now.
4. Our teacher ☐ found a source book.
5. You ☐ use it for your report.
6. Jake ☐ chosen turtles for his report.

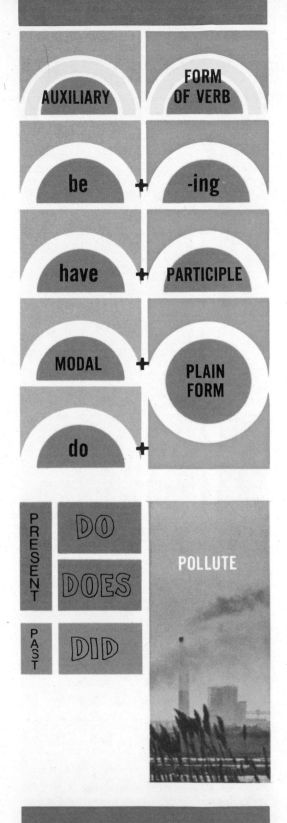

AUXILIARY + FORM OF VERB

be + -ing

have + PARTICIPLE

MODAL + PLAIN FORM

do +

PRESENT DO DOES

PAST DID

POLLUTE

155

LOOKING BACK AND CHECKING UP

Subjects and Predicates (pages 20-26)

A. As you write each sentence, divide it into subject **NP** and **VP**.

1. Catalogs give information.
2. Arthur found a card.
3. He was looking for a subject.
4. Henry worked in the library too.
5. One can help the other.
6. The cards were helpful.
7. Betty found some materials.
8. They were in the library.
9. The librarian had filed them.
10. Librarians can give assistance.
11. They are helpful.
12. We like our librarian.
13. She has helped us often.
14. I need information now.
15. She will find it for me.

B. List a proper noun for each of these:

1. lake   3. day   5. gulf   7. mountain
2. boy   4. month   6. girl   8. language

C. Write the plural of each of these nouns:

1. toy   4. mix   7. wife   10. country
2. gas   5. half   8. match   11. woman
3. ox   6. hobby   9. mouse   12. tomato

D. Which of the following makes up the subject **NP** in each sentence in A?

1. A proper noun
2. A common noun alone
3. A determiner followed by a noun
4. A personal pronoun
5. An indefinite pronoun

Words in the Verb Phrase (pages 58-62)

A. Tell whether the **VP** in each sentence below contains a verb or a verb followed by an **NP**.

1. Ruby chose the ruby as her topic.
2. She searched many book lists for her report.
3. She searched carefully.
4. She found *Birthstones.*
5. The book appealed to her.
6. It told about rubies.
7. Several countries produce them in quantity.
8. The color comes from an impurity.
9. Many people had a belief once.
10. A flame burned in the center.

B. Describe each **NP** used as an object in A.

C. Name the **VP** in each sentence below and tell whether it contains a form of *be* followed by an **NP** or a linking verb followed by an **NP**:

1. Jim Thorpe was an athlete at Carlisle Indian Industrial School.
2. The Carlisle Indians were footballers.
3. Thorpe became a star.
4. He remained a star for years.
5. He was a professional later.

More Words in the Verb Phrase (pages 88-93)

A. Point out the **VP** in each sentence and tell whether it is a form of *be* followed by an adjective or a linking verb followed by an adjective.

1. A rain forest is lush.
2. The forest is silent at noontime.
3. It seems empty.

4. It becomes noisy at dawn.
5. The animals grow restless then.

B. Write the **VP** from each of these sentences. Tell whether the adverbial is an adverbial of place, manner, or time.

1. One rain forest is in South America.
2. The forest grows in layers.
3. It has grown for many centuries.
4. Some trees soar high.
5. They overshadow others with their tops.

Tense in the Verb Phrase (pages 124-127)

A. Use the present form of the verb as you write each sentence:

1. Loons (outswim) fish.
2. A loon (catch) fish underwater.
3. The Arctic tern (fly) far.
4. Golden eagles (swoop) in dives.
5. An ostrich (run) fast.

B. Use the past form of the verb in each sentence.

1. I (see) a whale in the ocean.
2. It (break) through the water.
3. Its head (blow) a spout.
4. The whale (swim) on top for a while.
5. It (go) under again in a few minutes.

C. Use the proper form of *be* or *have* in each sentence.

1. Some whales ☐ toothless.
2. They ☐ baleen in their mouths.
3. Whales ☐ four legs once.
4. Two legs ☐ at the back.
5. A whale ☐ a mammal.

Auxiliaries (pages 152-155)

A. Write the **VP** from each sentence below. Show what kind of auxiliary is used and which form of the verb follows it.

1. This author has written about reptiles.
2. She is researching dinosaurs now.
3. Her books can teach us.
4. I do like them.
5. You will enjoy them.

B. Use an auxiliary in each sentence below:

1. You ☐ find encyclopedias in our library.
2. They ☐ teach you about reptiles.
3. I ☐ studied dinosaurs in them.
4. Roy ☐ writing about cats.
5. You ☐ find any subject in an encyclopedia.

UNIT 6 READING

LEO
July 23-Aug. 22

VIRGO
Aug. 23-Sept. 22

SAGITTARIUS
Nov. 22-Dec. 22

SCORPIUS Oct. 23-Nov. 21

ARIES
Mar. 21-Apr. 20

KINDS OF READING

DISCUSS IT. How are the signs of the zodiac used in "reading" the stars? Describe the type of reading performed in each of the following examples:

1. A hunter reading animal tracks
2. A sailor reading weather signs
3. A hiker reading a compass
4. An engineer reading a blueprint
5. A pupil reading a book

160

TAURUS
Apr. 21-May 22

PISCES
Feb. 20-Mar. 20

AQUARIUS

Jan. 21-Feb. 19

CAPRICORNUS
Dec. 23-Jan. 20

GEMINI
May 23-June 21

Sept. 23-Oct. 22
LIBRA

CANCER
June 22-July 22

What other kinds of reading can you think of? What skills are needed to perform some of the various kinds of reading?

This unit stresses the importance of reading and introduces you to various kinds of literature that we read for pleasure.

All civilizations have created myths and traditions to try to explain how human beings relate to their world. How do these pictures reflect the explanations that various groups of people have given?

What has replaced the explanations that are no longer used today? Which explanations are still used by some people? Why do you think people believe in these things? Why do you think it is, or isn't, a good idea for people to believe that some things and some persons have magic power?

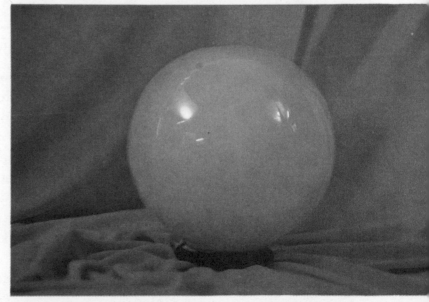

Solving a Mystery

The following selection is about the youngest and greatest detective in the world. Leroy Brown is the ten-year-old son of the chief of police of Idaville. Because Leroy has read more books than anybody and never forgets a word, everybody calls him Encyclopedia. Encyclopedia's favorite hobby is solving mysteries.

Match wits with Encyclopedia as you read the following case. Read carefully, look for clues, and find the solution to the mystery.

THE CASE OF THE RED BOAT

"All set for the fish, son?" asked Chief Brown.

Encyclopedia lifted his fishing pole. "All set," he answered smiling.

He didn't really feel like smiling. He felt like asking questions. He had seen his father slip a gun into the lunchbox.

During the drive to the docks, Encyclopedia finally got up courage to ask, "Are we really going fishing, Dad?"

"Of course," replied Chief Brown. "Why do you ask?"

"You brought a gun," said Encyclopedia.

"Oh . . ." said Chief Brown. "You saw it? Well, I don't expect we'll meet trouble. I brought it along just in case."

"In case of what?"

"Do you remember the robbery four days ago down in the islands?" Chief Brown said.

"Two armed men robbed one of the millionaires' homes," said Encyclopedia. "They got away with three hundred thousand dollars worth of jewels and furs."

"The robbers escaped by motorboat," said Chief Brown.

"That was four days ago. You don't think they're still at sea!" exclaimed Encyclopedia.

"It's possible," said Chief Brown. "About the time the robbers made their escape, a storm broke. The rains lasted only an hour or so. But there have been high winds until today."

"Do you believe the winds blew the robbers' boat out to sea?" asked Encyclopedia.

"The robbers could still be at sea, out of gas and drifting," said Chief Brown. "But let's forget about them. Let's think about fish."

At the docks, Encyclopedia helped his father unload the car. They bought ice and bait at the little store by the gas pumps. When everything was aboard, Chief Brown started the motor.

"Cast off," he called.

Encyclopedia undid the lines. The boat was a twenty footer with an outboard motor. Chief Brown rented her three or four Sundays each summer.

"We'll try our luck in the ocean first," said Chief Brown. "If nothing is biting, we can come closer to shore and try for snapper and flounder."

The boat moved smoothly across the calm waters of the bay. Once in the ocean, Chief Brown speeded up. As the shore fell farther and farther behind, Encyclopedia thought of the robbers.

What if he and his father met them at sea?

The robbers were armed. Would they try to come aboard like pirates? Or would they throw the stolen jewels and furs into the ocean and say they were harmless boatmen?

According to the newspaper stories, the two robbers had worn masks. No one knew what they looked like. As it had been dark, no one could be sure of what their boat looked like—only that it was not white.

Chief Brown slowed the motor. He handed Encyclopedia a fishing rod. "Time to try our luck," he said.

The fish were biting. Father and son had landed ten beauties when Chief Brown suddenly put aside his rod. For several minutes he looked through field glasses at a small red boat in the distance.

Then he called the Coast Guard on the ship-to-shore radio.

Within forty minutes a Coast Guard cutter came alongside. It carried a big gun on the front deck.

Chief Brown greeted the captain. "I think that's the one we've been looking for," he said, pointing to the red boat. "I would have moved closer, but my son is with me."

"Better drop anchor and come aboard," said the captain. "This will be the safest place if there is shooting."

Chief Brown put over the anchor. He and Encyclopedia climbed aboard the cutter. The captain shouted orders. The cutter headed for the small red boat.

At first the red boat seemed empty. Then Encyclopedia saw a man. He came out of the tiny cabin and waved.

The cutter swung alongside. A rope ladder was dropped, and the man reached for it weakly. Three Coast Guardsmen helped him aboard.

"Thank goodness you saw us!" the man gasped, stepping onto the deck of the cutter. He took off his cap. With a handkerchief he wiped the heavy sweat from his bald head and face. "Water, please," he said. "Water!"

Water was brought. The man drank it in great gulps.

"I'm Roger Ascot," he said at last. "Ben Page and I

166

were out for a day's fishing when the storm hit us. The waves were terrible. The radio went dead right away. Sea water got into the gas, and the engine quit."

Again he dried the sweat from his head and face with his handkerchief.

"We've been drifting four days without food and water," he went on. "We had some food in a chest, but it was washed overboard with our fishing things. Ben passed out yesterday from thirst. He's in the cabin."

Ben Page was immediately brought onto the cutter and taken below. Roger Ascot followed him.

Chief Brown climbed down the rope ladder. For a few minutes he looked carefully around the red boat.

"There's water in the gas, all right," he said. "The radio doesn't work, and I don't see any food or drinking water."

"How about guns?" said Encyclopedia. "And the stolen jewels and furs?"

"The boat is clean," said Chief Brown. "I may have made a mistake. Roger Ascot and Ben Page don't appear to be the robbers."

"Don't believe Roger Ascot's story," warned Encyclopedia. "He has the face of a liar!"

WHAT DID ENCYCLOPEDIA MEAN?
Donald J. Sobol

The solution to "The Case of the Red Boat" is printed upside down at the bottom of page **168**.

DISCUSS IT. Discuss answers to the following:

1. Why did Chief Brown think the robbers would still be at sea four days after the robbery?
2. What was stolen?
3. Why didn't anyone know what the robbers looked like?
4. What happened to the stolen items?
5. How did Encyclopedia know that Roger Ascot was not telling the truth?

Capital Letters

Why do the words in bold letters begin with capital letters?

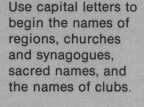

Use capital letters to begin the names of regions, churches and synagogues, sacred names, and the names of clubs.

1. Encyclopedia and his father went to the **South** to solve a case.
2. Some silver had been stolen from **St. Mark's Chapel.**
3. "Thank **God** you have come," exclaimed the priest.
4. Encyclopedia received an award from the **Detective Club.**

Solution to *The Case of the Red Boat*

Roger Ascot said he and Ben Page had been without drinking water for four days.

Yet when he came aboard the Coast Guard cutter, he made a mistake—and Encyclopedia caught it right away.

Roger Ascot wiped the sweat off his head and face.

After four days without a drink, Roger Ascot's body would have been dried out. He couldn't have sweated one drop!

Trapped by his lie, Roger Ascot confessed.

When he and Ben Page saw the Coast Guard cutter, they threw everything overboard—the stolen jewels and furs and their guns. To help their story of being two fishermen caught in a sudden storm, they threw their food and water overboard, too.

Then they made believe they were weak from hunger and thirst.

168

FOLLOW THROUGH. Copy the following sentences and add capital letters where necessary:

1. Angela is a member of the church of god.
2. People came from the east and the west to attend the conference.
3. Is jehovah another name for god?
4. The angel gabriel is always shown holding a horn.
5. Are you planning to attend the meeting of the camera club?

KINDS OF LITERATURE

You have been reading different kinds of stories for several years. What are some of the different kinds of stories that are written? What are the characteristics of each kind of story?

FOLLOW THROUGH. Tell which of the following kinds of literature is described by each definition below:

a. biography   c. fable   e. ballad
b. fairy tale   d. tall tale   f. myth

1. A narrative poem suitable for singing
2. A written story of a person's life
3. A legendary story used to explain a natural event or to describe a supernatural being
4. A short story, usually about animals, that teaches a lesson
5. An exaggerated story that is obviously not true
6. A make-believe story told to entertain children

FOLLOW THROUGH. All stories contain the four parts listed below. See whether you can tell which of the following definitions describes each story part. Check the dictionary to make sure of your answers.

a. beginning   b. buildup   c. climax   d. ending

1. The most exciting part of the story
2. Events that keep you interested in what is about to happen
3. A brief statement that follows the climax
4. The part that tells about the characters and the setting

169

THE FABLE

You know that animals cannot talk. So did Aesop, the Greek slave who wrote many fables. But he wanted to point out human faults without hurting feelings. For that reason, in his stories he used animals that talked and behaved like people.

THE FOX AND THE CROW

One morning a crow got hold of a piece of cheese.

"What luck!" she thought, and flew up on a dead branch to enjoy it.

Now a fox was just then passing the spot. At the sharp smell of cheese he stopped dead in his tracks and sniffed all around the tree. Then he looked up. There sat the crow with the cheese in her beak.

"How nice it would be to start my breakfast with a piece of cheese!" thought the fox.

"The Fox and the Crow" from *Aesop's Fables*, retold by Anne Terry White. Copyright © 1964 by Anne Terry White. Reprinted by permission of Random House, Inc.

His mouth watered for the tidbit. But he couldn't climb up and take the cheese away, for foxes don't climb trees. And anyway the crow would fly off before he got there. "No, my wits will have to get the cheese for me," he said to himself. And in his friendliest tone he called out to the crow:

"Good morning!"

The crow knew better than to answer. If she opened her mouth, she would drop the cheese. So she just sat and listened.

"My dear," the fox went on, "how lovely you are! Your eyes are so bright, your tail is so perky! Your plumes shine like the morning sun. Tell me, Beautiful Creature, can you also sing? Now don't be bashful. Just let me hear you. If your voice matches the rest of your charms, I will say you are the finest bird in these woods."

Up on her dead branch the crow was dizzy with joy. Nobody had ever said such wonderful things to her before. She wanted very much to show the fox that she could also sing. So she opened her beak and gave out a loud, harsh "Caw."

That was all the fox was waiting for. He snapped up the cheese even before it reached the ground.

"I'll give you a piece of advice," he said as he turned to go. "Don't let flattery make a fool of you!"

Take care! Flattery works—more or less—on nearly all of us.

DISCUSS IT. There are certain characteristics that help you to identify fables. By answering the following questions, you will learn some of these characteristics:

1. Who are the main characters of the story?
2. What opinion does the author cause you to form of the fox? the crow?
3. Around what single episode is the fable built?
4. What is the moral, or lesson, of the story?
5. Why did the author keep the story so short and simple?

171

WRITE IT. Write a definition of a fable, using the answers to the previous questions as a guide.

Reread the fable and find the answers to these questions:

1. In which paragraph is the beginning of the story?
2. With what paragraph does the buildup begin?
3. With what paragraph does the buildup end?
4. What two paragraphs make up the climax of the story?
5. What paragraph contains the ending?

Most of the fables that we read today were written hundreds of years ago. Yet there are some fables written by modern authors. James Thurber was a popular American humorist who wrote modern fables. Notice the characteristics that make the following story a fable:

THE WEAVER AND THE WORM

A weaver watched in wide-eyed wonder a silkworm spinning its cocoon in a white mulberry tree.

"Where do you get that stuff?" asked the admiring weaver.

"Do you want to make something out of it?" inquired the silkworm, eagerly.

Then the weaver and the silkworm went their separate ways, for each thought the other had insulted him. We live, man and worm, in a time when almost everything can mean almost anything, for this is the age of gobbledygook, doubletalk, and gudda.

MORAL: *A word to the wise is not sufficient if it doesn't make any sense.*

Copr. © 1956 James Thurber. From *Further Fables for Our Time*, published by Simon and Schuster. Originally printed in *The New Yorker.*

DISCUSS IT. Compare the two fables you have read by discussing the questions below:

1. How were the fables alike?
2. How were they different?
3. How would you compare the morals of the two fables?
4. Why may each of these stories be classified as fables?
5. What clues help you to realize that one of the fables is a modern fable?

TELL IT. Explain what is meant by the moral of each fable. From your own experience, give an example in which you have seen flattery work on someone. Then give an example in which someone has not understood the words of another.

WRITE IT. Each of the following fables contains a beginning and a buildup. State the ending in the form of a moral.

The Rich Dog and the Poor Dog

A rich dog lived in a big house. He had more of everything than he could use. One day he had eaten from the big bowl in his yard until he was stuffed. There was still much food left in his bowl. A skinny, hungry dog came along and asked for something to eat. "Get out of here," barked the rich dog. "This is my food." The hungry dog left the yard.

Later in the day the rich dog was in another part of the neighborhood. He was attacked by a large, mean dog. Just then the hungry dog came up the street. . . .

173

A fox sat every day on a riverbank telling the fish, ducks, turtles, and other animals how to swim. No matter how well they swam, the fox told them how they could swim better.

One day the animals decided to play a trick on the fox. Two turtles painted their shells with mud so that they looked like rocks. They waited for the fox on the riverbank. The fox thought the shells were rocks and sat on them. The turtles crawled toward the river and dumped the fox into the water. . . .

DISCUSS IT. Take turns reading your endings to the class. Notice whether the ending and the moral of each fable seem to be closely related. Select the endings that you think are best and be prepared to explain why.

WRITE IT. Select a moral, animal characters, and a plot that you will use in a fable. Add a beginning, a buildup, a climax, and an ending. The morals below may help you to get started. Write the fable in such a way that it can be dramatized, or acted out, by two persons. The characters should tell much of the story through their conversation.

1. Haste makes waste.
2. Waste causes hardships.
3. Good advice is wasted on fools.
4. Good health is more important than great wealth.
5. We often despise what is most useful to us.

174

EDIT IT. Read your fable to be sure that you have enclosed the direct words of each speaker in quotation marks. Check also that you have set off the words of the speaker from the rest of the sentence by a comma or commas.

Select a partner to work with you in dramatizing your fable. Practice until you are both ready to dramatize your fable.

Notice that in the following sentence there is a cause that creates a particular effect. What are the cause and the effect?

If I open my mouth, then I'll drop the cheese.

What words give you clues that the sentence is a cause-and-effect sentence? Why are cause-and-effect sentences often used in fables?

The following words help you to identify cause-and-effect sentences:

if — then   because   since   either — or

FOLLOW THROUGH. Make up four cause-and-effect sentences, using one of the items above in each.

THE BALLAD

Billy the Kid has become a regular part of American folklore. He was born William H. Bonney in New York City in 1859. His family moved west; and when he was a young boy, he shot a man in Silver City, New Mexico. He lived the life of killing and stealing until he was shot at the age of 21 by a former friend, Sheriff Pat Garrett. Although he was a small, stoop-shouldered man who was generally known as a coward, his life became the subject of folk songs and stories. Many books, movies, TV programs, and songs have been written about Billy.

The ballad on the next page tells about Billy's life.

Billy the Kid

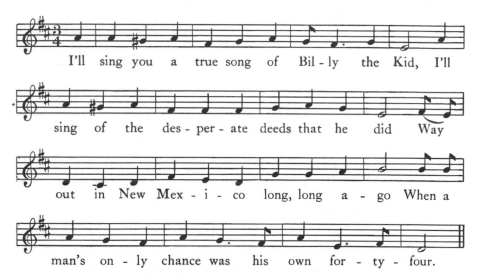

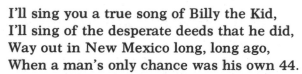

I'll sing you a true song of Billy the Kid,
I'll sing of the desperate deeds that he did,
Way out in New Mexico long, long ago,
When a man's only chance was his own 44.

When Billy the Kid was a very young lad,
In old Silver City he went to the bad;
Way out in the West with a gun in his hand
At the age of twelve years he first killed his man.

Fair Mexican maidens play guitars and sing
A song about Billy, their boy bandit king,
How ere his young manhood had reached its sad end
Had a notch on his pistol for twenty-one men.

'Twas on the same night when poor Billy died
He said to his friends: "I am not satisfied;
There are twenty-one men I have put bullets through
And Sheriff Pat Garrett must make twenty-two."

Now this is how Billy the Kid met his fate:
The bright moon was shining, the hour was late,
Shot down by Pat Garrett, who once was his friend,
The young outlaw's life had now come to its end.

176

There's many a man with a face fine and fair
Who starts out in life with a chance to be square,
But just like poor Billy he wanders astray
And loses his life in the very same way.

DISCUSS IT. Read the ballad and tap your foot lightly with the rhythm of the poem. How many beats are in each line? What story is told by the ballad?

FOLLOW THROUGH. Arrange the events below according to the paragraph on page 175 and the ballad:

A narrative poem that has a strong rhythm and is suitable for singing is called a *ballad*.

> Billy decided to shoot Pat Garrett.
> Billy was shot and killed.
> Billy killed a man in Silver City.
> Billy moved to the West.
> Billy shot twenty-one men.

Sometimes events are told in time order:

1. He wrote a letter during class.
2. After I finish my homework, I watch TV.

In which sentence do two events happen at the same time? What word in each sentence helps you know the order in which the events occurred? What other words help you to know the time order of events?

Words like *before, after, first, then, while,* and *during* are time words. Notice that the time order can be changed by changing only one of these words:

1. Cora talked to me **while** she ate her lunch.
2. Cora talked to me **before** she ate her lunch.
3. Cora talked to me **after** she ate her lunch.

FOLLOW THROUGH. The two events in the sentences below happen at the same time. Substitute one word in each sentence to show that the first event happened *before* the other. Then substitute one word to show that the first event happened *after* the other.

1. During dinner Uncle Matt told us about his trip.
2. The ladies talked while they rode on the bus.
3. Debbie slept during the program.
4. The carpenter sang while he built the shelves.
5. A strong wind blew during the storm.

Think of a jingle used on TV or radio to advertise a product. How are you able to remember the words of the jingle?

Using music as a memory aid is an old practice. Before writing was invented, historical records were passed down orally. To help people remember events accurately, the events were often sung in the form of ballads. Some ballads were about famous persons; some were about places; some were about events; and others, like the one below, were about occupations.

DARK AS A DUNGEON

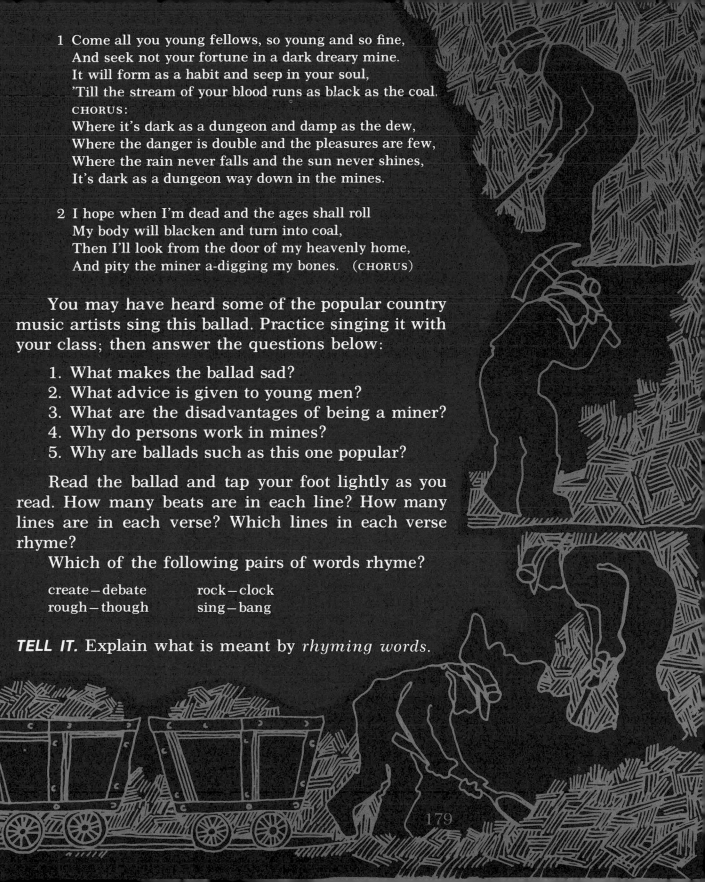

1 Come all you young fellows, so young and so fine,
And seek not your fortune in a dark dreary mine.
It will form as a habit and seep in your soul,
'Till the stream of your blood runs as black as the coal.
CHORUS:
Where it's dark as a dungeon and damp as the dew,
Where the danger is double and the pleasures are few,
Where the rain never falls and the sun never shines,
It's dark as a dungeon way down in the mines.

2 I hope when I'm dead and the ages shall roll
My body will blacken and turn into coal,
Then I'll look from the door of my heavenly home,
And pity the miner a-digging my bones.   (CHORUS)

You may have heard some of the popular country music artists sing this ballad. Practice singing it with your class; then answer the questions below:

1. What makes the ballad sad?
2. What advice is given to young men?
3. What are the disadvantages of being a miner?
4. Why do persons work in mines?
5. Why are ballads such as this one popular?

Read the ballad and tap your foot lightly as you read. How many beats are in each line? How many lines are in each verse? Which lines in each verse rhyme?

Which of the following pairs of words rhyme?

create – debate   rock – clock
rough – though   sing – bang

TELL IT. Explain what is meant by *rhyming words*.

FOLLOW THROUGH. Think of at least two words that rhyme with each of the words below:

1. drum	6. fact	11. past
2. blur	7. sale	12. brown
3. hurt	8. grain	13. fence
4. made	9. sand	14. cream
5. take	10. gang	15. park

WRITE IT. Select a person, a place, or an event about which to write a ballad. Arrange the information you wish to present in the appropriate time order. You may wish to fit the words to a tune that you already know. Be sure that the lines have a consistent rhythm and rhyme. You may use a make-believe event to write about if you wish.

EDIT IT. Read your ballad and tap your foot lightly to make sure that your rhythm is consistent. Check the rhyming words to be sure that the sounds are the same. Begin each line with a capital letter and be sure that each sentence ends with the proper punctuation mark.

Select volunteers to lead the class in singing the ballads.

TALL TALES

The tall tale is a form of literature that was developed in the United States. Our country was settled with people who had a great spirit of adventure, imagination, and humor. The pioneers who moved west were rough and boastful. Ordinary descriptions weren't enough for them. They needed to exaggerate. Their heroes were part man, part tiger, and part alligator. They could lick a cage full of wild gorillas single-handed and tame a mountain lion to ride. Even their crops were far from ordinary.

Have you ever seen a tall tale about a woman? During what period in our country's history were most of the tall tales written? What roles were women expected to play at that time? Why do you think there are very few tall tales about women?

In the following selection, identify some of the characteristics that label it as a tall tale:

THE POPCORN PATCH

"I had an old mule once upon a time that fooled himself clean to death," said Hank Huggins. "It happened down in Cade's Cove where I had planted me a little patch of corn, the kind that's used for popping. It was a hot day. I didn't want to go out plowing that morning, but my old lady got after me.

" 'Hank,' she said, 'If you don't get out and plow that field of popcorn, the weeds will take it and the young'uns won't have any corn to pop at Christmas time.'

An exaggerated story that obviously is not true is called a *tall tale*.

"I wasn't in the notion, I can tell you that. I saw the day was going to be a scorcher. But once my old lady has set her mind to something, there's no peace until it's done. So I went out, hitched up the mule, and set off to plow the cornfield.

"Heavens to Betsy, it was hot in that cove! The mountains standing up all around kept out every breath of breeze. The place held the heat like an oven. July flies were a-droning in the trees and the leaves hung as limp as a dog's tongue. It would be hard to say which was hotter, me or that old mule. Up and down the rows we went, a-toiling and a-sweating.

"Along towards noon it was broiling for certain. Even the old logs and stumps began to crawl off in the shade. Suddenly I heard a crackling sound in the air. Before I could figure out what happened, white flakes were a-flying all around. At first, I thought it was a snowstorm. Then I realized what it was: The blazing sun had set that corn a-popping, and it was falling like a snowstorm.

"That old mule, he stopped and looked around. Then he began to shiver. He thought for sure he'd been overtaken by a howling blizzard. He stood there and squinched himself all up, like critters do when it's real cold.

"'Get along there!' I hollered at him. 'It's nothing but popcorn!'

"But the poor thing couldn't understand. He'd never seen any popcorn before and he thought it was snow. He just stood there, shaking and shivering in every limb. I couldn't do a thing with him. It was a crying shame. Before I could get that critter unhooked from the plow and out of there, he gave right up. He lay down in the row and froze to death—all covered with popcorn."

Ellis Credle

How can you tell that the writer of the tall tale does not really expect you to think that the story is true? What are some other tall tales that you know? What do all tall tales seem to have in common?

Which of the sentences below is exaggerated?

1. Bill was a good fighter who was clever, strong, agile, and mean.
2. In a fight Bill was cunning as a fox, strong as an elephant, quick as a gazelle, and mean as a hungry bear.

Why would sentence 2 probably be included in a tall tale?

FOLLOW THROUGH. Rewrite each sentence below so that it is obviously not true:

1. The mosquitoes at our picnic were quite large.
2. Paul Bunyan could chop trees down quickly.
3. Riverboat Ray could paddle a canoe quite efficiently.
4. Deadeye Dick was an excellent shot with his pistol.
5. The grapefruit in Texas are quite large.

WRITE IT. Think of an occupation or an event that you could use as a topic of a tall tale. Follow the steps below in developing your tall tale:

1. List the events in the order that they take place.
2. Decide what you will exaggerate so that your readers will know the story is not true.
3. Decide how you will exaggerate the character or event.
4. Plan a beginning, a buildup, a climax, and an ending for the tale.
5. Write the tall tale.

EDIT IT. Read each sentence in your tall tale. Is it exaggerated? Should it be? Be sure that enough of the sentences are exaggerated so that the tale is obviously untrue.

TELL IT. Take turns telling your tall tales to the class. Select the tales that you like best. Explain why you like them best.

Look at the illustration on page 181. Draw your own illustration of that or any other tall tale. If you wish, you may use a tall tale you have read or any of those told by members of your class.

Myths

Notice the characteristics of a myth as you read this one. Decide why you think the myth was told.

Proserpine and Pluto

Pluto, the wicked god of the underworld, was forbidden to visit Olympus, the home of the chief gods of ancient Greece. He lived in a deep palace in the underworld. One day he met Jupiter while they were both walking on earth. "I have fallen in love with Proserpine, the daughter of your sister Ceres," he said. "May I have your permission to marry her?"

Jupiter was afraid to offend either Pluto or Ceres by answering the question, so he winked. The wink was all the encouragement Pluto needed.

One sunny afternoon Proserpine was picking flowers and wandered away from her friends. Pluto had been waiting for such an opportunity. He galloped up in his carriage, seized her, and carried her deep inside the earth.

Pluto took Proserpine into his palace and placed her on a throne next to his. "I am Pluto, king of the underworld," he explained. "I have watched you and fallen in love with you. I want you to be my wife." Proserpine could do nothing but cry.

Ceres was heartbroken. Day after day she roamed the earth searching for Proserpine. She forgot her work as goddess of the harvest. The flowers did not bloom. Crops did not ripen.

Finally, Jupiter sent for her and asked why the plants were not growing.

"You are king of the gods," replied Ceres. "Return my daughter, and I will cause things to grow again."

Jupiter explained that Proserpine was with Pluto. He said that if she had eaten any food of the underworld, she could not return to earth. Then he agreed to send Mercury, his messenger, to the underworld to see whether she had eaten.

At that very moment Pluto had given Proserpine a pomegranate. She had never seen a pomegranate before. It looked good and she was hungry. She took a bite but found that the pomegranate was full of seeds. "I don't want any more," she said. "I swallowed some seeds."

Just then Mercury appeared at the castle. He learned that Proserpine had eaten, so he returned to Jupiter.

Ceres refused to let anything grow until her daughter was returned. Jupiter was forced into a decision. He went to visit Pluto and told him everyone would starve if Ceres could not have Proserpine back.

Pluto answered, "I love Proserpine and want her with me always. But she is not happy here. Since she swallowed only seven seeds, I will keep her here with me seven months of the year. She may spend the other five months with Ceres on earth."

Proserpine and Pluto were married. Each spring she returns to earth with Ceres. The flowers and trees grow. In the fall she returns to the underworld. Then Ceres is sad and nothing grows.

What causes our four seasons? When this myth was told, did people know that the seasons are caused by the earth's revolving around the sun? How were the seasons explained in the myth? Why do you think some gods were portrayed as being evil? Why do you think women were included in myths but not in tall tales? What was the purpose of this myth?

How do you suppose Proserpine felt when she arrived at Pluto's gloomy underworld castle? How did Jupiter feel when Ceres did not allow crops to grow and Pluto insisted on keeping Proserpine in the underworld? How did Ceres feel when she realized her daughter had been stolen?

TELL IT. Pretend that you are a TV reporter. Select one of the characters in the myth and prepare to interview her or him. Plan carefully the questions that you will ask. Other members of the class will study the characters in the myth and decide how they would answer various questions about their feelings. Conduct several interviews during class time.

As the interviews are conducted, decide whether the questions are appropriate. Then determine whether the answers seem in keeping with each character. Discuss these issues after each interview.

A legendary story used to explain a natural event or to describe a supernatural being is called a *myth*.

185

Happenings in Your Language

Do you know how many words are in our language? Have there always been the same number of words in English? Linguists estimate that at one time there were fewer than 10,000 words in English. Now there are approximately 800,000.

How do new words come into our language? Some words are made up, or coined. Some are taken from other languages. Sometimes two words are blended into one, as in *smog*. Other words come from people's names.

Some words that have come into our language are the names of gods and goddesses from mythology. Although all cultures have myths, our language has been most affected by the Greek and Roman myths. The Greeks and Romans had the same gods, but they gave them different names. For example, the god of the sea was called Poseidon by the Greeks and Neptune by the Romans. Below are the names and titles of some famous Greek and Roman gods and goddesses:

Vulcan—god of fire
Faunus—god of animals
Pomona—goddess of fruit
Iris—goddess of the rainbow
Ceres—goddess of agriculture

Polyhymnia—goddess of religious music
Hygeia—goddess of health
Flora—goddess of flowers
Somnus—god of sleep
Titans—a family of giants

FOLLOW THROUGH. Using the names and titles of these gods and goddesses, try to figure out the meanings of the words in bold letters.

1. His **somnolence** was obvious because of his frequent yawning.
2. Our choir bought new **hymnals.**
3. Rubber is **vulcanized** to make it strong and elastic.
4. The center of our basketball team is a **titan.**
5. We are studying **hygiene** in school.
6. My cousin is an expert on the **fauna** of the Pacific Northwest.
7. Those colorful flowers belong to the **iris** family.
8. Have you read about the **flora** of Hawaii?
9. My favorite breakfast food is **cereal.**
10. My brother is studying to be a **pomologist.**

Using Your Language

Notice the words in bold letters in these sentences:

By the end of autumn most of the leaves had **fallen** from the trees. Some of them had **flown** miles from their trees on the wind. Soon the winter winds **froze** all the unprotected plants.

What are the forms of each word in bold letters? Use your dictionary if you do not know.

FOLLOW THROUGH. Use the appropriate form of the word in parentheses in each sentence below:

(fly)   1. Have you ever ☐ in an airplane?
(fall)   2. Snow has ☐ for three days.
(freeze) 3. The drop in temperature ☐ our plants.
(fall)   4. My sister has ☐ down our stairway twice.
(freeze) 5. Dad ☐ flavored ice in our freezer.
(fly)   6. Bruce hasn't ☐ his model plane yet.
(fall)   7. The deer had ☐ into that pit.
(fly)   8. That bird has ☐ around in our yard all day.
(freeze) 9. Our wash ☐ on the clothesline.
(fall)   10. My sister has ☐ in love many times.

187

CHECK UP ON YOURSELF

Types of Literature (pages 169–185)

Which of the following types of literature is identified by each of the definitions below?

ballad	fable	myth
biography	fairy tale	tall tale

1. A narrative poem set to music
2. A short story, usually about animals, that contains a moral, or lesson
3. A true account of a person's life
4. An exaggerated story about a true or fictional character
5. A legendary story used to explain natural happenings or to describe supernatural beings
6. A story about make-believe people used to entertain children

Cause-and-Effect Sentences (page 175)

Tell which word helps you to identify each of the following as a cause-and-effect sentence:

1. Because she was hurt, the small child cried.
2. If you win a race, then you receive a ribbon.
3. Since she was happy, she was fun to be with.
4. Either you finish your work now, or you cannot go.
5. He put on his coat because he was cold.

Time-Order Sentences (page 177)

Each of the sentences below describes two events that happened at the same time. Rewrite each sentence and substitute one word so that the events happened at different times.

1. While she was reading, the phone rang.
2. During the baseball game, it began to rain.
3. The ladies ate while they planned the program.
4. They went boating during the storm.
5. Mother cried when she heard the news.

Rhyming Words (page 179)

Copy the words below in a single column. After each word, write at least two other words that rhyme with it.

1. strum	4. work	7. plane	10. fair	13. hope
2. jump	5. grab	8. flash	11. cent	14. you
3. purr	6. slack	9. skate	12. think	15. play

Using Exaggeration (pages 182–183)

Rewrite each factual statement below so that it becomes an exaggerated statement:

1. High winds blew through our neighborhood last night.
2. The mechanic who repairs our car is really strong.
3. My uncle is so lazy that he doesn't get anything done.
4. It was so cold that mechanical objects wouldn't work.
5. Carl was the fastest carpenter I have ever seen.

Words from the Myths (pages 186–187)

Write the sentences below, using one of the following words for the blank in each sentence:

pomologist   fauna   iris   somnolence   titan

1. An ☐ is a beautiful flower.
2. The ☐ of the island were starving because of the snow.
3. His ☐ caused him to go to bed early.
4. A scientist who specializes in the growing of fruit is a ☐.
5. He was as large as a ☐.

Using Your Language (page 187)

Use the appropriate form of the word in parentheses for each sentence below:

(fly)   1. My father has ☐ over 30,000 miles.
(freeze) 2. One time the wings of the plane ☐.
(fall)   3. The plane might have ☐.
(fly)   4. The pilot had not ☐ in such temperatures before.
(freeze) 5. He almost ☐ at the controls.

189

LOOKING BACK AND CHECKING UP

Identifying Types of Listening (pages 8–14)

Match each type of listening below with its definition.

Marginal Listening   Analytical Listening
Attentive Listening   Appreciative Listening

1. Listening to see whether information is complete and accurate
2. Listening in such a way that you hear only those things that interest you
3. Listening that encourages you to establish a certain mood or form mental images
4. Listening carefully so that you can remember what has been said

Using Commas (pages 41, 71, and 106)

Use commas where they are needed as you write each sentence.

1. Yes that is the man I saw.
2. Darlene did you win an award?
3. Dr. Albert Norris president of the association opened the meeting.
4. No I did not call you this morning.
5. My teacher likes me Mom.

Writing a Bibliography (page 136)

Arrange the following items as a bibliography. List the parts in the right order and punctuate them correctly.

A matter of miracles by e b fenton. Holt, Rinehart and Winston, Inc. 1967 New York.

Zilpha k. snyder. The egypt game. Atheneum Publishers 1967 New York.

Adam Bookout by Louisa r shotwell. The Viking Press New York 1967.

Bawden, Nina. J. B. Lippincott Company Philadelphia, 1967. A handful of thieves.

The flight of the doves by Walter Macken, The Macmillan Company 1968, New York.

More Ideas For You!

1. See how many different types of reading you can identify. Prepare a bulletin-board display or another display that shows the different types.

2. Read another Encyclopedia Brown mystery to the class and ask them to solve it.

3. Find some information on astronomy and present a report to the class.

4. Many common expressions, such as "Don't count your chickens before they are hatched" and "He is a wolf in sheep's clothing," come from fables. Make a list of common expressions and show the fables from which they are taken.

5. Read some tall tales until you find one that appeals to you. Read the tale aloud and record it on a tape recorder. After you have a recording that satisfies you, play it for the class.

6. Mythology has been an important part of other cultures besides Greek and Roman. Read some myths from another culture and present an oral report on the major gods and goddesses.

7. Bring in some records or tapes of ballads by your favorite performer and play them for the class.

8. If you have friends who play musical instruments, you may want to record your own performance of some ballads and play them for the class.

9. Many words in our language have come from Greek and Roman gods and goddesses. Choose ten gods and goddesses and make a poster listing as many words as you can find that were taken from their names.

191

LOOKING AT YOUR LANGUAGE

NP + VP

PRESENT TENSE

PLURAL NOUN

(Those) books
(Our) friends

CERTAIN PERSONAL PRONOUNS

I
You
We
They

PLAIN

tell
have
look

FORM

SOME PROPER NOUNS

Mexicans
The Great Lakes

THE BASIC SENTENCE

Tense Forms

You know that a verb has two present tense forms. What are they? If you have forgotten, look back at page 124.

Look at the Language Strip. With what kinds of subject **NP**'s is the plain form of each verb used?

The plain form is used when the subject **NP** is one of the following:

1. A plural form of a noun — with or without a determiner

    a. Card catalogs + **give** information.
    b. These three cards + **tell** about *The Hudson.*

2. The personal pronouns *I, you, we,* and *they*

    a. I + **have** the book.
    b. You + **have** another book in your apartment.
    c. We + **gather** facts.
    d. They + **go** into our report.

3. Some proper nouns

    a. The Rocky Mountains + **tower** above us.
    b. The Burnses + **travel** every year to the West.

Look at the Language Strip. With what kind of subject **NP**'s is the *-s* form of the verb used?

The *-s* form of a verb is used when the subject **NP** is one of the following:

1. A singular form of a noun—with or without a determiner

    a. A dictionary + **gives** much information.
    b. Patience + **helps**.

2. The personal pronouns *he, she,* and *it*

    a. He + **finds** spellings.
    b. She + **sees** synonyms.
    c. It + **has** pronunciations.

3. The indefinite pronouns listed in the Language Strip on page 26.

    a. Someone + **looks** for compounds.
    b. Everyone + **uses** a dictionary.
    c. Nobody + **writes** without one.

4. Some proper nouns

    a. Angela + **reads** fast.
    b. Herbert S. Zim + **writes** for young people.

FOLLOW THROUGH. Use the plain form or the *-s* form of the verb as you write each sentence.

    1. My friends (read) comic books.
    2. Rolando (like) mysteries.
    3. He (borrow) them from the library.
    4. My parents (borrow) from the bookmobile.
    5. Everyone (want) that book.

NP + VP

PRESENT TENSE

SINGULAR NOUN

(A) book
(One) boy

CERTAIN PERSONAL PRONOUNS

He
She
It

-S FORM

tells
has
looks

CERTAIN INDEFINITE PRONOUNS

Something
Anyone
Everybody

SOME PROPER NOUNS

The Alamo
John Doe

Study the following chart. Then complete the two Follow Through's.

SUBJECT NP	PRESENT TENSE FORMS	PAST TENSE FORMS
The personal pronoun *I*	am	was
The personal pronouns *he*, *she*, and *it*	is	was
Certain indefinite pronouns	is	was
A singular noun	is	was
Some proper nouns	is	was
The personal pronouns *we*, *you*, and *they*	are	were
A plural noun	are	were
Some proper nouns	are	were

NP + be	CONTRACTION
I am	I'm
You are	You're
He is	He's
She is	She's
It is	It's
We are	We're
They are	They're

FOLLOW THROUGH. Use the present tense form of *be* as you write each sentence.

1. Myths ☐ legends.
2. A fable ☐ untrue.
3. Fairy tales ☐ untrue.
4. I ☐ interested in them.
5. They ☐ enjoyable.

FOLLOW THROUGH. Use the past tense form of *be* as you write each sentence.

1. Selma ☐ my buddy last year.
2. She ☐ in my class.
3. The Beims ☐ coauthors.
4. One title ☐ *Two Is a Team.*
5. Something ☐ special about it.

194

When a personal pronoun and a present tense form of *be* are used in a sentence, how are they often written? Look at the Language Strip on page 194. What do we call words like *I'm?*

I'm in school.

FOLLOW THROUGH. As you write each sentence, use a contraction in place of the words in parentheses.

1. (I am) interested in many subjects.
2. (He is) interested in mysteries only.
3. (They are) his hobby.
4. (You are) happy with mathematics.

CHECK UP ON YOURSELF

A. Use a present tense form as you write each sentence.

1. Myths (explain) beliefs.
2. A fable (present) a moral.
3. I (enjoy) fables.
4. Ella (sing) ballads.

B. Use a present tense form of *be* as you write each sentence.

1. These books ☐ fiction.
2. They ☐ from my shelf.
3. Mother ☐ my buyer.
4. This title ☐ *Necessary Nellie.*

C. Use a past tense form of *be* as you write each sentence.

1. The dog ☐ necessary to the children.
2. The children ☐ Mexican-Americans.
3. Everyone ☐ happy with that dog.
4. She ☐ a stray.

THE LANGUAGE OF SYMBOLISM

SIGNS COMMUNICATE

Symbols are rapidly replacing signs in the National Park System. Some of the symbols used are shown above. Basically, they are signs without words. For instance, a fish with a hook dangling above it tells the sportsman that fishing is permitted. The same sign with a red slash through it indicates that fishing is not permitted. All the signs with an asterisk (*) beside them are available with a red slash. In all, there are seventy-seven symbols plus the slash mark to be used in United States parks.

FOLLOW THROUGH. Other symbols being used in our National Park System are shown below. Match each symbol with the idea it expresses.

1. Ranger Station
2. Pets on Leash
3. Post Office
4. First Aid
5. Tunnel
6. Sledding
7. Telephone

8. Airport
9. Bus Stop
10. Gas Station
11. Showers
12. Lodging
13. Campfires
14. Picnic Shelter

15. Kennel
16. Sailboating
17. Bicycle Trail
18. Lighthouse
19. Swimming
20. Horse Trail
21. Playground

IMPRESSIONS

All the pictures below are from magazine advertisements. What products or companies do you think the pictures are advertising?

What kind of words (called "copy") would you put with each picture? Why do you think the advertisers decided to keep the copy outside the picture part of the ads? Why are ads like these more, or less, effective than ads that feature the product or the company?

Kelly Services

Metropolitan Life

198

Piedmont Airli

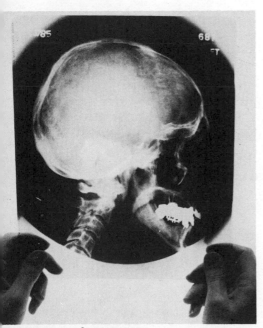

General Telephone & Electro

Hammermill Paper Co.

WORDS, WORDS, WORDS

Any word can stand for any idea as long as the people using that word agree on its meaning.

You know that symbols stand for ideas. Are words symbols? How were certain words selected to stand for particular ideas? Why do persons in other parts of the world express the same ideas with words different from ours?

The following selection presents some interesting ideas about the origin and use of words. It also demonstrates that many different words may be used to express the same idea.

You remember that words having the same or nearly the same meaning are called **synonyms.** *There are several groups of synonyms in the following selection. Some of the synonyms are hard words. But, if you remember that synonyms have nearly the same meanings, you can figure out the meanings of most of the hard words.*

THE WORD MARKET

And, from across the square, five very tall, thin gentlemen regally dressed in silks and satins, plumed hats, and buckled shoes rushed up to the car, stopped short, mopped five brows, caught five breaths, unrolled five parchments, and began talking in turn.

"Greetings!"

"Salutations!"

"Welcome!"

"Good Afternoon!"

"Hello!"

"The Word Market" from *The Phantom Tollbooth*, by Norton Juster. Copyright © 1961 by Norton Juster. Reprinted by permission of Random House, Inc. and Collins, Publishers.

Milo nodded his head, and they went on, reading from their scrolls.

"By order of Azaz the Unabridged——"

"King of Dictionopolis——"

"Monarch of letters——"

"Emperor of phrases, sentences, and miscellaneous figures of speech——"

"We offer you the hospitality of our kingdom,"

"Country,"

"Nation,"

"State,"

"Commonwealth,"

"Realm,"

"Empire,"

"Palatinate,"

"Principality."

"Do all those words mean the same thing?" gasped Milo.

"Of course."

"Certainly."

"Precisely."

"Exactly."

"Yes," they replied in order.

"Well, then," said Milo, not understanding why each one said the same thing in a slightly different way, "wouldn't it be simpler to use just one? It would certainly make more sense."

"Nonsense."

"Ridiculous."

"Fantastic."

"Absurd."

"Bosh," they chorused again, and continued.

"We're not interested in making sense; it's not our job," scolded the first.

"Besides," explained the second, "one word is as good as another—so why not use them all?"

"Then you don't have to choose which one is right," advised the third.

"Besides," sighed the fourth, "if one is right, then ten are ten times as right."

"Obviously you don't know who we are," sneered the fifth. And they presented themselves one by one as:

"The Duke of Definition."

"The Minister of Meaning."

"The Earl of Essence."

"The Count of Connotation."

"The Undersecretary of Understanding."

Milo acknowledged the introduction and, as Tock growled softly, the minister explained.

"We are the king's advisers, or, in more formal terms, his cabinet."

"Cabinet," recited the duke: "1. a small private room or closet, case with drawers, etc., for keeping valuables or displaying curiosities; 2. council room for chief ministers of state; 3. a body of official advisers to the chief executive of a nation."

"You see," continued the minister, bowing thankfully to the duke, "Dictionopolis is the place where all the words in the world come from. They're grown right here in our orchards."

"I didn't know that words grew on trees," said Milo timidly.

"Where did you think they grew?" shouted the earl irritably. A small crowd began to gather to see the little boy who didn't know that letters grew on trees.

"I didn't know they grew at all," admitted Milo even more timidly. Several people shook their heads sadly.

"Well, money doesn't grow on trees, does it?" demanded the count.

"I've heard not," said Milo.

"Then something must. Why not words?" exclaimed the undersecretary triumphantly. The crowd cheered his display of logic and continued about its business.

"To continue," continued the minister impatiently. "Once a week by Royal Proclamation the word market is held here in the great square and people come from everywhere to buy the words they need or trade in the words they haven't used."

"Our job," said the count, "is to see that all the words sold are proper ones, for it wouldn't do to sell someone a word that had no meaning or didn't exist at all. For instance, if you bought a word like *ghlbtsk*, where would you use it?"

"It would be difficult," thought Milo—but there were so many words that were difficult, and he knew hardly any of them.

"But we never choose which ones to use," explained the earl as they walked toward the market stalls, "for as long as they mean what they mean to mean we don't care if they make sense or nonsense."

"Innocence or magnificence," added the count.

"Reticence or common sense," said the undersecretary.

"That seems simple enough," said Milo, trying to be polite.

"Easy as falling off a log," cried the earl, falling off a log with a loud thump.

"Must you be so clumsy?" shouted the duke.

"All I said was——" began the earl, rubbing his head.

"We heard you," said the minister angrily, "and you'll have to find an expression that's less dangerous."

The earl dusted himself off as the others snickered audibly.

"You see," cautioned the count, "you must pick your words very carefully and be sure to say just what you intend to say. And now we must leave to make preparations for the Royal Banquet."

"You'll be there, of course," said the minister.

But before Milo had a chance to say anything, they were rushing off across the square as fast as they had come.

"Enjoy yourself in the market," shouted back the undersecretary.

"Market," recited the duke: "an open space or covered building in which——"

203

And that was the last Milo heard as they disappeared into the crowd.

"I never knew words could be so confusing," Milo said to Tock as he bent down to scratch the dog's ear.

"Only when you use a lot to say a little," answered Tock.

Milo thought this was quite the wisest thing he'd heard all day. "Come," he shouted, "let's see the market. It looks very exciting."

Norton Juster

FOLLOW THROUGH. In our language, to be "in" means often to be "in style," to be "with it." See how "in" you are in your knowledge of words. Substitute one of the *in-* words below for its synonym in each of the following sentences. Use your dictionary or thesaurus if you need help.

| inborn | insipid | incident | insurgent | inform |
| inane | incision | indigent | infuriate | involve |

1. Where were you when the *event* in question took place?
2. When will you *tell* me of my test score?
3. Please don't *engage* me in the argument.
4. The *rebelling* group waved fists at the speaker.
5. Those last remarks *enrage* me.
6. Some people believe that coordination is *natural* ability.
7. The doctor made a small *cut* in the patient's chest.
8. That story is *dull*.
9. The money was divided among several *needy* families.
10. That argument is *silly*.

What did the earl mean when he made the following statement?

"But we never choose which ones to use, for as long as they mean what they mean to mean we don't care if they make sense or nonsense."

Does the statement mean that as long as people agree on the meaning of a word, any word would be satisfactory? If we all agreed that *forp* could represent a chair, could we substitute *forp* for *chair*?

204

TELL IT. Below are some new words to represent old ideas. Pretend that all other words in our language are the same.

clib — friend	fip — show	mu — he
pont — tree	nuff — approach	mus — his
giff — boy	glum — fall	
conkle — picnic	konk — break	slif — tall
tobel — message	dorp — cover	feeper — loyal
porp — cast	glim — climb	
mip — foot	zong — slip	posily — skillfully
rilk — top	crim — write	orik — later

Using the new language described above, decode the following story:

> At the conkle a giff was fipping how posily mu could glim a slif pont. As mu nuffed the rilk, mus mip zonged. Mu glummed. Orik, mus feeper clibs were crimming tobels on the porp dorping mus konked mip.

WRITE IT. Choose a partner and make up a small sample of a new language similar to the one above. Write a short story using your new language. Exchange stories with another pair of pupils. Decode the ideas expressed in the story.

DISCUSS IT. How would you answer the following?

1. How is the language you made up different from English?
2. How is the language you made up similar to English?
3. Why didn't you make up words beginning with letter combinations such as *zx*, *dh*, *rp*, and *bd*?
4. Why might speakers of another language make up words with letter combinations different from those used by members of your class?
5. What three things have you learned about languages in general from making up a small part of a language?

FOLLOW THROUGH. The following sentences contain the same message written in two different codes. Try to figure out the pattern of both codes.

B dpef jt b tfsjft pg tzncpmt sfqsftfoujoh xpset.

1 3,15,4,5 9,19 1 19,5,18,9,5,19 15,6 19,25,13,2,15,12,19 18,5,16,18,5,19,5,14,20,9,14,7 23,15,18,4,19.

FOLLOW THROUGH. Think of a one-sentence message. Make up any type of code that you would like to use and write your message in that code. Exchange your message with a classmate. Try to decode your classmate's message.

Why may codes be considered language? How is the English language like a code? How is it different from a code?

ACRONYMS

Notice the words in bold letters below:

1. Use the **ZIP** Code on all mail.
2. Mick's dad has a new **scuba** outfit.

What is *ZIP*? What does *scuba* mean? How are these words formed? Words such as these might be considered codes. They are formed by combining the initial letter or letters of words. *ZIP* stands for *Z*oning *I*mprovement *P*lan. *Scuba* stands for *s*elf-contained *u*nderwater *b*reathing *a*pparatus. Word symbols such as these are called *acronyms*.

TELL IT. Tell what the following acronyms stand for. Use a dictionary or an encyclopedia if you need help.

| Anzac | SAC | jato | NATO | AWOL |
| snafu | WHO | PAL | POW | radar |

WRITE IT. Think of some humorous acronyms for pretend organizations, such as LOSERS—*L*eague *o*f *S*tudents *E*ncouraging *R*ash *S*tatements. Share your acronyms with your classmates.

A word formed from the beginning letter or letters of a group of words or parts of words is called an *acronym*.

206

RESPONDING TO SYMBOLS

Look at the symbols below to see which of them gives you a pleasant feeling; an unpleasant feeling; a neutral feeling.

TELL IT. Tell how each of the symbols makes you feel. Listen as other members of the class tell how they feel about the symbols.

DISCUSS IT. Discuss answers to the following questions:

1. Why do the symbols cause different feelings in different people?
2. What causes people to feel the way they do?
3. Why are words considered symbols?
4. For what are words symbols?
5. Why do words cause different feelings in different people?

Past experiences cause people to develop particular feelings about certain signs and symbols.

207

Word Symbols as PROPAGANDA

Any organized approach to spreading particular ideas, beliefs, or information is called *propaganda*.

If you were planning to buy a new car, why would you rather have a Panther than a Goat? Why would you rather live in Holly Hill than Skunk Hollow? Why would you rather drink a glass of Zing than a glass of Blop?

Many persons earn their living trying to influence you to buy a certain product, think a certain way, or vote for a particular candidate. These persons are writers of *propaganda*.

Loaded Words

How do writers of propaganda use word symbols to influence your thinking? What are some examples of propaganda that you see every day? Why is it important that you learn to recognize propaganda techniques?

TELL IT. What emotional words are found in this newspaper ad?

HERE'S A NICE, CLEAN LITTLE NUMBER. GOOD, SOLID, DEPENDABLE TRANSPORTATION. ONLY ONE OWNER; A LITTLE OLD LADY IN PASADENA DROVE IT ONLY ON SUNDAY — WHY, I DON'T SELL ANYTHING I WOULDN'T BUY MYSELF!

Why would this ad be appealing to a person looking for a job? What words are used to flatter the person who would apply for the job? What questions would you like to ask about the job that are not answered in the ad?

WRITE IT. Make up an advertisement of 25 words or fewer to appear in the classified section of a newspaper. Use favorable emotional words designed to sell a particular item. If you cannot think of an item to sell, the following may give you some ideas:

1. An expensive folk guitar
2. Five German shepherd puppies
3. A one-speed boy's bicycle
4. An aquarium with stand, light, heater, plants, and fish
5. A scout tent

EDIT IT. Read your ad to be sure that the describing words you used are favorable emotional words.

Name-Calling

Notice the emotional words in the sentence below:

Their leader is a repulsive, long-haired rabble-rouser.

What words have unpleasant emotional feelings for you? Why do you think the statement might have been made by an adult? How could the statement cause readers to have a bad feeling about the person described? What facts are presented to indicate that the person is undesirable?

Notice how the sentences below are different:

1. The spoiled brat cried all afternoon.
2. The small child cried all afternoon.

Why does sentence 1 give you an unfavorable feeling? Why is sentence 2 considered a neutral statement? Explain how a person can describe an event a number of different ways by selecting his words carefully.

Favorable or unfavorable emotional words used in propaganda are called *loaded words.*

Propaganda that uses smear words, not facts, to discredit a person or an idea is called *name-calling.*

TELL IT. Identify the smear words in each of the following sentences:

1. The ugly old woman shrieked at us.
2. The clumsy oaf stumbled across the stage.
3. A cowardly soldier ran from the dog.
4. A hippie wordmonger made a speech.
5. A smart aleck entertained the crowd.

WRITE IT. Substitute neutral words for the smear words in each sentence above.

EDIT IT. Read your sentences to be sure that you have removed all the smear words.

Slogans

Which of the statements below has more appeal for you?

1. Buy the dandy candy with the name of Fame.
2. Fame candy is tasty and nutritious.

Why will you be able to remember sentence 1 easier than sentence 2? Think of some advertising sentences that you remember. What characteristic about these advertisements helps you to remember them?

A simple, catchy, and easily remembered statement is called a slogan.

WRITE IT. Make up at least five advertising statements that may be considered slogans. If you cannot think of products to advertise, these suggestions may give you some ideas:

1. Sweetbreath Chewing Gum
2. Celebrity Hair Dressing
3. Champion Breakfast Cereal
4. Speedstreak Bicycle
5. Sparkle Toothpaste

SNAPPY GUM
HAPPY GUM!

EDIT IT. Make sure your slogan is short. Check to see whether you have used rhyming words, or catchy words, to make the slogan easy to remember.

210

TELL IT. Read your slogans to the class. Decide which slogans are most appealing. Discuss why these slogans are more effective than the others. Try to list four or five guidelines for writing good slogans.

FOLLOW THROUGH. Tell which of the following propaganda techniques is used in each of the ads below:

    A. Loaded words   B. Name-calling   C. Slogans

1. Wear Cowhide—the classy belt with the brassy buckle.
2. Our sneaky major has been accused of dishonesty.
3. Enjoy the warm, carefree, relaxed atmosphere of our hotel.
4. Drink Silk Soda—the sophisticated soft drink that's smooth as silk.
5. Anyone who votes against this bill is a Communist.

Most of us are concerned about what others think and do. What are some propaganda techniques that are based on this concern? Notice how the writers of the ads below use other persons to try to influence us:

1. Doctors agree that Adams Aspirin is an effective pain reliever.
2. Mauler Martin, linebacker for the Topeka Terrors, has this to say about Adams Aspirin: "Whenever I have a tension headache before a big game, I take Adams Aspirin. Before the opening kickoff, I feel great."
3. Adams Aspirin is the tension reliever of executives on the go.
4. More people take Adams Aspirin than any other brand of aspirin.
5. Adams Aspirin is the best aspirin that money can buy.

What characteristic do all the ads above have in common? Why do advertisers often try to convince their audience that other persons are using the product? What persons are mentioned in the ads above? Which ad attempts to convince you that qualified authorities recommend Adams Aspirin? What evidence does the ad present to indicate that doctors prefer the product? How is the reference to the doctors intended to deceive you?

A propaganda technique that implies that certain professional groups use a product or support an idea is called *appeal to authority.*

211

In which of the ads does a well-known personality endorse the product? How does the fact that a football player uses the product affect the quality of the product? What other ads can you think of in which a famous personality endorses a product? Why do famous people endorse products? How are such ads misleading?

Which ad tries to make you feel that if you use the product, you join the ranks of big business executives? Why is this idea an appealing one? Why is the ad not true?

Which ad tries to convince you that everybody is using the product? What is the purpose of such an ad? What evidence could be presented to support the statement? Why do you think the evidence is not presented?

Which ad states a conclusion without giving any proof? What other ads do you know that state a product is best? Is it possible for every brand of every product to be the best? Why, then, do you think advertisers make such statements?

TELL IT. Which of the following propaganda techniques is used in each of the ads below? Be prepared to defend your choice.

Appeal to authority   Image making   Bandwagon technique
Testimonial   Glittering generality

1. Twig Dresses make all women look twenty pounds lighter.
2. Maxine Moviestar says, "For beautiful lips use Luscious Lipstick."
3. Everybody in town is playing miniature golf.
4. Men of distinction wear Wowie Shirts.
5. Alfred Astronaut says, "I drink Sunny Orange Juice every morning."
6. Gentry Jewelry is only for those who can afford it.
7. The President of the United States recommends our candidate.

8. Students everywhere use Perry Pencils.
9. Lumpy Bread is the best bread baked anywhere.
10. Nine out of ten dentists use Smiley Toothpaste.

Why do the following words from the sentences above begin with capital letters?

Twig Dresses   Gentry Jewelry
Luscious Lipstick   Perry Pencils
Wowie Shirts   Lumpy Bread
Sunny Orange Juice   Smiley Toothpaste

Trade names begin with capital letters.

FOLLOW THROUGH. Write these sentences, using capital letters where necessary:

1. Buy dandy candy.
2. For large muscles eat strongheart cereal.
3. Chew gleaming gum for gleaming teeth.
4. Most football coaches shave with keeno blades.
5. Have smooth sailing with rockaby boats.

WRITE IT. Make up an advertisement using each of the propaganda techniques found in the ads above.

EDIT IT. Read your ads to be sure you have begun each trade name with a capital letter.

TELL IT. Read your ads to your classmates and ask them to tell which propaganda technique is used in each ad. Decide which ads are most convincing, and tell why you think they are convincing.

Using Your Language

Notice the words in bold letters in these sentences:

1. Jim and **I** saw Marie.
2. Marie saw Jim and **me**.
3. Marie walked behind Jim and **me**.

What do we call groups of words like *Jim and I* and *Jim and me*? These groups make up *compound parts. Compound* means "anything that is formed by combining two or more parts."

213

You can check the word forms used in a compound part by reading the sentence and dropping out the first part of the compound.

Now read each sentence again, omitting the words *Jim and*. Why do the sentences sound right? You would not say anything like the following:

1. *Me* saw Marie.
2. Marie saw *I*.
3. Marie walked behind *I*.

FOLLOW THROUGH. Use the right word for the box as you copy each sentence below:

(he, him) 1. Arlene and ☐ went on a hike.
(he, him) 2. We saw Joe and ☐ at the circus.
(they, them) 3. The judge gave the prize to Gail and ☐.
(she, her) 4. Father scolded Susie and ☐.
(he, him) 5. The soldier walked toward Bob and ☐.
(we, us) 6. Our friends and ☐ watched the game.
(I, me) 7. Mark found his cousin and ☐.
(I, me) 8. The dog ran after my teacher and ☐.
(I, me) 9. He and ☐ washed the windows.
(she, her) 10. Our flag was designed by Sherry and ☐.

The Way Your Language Changes

Propaganda sometimes contains cleverly worded statements that hide the truth. Which statement below is more truthful?

1. There were fifty people dancing in a 20′ x 20′ room.
2. The room was large enough to accommodate our dance.

Why would statement 2 be considered an unproved generality? Why is statement 1 a truthful statement?

TELL IT. Restate each of the following statements so that it can be tested for accuracy:

1. He is too fat.
2. John is a remarkable pupil.
3. Squirrels cause damage.
4. My uncle drives too fast.
5. Our garage is too small.

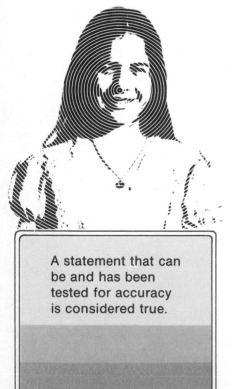

A statement that can be and has been tested for accuracy is considered true.

214

With which statement below would most people agree?

1. Abraham Lincoln was our greatest President.
2. Abraham Lincoln was a great man.

Why would most people agree that Lincoln was a great man? Why might they not all agree that he was the greatest President?

Something that most people feel the same way about is considered true.

WRITE IT. Write five sentences that would be considered true because most people would feel the same way.

EDIT IT. Read your statements carefully to be sure they are statements with which most people would agree and not just your opinion.

With which of the following do you agree?

1. We should never worry about the rights of others.
2. We should all respect the rights of others.

Why would most persons agree with statement 2? Why would this statement be considered a directive or an order?

A directive that we believe should be obeyed is considered true.

FOLLOW THROUGH. Tell which of the following statements are true. Be prepared to explain how you decided they are true.

1. a. Sharon is a great athlete.
   b. Sharon can run a mile in four minutes and three seconds.
2. a. People should be free to seek the truth.
   b. People should do whatever they want to do.
3. a. Margaret is 4' 8" tall and weighs 140 pounds.
   b. Margaret is a fat slob.
4. a. We should agree with all our President's decisions.
   b. We have the right to disagree with our President's decisions.
5. a. David and I disagree on many issues.
   b. David is stupid.

CHECK UP ON YOURSELF

Relating Meaning to Symbols (pages 196–197)

Tell what idea is expressed by each symbol shown
below. Match the numerals and the letters.

a. Falling Rocks	i. Water Skiing
b. Dam	j. Restrooms
c. Fish Hatchery	k. Diving
d. Information	l. Mechanic
e. Marina	m. Handicapped
f. Food Service	n. Recreation Vehicle Trail
g. Grocery Store	o. Amphitheater
h. Rowboating	p. Parking

Identifying Acronyms (page 206)

Tell what each of the acronyms below represents:

jato   SAC   NATO   PAL   WHO

Propaganda Techniques (pages 208–212)

Tell which of these propaganda techniques is described in each numbered definition:

loaded words	testimonial
name-calling	image-making
slogans	bandwagon technique
appeal to authority	glittering generality

1. Leads the reader to believe that everybody is using the product advertised
2. Uses smear words but not facts to discredit something
3. Uses words that are filled with emotional meanings
4. Is a simple, catchy, easy-to-remember statement
5. States that something is true but presents no evidence
6. Implies that professional people who really know use the product advertised
7. Has a well-known personality tell why he uses the product
8. Associates a desirable image with the product

Recognizing True Statements (pages 214–215)

Tell which of the following statements are true and defend your choices:

1. People should keep themselves in good physical condition.
2. The cost of the movie was too expensive.
3. Dill pickles are too salty.
4. The guitar is a popular musical instrument today.
5. There were 200 persons in the audience.

LOOKING BACK AND CHECKING UP

Nature of Language (pages 16–17)

Make up two sentences using each word below. Be sure the word has a different meaning in each.

bread	rock	camp	straight	boy
rap	split	pad	cool	hip

Using Homophones (page 43)

For each word below, write another word with the same pronunciation:

break	pear	stare	shoot	fowl
hare	baste	mourning	peak	air

Feeling and Opinion (pages 113–114)

Tell which of the following statements are feelings and which are opinions:

1. You are a liar.
2. I am embarrassed because you made fun of me.
3. Harold is a very selfish person.
4. Sara made me angry when she didn't show up.
5. I am sad because Paul yelled at me.

Using Your Language (Index)

Use the appropriate form of the word in parentheses in place of the blank in each sentence below:

(ride)　　1. Sam has never ☐ on a horse.
(speak)　 2. Have you ever ☐ into a tape recorder?
(fall)　　 3. The leaves have ☐ from that tree.
(fly)　　　4. My aunt has ☐ all over the world.
(freeze)　5. The water ☐ into ice.
(ride)　　6. Ann has ☐ so well that she won the prize.
(speak)　 7. Our president has ☐ on that topic often.
(fall)　　 8. The Indian chief has ☐ from his horse.
(fly)　　　9. Mother has ☐ only once in an airplane.
(freeze)　10. I ☐ our flavored water.

218

More Ideas For You

1. Investigate and describe to the class a symbol system such as a code, a dance, a storm warning, or a map.

2. Compile a list of acronyms from newspapers and magazines. See how many acronyms you can list during a given period of time.

3. Make a colorful poster using the signs of the zodiac as the theme.

4. Prepare a report explaining astrology.

5. Construct a bulletin-board display for your school or classroom explaining the various propaganda techniques. Use examples from newspapers and magazines to demonstrate the various techniques.

6. Copy or record on tape examples of propaganda from TV commercials, speeches, or newscasts. Read or play the examples to the class and have them identify each technique used.

7. With a group, make up several examples of propaganda. Dramatize the propaganda for the class and have the members identify the various techniques.

8. Prepare a bulletin-board display to demonstrate the different types of truthful statements. Include examples of each type of statement.

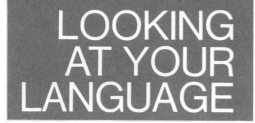

LOOKING AT YOUR LANGUAGE

BASIC SENTENCES

What does this rule tell us?

This rule describes **basic sentences**.

Study the seven basic sentence patterns that follow. Where do the patterns differ—in the **NP** or in the **VP?** If you have trouble recalling any kind of **VP,** turn back to the page referred to in parentheses.

Basic Sentence Pattern 1 (page 58)

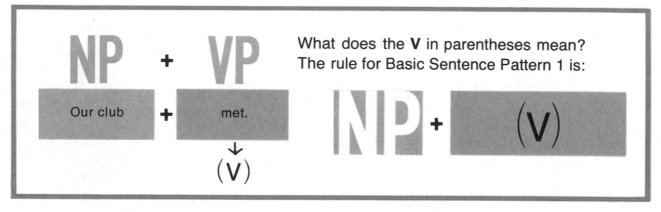

What does the **V** in parentheses mean? The rule for Basic Sentence Pattern 1 is:

Basic Sentence Pattern 2 (page 58)

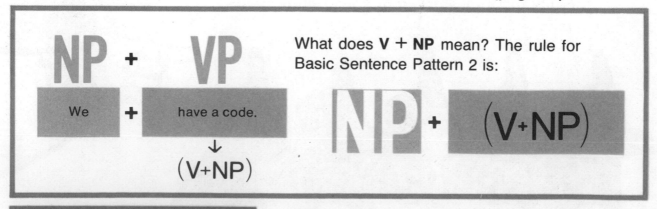

What does **V + NP** mean? The rule for Basic Sentence Pattern 2 is:

220

FOLLOW THROUGH. Show whether each sentence below is an example of BSP 1 or BSP 2. Write the rule as your answer.

1. The code uses symbols.
2. The symbols communicate.
3. They form a message.
4. Codes fascinate us.
5. We think hard.
6. This book discusses codes.
7. It breaks some codes.

Basic Sentence Pattern 3 (page 61)

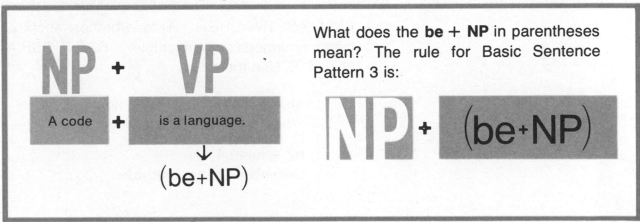

What does the **be + NP** in parentheses mean? The rule for Basic Sentence Pattern 3 is:

Basic Sentence Pattern 4 (page 88)

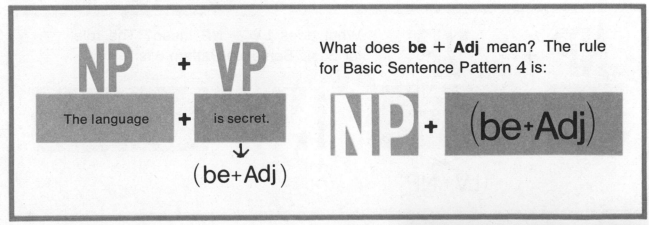

What does **be + Adj** mean? The rule for Basic Sentence Pattern 4 is:

Basic Sentence Pattern 5 (page 90)

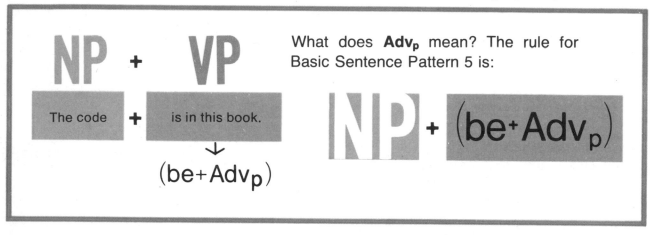

What does **Adv_p** mean? The rule for Basic Sentence Pattern 5 is:

$$NP + (be + Adv_p)$$

FOLLOW THROUGH. Write whether each of these sentences is an example of BSP 3, BSP 4, or BSP 5. Use the rule.

1. All my classmates are members.
2. We were on a field trip yesterday.
3. Our teacher is our adviser.
4. He is helpful.
5. Our meetings are enjoyable.

Basic Sentence Pattern 6 (page 62)

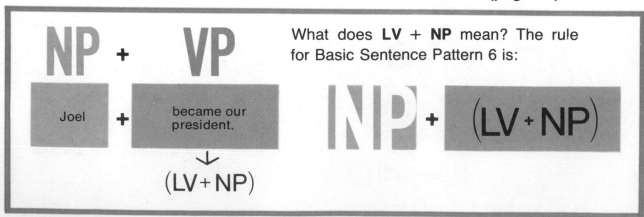

What does **LV + NP** mean? The rule for Basic Sentence Pattern 6 is:

$$NP + (LV + NP)$$

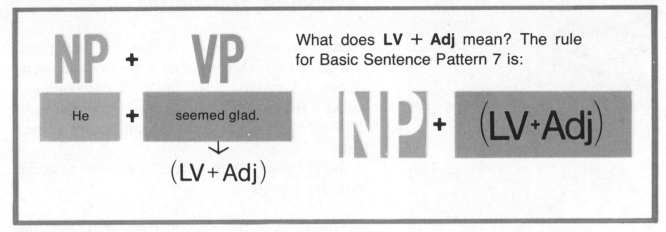

What does **LV + Adj** mean? The rule for Basic Sentence Pattern 7 is:

FOLLOW THROUGH. Which basic sentence pattern does each of these sentences represent? Write the rule as your answer.

1. Our club studies codes.
2. Some of them seem hard.
3. Deciphering can be fun.
4. We concentrate.
5. A code can become a challenge.
6. The club studies for hours.
7. Our method is scientific.
8. One book has helped us.
9. It is in a strongbox.
10. *Secrets with Ciphers and Codes* is its title.

FOLLOW THROUGH. Write a sentence that is an example of each of the seven basic sentence patterns:

1. NP + (V)
2. NP + (V + NP)
3. NP + (be + NP)
4. NP + (be + Adj)
5. NP + (be + Adv$_p$)
6. NP + (LV + NP)
7. NP + (LV + Adj)

BSP 2 George + broke the code.

BSP 2 Charlie + broke the code.

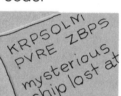

Transform

George and Charlie broke the code.

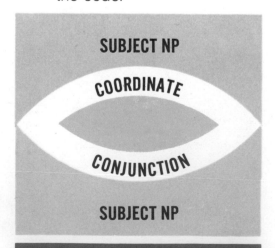

SUBJECT NP

COORDINATE

CONJUNCTION

SUBJECT NP

TRANSFORMS

Compound Transforms

Basic sentences can be changed, or transformed, into sentences that are not basic sentences. A sentence that is not a basic sentence is called a **transform.** You will now explore several different ways to produce a **compound transform.**

The sentences in the Language Strip tell about breaking a code.

1. What part of the second basic sentence has been put into the first basic sentence?
2. In the transform, what word is used to join the two **NP**'s?
3. Now look at this transform and tell what word has been used to join the two **NP**'s:

> BSP 2: George broke the code.
> BSP 2: Charlie broke the code.
> Transform: George or Charlie broke the code.

A compound transform may be made by putting the subject **NP** of one basic sentence into the subject **NP** of another basic sentence. The two subject **NP**'s may be joined by *and* or *or.*

Look at the Language Strip. What are words like *and* and *or* called?

FOLLOW THROUGH. Transform these pairs of sentences by using compound subject **NP**'s:

1. Linda invented a code. Ed invented a code.
2. Hank studied the code. I studied the code.
3. Hank studied for hours. I studied for hours.

224

4. Linda seemed pleased. Ed seemed pleased.
5. Hank looked puzzled. I looked puzzled.
6. Ed had an idea. Linda had an idea.
7. He gave clues. She gave clues.
8. Clues are helpful. People are helpful.
9. Hank used the clues. I used the clues.
10. The code became clear. The message became clear.

Coordinate conjunctions are used also to put other parts of one basic sentence into another basic sentence. Look at the Language Strip and answer these questions:

1. In the sentences about Joe, what part of the second basic sentence has been put into the first basic sentence?
2. In the sentences about Myra, has the whole **VP** or part of the **VP** of the second basic sentence been put into the first basic sentence?

> A compound transform may be made by putting the whole **VP** or part of the **VP** of one basic sentence into another basic sentence.

FOLLOW THROUGH. Transform each pair of sentences by using a compound:

1. Linda helped us. Linda encouraged us.
2. Ed presented a book. Ed talked about it.
3. I invented a code. I showed it to them.
4. The code used symbols. The code used signs.
5. I gave the code to them. I challenged them.
6. They solved the code. They gave the answer.
7. Hank borrowed the book. Hank read it.
8. He studied hard. He asked questions.
9. We were patient. We were helpful.
10. Everyone knew the code now. Everyone was pleased.
11. The time came. The time went.
12. We turned to another one. We started.

BSP 2 | Joe called the operator.

BSP 2 | Joe checked the time.

Transform

Joe called the operator
    and checked the time.

BSP 7 | Myra seems quick.

BSP 7 | Myra seems alert.

Transform

Myra seems quick and
    alert.

BSP COORDINATE **and or but** CONJUNCTION **BSP**

1

BSP 3 Sally is secretary.

BSP 3 Pam is treasurer.

Transform

Sally is secretary and Pam is treasurer.

2

BSP 1 We should start now.

BSP 4 We will be late.

Transform

We should start now, or we will be late.

3

BSP 1 Don arrived at the club early.

BSP 1 Paul came later.

Transform

Don arrived at the club early, but Paul came later.

Look at the Language Strip and answer these questions:

1. In the sentences in 1, has part of one basic sentence been put into another basic sentence, or have the two basic sentences been joined by *and*?
2. In the second transform, how have the two basic sentences been joined?
3. What coordinate conjunction is used in the third transform?
4. Besides the coordinate conjunction in two of the transforms, what mark of punctuation do you see?

A compound transform may be made by joining two basic sentences with a coordinate conjunction. A comma is used before the conjunction unless the parts of the compound are very short.

WRITING HINT: Knowing how compound transforms are made will help you with certain writing skills.

FOLLOW THROUGH. Join each pair of basic sentences below with a coordinate conjunction. When you make the transform, remember to punctuate it.

1. a. Summer came.
   b. I went to the beach.
2. a. You should go to bed now.
   b. You will be tired tomorrow.
3. a. Greg likes candy.
   b. It is bad for his teeth.
4. a. June goes to camp.
   b. Her brother joins her.
5. a. The book is exciting.
   b. It is long.

226

6. a. It rained all day.
   b. Bill stayed indoors.
7. a. Parties can be fun.
   b. They can be dull.
8. a. Everyone stayed late.
   b. Ann went home.

Look at the Language Strip on this page.

1. Study the first transform. What form of the verb is used in the first basic sentence? in the second? What form of the verb is used in the transform?
2. Study the second transform. What form of *be* is used in the first basic sentence? in the second? What form of *be* is used in the transform?
3. Now substitute *was* for *is* in the basic sentences referred to in item 2 above. What form of *be* would be used in the transform?
4. In the third transform, what form of the verb is used in the first basic sentence? in the second? What form of the verb is used in the transform?

FOLLOW THROUGH. Use a compound transform to join each pair of basic sentences. Remember to think about the form of the verb.

1. a. George is early.
   b. Laura is early.
2. a. Grace lives on our block.
   b. Her sister lives on our block.
3. a. Al tries hard.
   b. Ed tries hard.
4. a. Ron plays softball.
   b. Linda plays softball.
5. a. Jerry was successful.
   b. Meg was successful.
6. a. The dog likes the food.
   b. The cat likes the food.
7. a. He studies the book.
   b. She studies the book.
8. a. Steve is happy.
   b. I am happy.

227

1

BSP 2 George uses our book.

BSP 2 Laura uses our book.

Transform

George and Laura use our book.

2

BSP 5 Eve is in our club.

BSP 5 Charlie is in our club.

Transform

Eve and Charlie are in our club.

3

BSP 2 Susan likes codes.

BSP 2 I like codes.

Transform

Susan and I like codes.

1

BSP 2 | Susan studied the code.

BSP 2 | I studied the code.

Transform

Susan and I studied the code.

2

BSP 2 | The boys asked Susan for help.

BSP 2 | The boys asked me for help.

Transform

The boys asked Susan and me for help.

3

BSP 2 | We found articles for them.

BSP 2 | We found articles for us.

Transform

We found articles for them and us.

Look carefully at the transforms in 1, 2, and 3 in the Language Strip. How will they help you to avoid mistakes like "Joe and me went," "He helped Tom and I," and "They gave it to Sue and I"?

FOLLOW THROUGH. Use a compound transform to join each pair of basic sentences. Remember to watch the pronoun forms.

1. a. Ed wrote a story.
   b. She wrote a story.
2. a. Ed gave the story to Tom.
   b. Ed gave the story to me.
3. a. The group invited him to the club.
   b. The group invited me to the club.
4. a. Tom read it.
   b. I read it.
5. a. I spoke about the story.
   b. I spoke about him.
6. a. Tom gave a book to him.
   b. Tom gave a book to her.
7. a. They sang for you.
   b. They sang for us.
8. a. Sally signed for them.
   b. Sally signed for me.

CHECK UP ON YOURSELF

A. Show which of the basic sentence patterns is represented by each of these sentences. Use the rule in writing your answer.

1. The flowers smelled good.
2. The candidate became President.
3. The man fell heavily.
4. We will pledge some money.
5. The baby was hungry.
6. His father fed him.
7. The man left quickly.
8. He was a salesman.
9. Sally is in school.
10. She will become a doctor.

228

B. Write the compound transform that results from putting part of one basic sentence into another basic sentence.

1. That note is peculiar. This note is peculiar.
2. The message seems unclear. The message seems odd.
3. Angela studied the note. Angela studied the handwriting.
4. She put it over light. She found another message.
5. She studies such messages. Jan studies such messages.

C. Join each pair of basic sentences with a coordinate conjunction. When you make the transform, remember to punctuate where necessary.

1. a. The race is over.
   b. John has won.
2. a. The sky is cloudy.
   b. The weather forecaster predicts sunshine.
3. a. I may go to the beach.
   b. I may play tennis.
4. a. I'll take my raft.
   b. Joe will take his goggles.
5. a. Joe will dive.
   b. I am tired.

D. Transform each pair of sentences into one sentence. Watch the pronoun forms.

1. a. Sid studies plants.
   b. I study plants.
2. a. Our findings interest our teacher.
   b. Our findings interest us.
3. a. He checks our findings.
   b. We check our findings.
4. a. He speaks to the group.
   b. He speaks to us.
5. a. The teacher guides Sid.
   b. The teacher guides me.

Dennis Stock: Magnum Photos

A writer uses various words and forms to present his information in a particular way. A photographer uses lenses, filters, and exposures to present his information in a particular way. Skill in both writing and photography depends on how well you can present information in an interesting way. Notice how the photographers presented information in an interesting way in the photographs on these two pages.

The photographer of this picture observed a scene that he thought would make an unusual photograph. How did he position himself to create the desired effect?

and Writing

Camilla Smith, courtesy *Camera 35*

What is the effect created by painting a scene on a car door?

How is color used to create an effect in photography? Notice how the blue emphasizes the cold foggy day on which the trees were photographed. Notice also how color is used to create an unusual effect in the photograph of the fountain.

Roger Miller, courtesy *Camera 35*

Mitchell Funk, courtesy *Camera 35*

DISCUSS IT. Talk about the following:

1. Explain why the photographer took the picture of the man carrying the fish. What special effect is created in this photograph?
2. Tell how the photograph of the scene on the car door makes a more interesting photograph than the scene alone would have made.
3. Why is the blur in the picture on page 232 good photography, while blurs in other photographs are considered bad photography? Explain how blurred or incomplete details can be good in some types of writing and poor in other types.
4. How would the photographs of the trees and the fountain have been different if the colors were different? Compare the use of color in photography and colorful words in writing.
5. How do the photographs show that ordinary information can be presented in a novel and interesting way? Can the same information be presented in a dull and uninteresting way? How is this idea true also of presenting information in writing?

WRITE IT. Write a few sentences explaining at least three techniques a writer can use to present ordinary information in an interesting way.

IMPRESSIONS

Dreaming is one way that your mind helps you deal with the many things that happen in your life: your fears, wishes, worries, joys. Sometimes dreams seem real; but usually something is not quite right, because the mind often changes details to make the dream easier to accept.

Have you ever awakened from a dream screaming or crying or laughing? Which dreams do you remember better, bad ones or good ones? Think back to a dream that you

Union Pacific Railroad Colorphoto

234

especially remember. What was your day like before you had the dream? In the dream were there any things like something that happened to you or that you thought about during the day? What do you think you can learn about yourself from remembering and thinking about your dreams?

THINKING ABOUT STORIES

The bell to Connie's apartment woke her family late one night. In the hallway in front of their door was a little kitten in a basket. Writing a story about this event, Connie considered each of the following six titles:

The Kitten	Our New Pet
A Midnight Visitor	The Ringing Doorbell
The Surprise	Kitten in a Basket

DISCUSS IT. Rank the titles, using 1 as the title you like best and 6 as the one you like least. Discuss the strengths and weaknesses of each title.

Notice the words that begin with capital letters in the titles above.

Remember that the first, last, and all important words in a title begin with capital letters.

FOLLOW THROUGH. Write the following story titles correctly on your paper:

1. my trip to hawaii
2. adventure in the woods
3. treasure at the seashore
4. building an aquarium
5. my happiest day

Make up an interesting title that explains the action taking place in each of the pictures on the next page.

a.

b.

c.

d.

e.

TELL IT. Tell your titles to the class. Notice how the different titles cause persons to think about the pictures from different points of view.

EXPERIENCE WRITING

For most of us it is easier to write about our own experiences than any other subject. In the paragraphs that follow, George Herman "Babe" Ruth tells about an experience that caused him to become a baseball pitcher.

Occasionally Brother Matthias would move me around to various positions, infield and outfield. But the first time he put me in the box to pitch came when I displeased him. He put me in to show me up. I was 14 or 15 and we were playing a game in which we were taking a terrific beating. One pitcher after another was being knocked out of the box and finally it seemed funny to me. When our last pitcher began to be hit all over the lot, I burst out laughing at him. I guess I said a few things too.

Brother Matthias called time immediately and walked over to the catcher's box.

"What are you laughing at, George?" he asked me in his strong but gentle way.

"That guy out there—getting his brains knocked out," I howled, doubled over with laughter.

Brother Matthias looked at me for a long time.

"All right, George, *you* pitch," he said.

I stopped laughing.

"I never pitched in my life," I said. "I can't pitch."

"Oh, you must know a lot about it," he said, casually. "You know enough to know that your friend isn't any good. So go ahead out there and show us how it's done."

I knew he meant business. I put aside my mask and catcher's mitt, borrowed a finger mitt, and walked out to the mound. I didn't even know how to stand on the rubber, or how to throw a curve or even how to get the ball over the plate.

Yet, as I took the position, I felt a strange relationship between myself and that pitcher's mound. I felt, somehow, as if I had been born out there and that this was a kind of home for me. It seemed to be the most natural thing in the world to start pitching—and to start striking out batters.

Selection from the book *The Babe Ruth Story* as told to Bob Considine. Copyright, 1948, by George Herman Ruth. Published by E. P. Dutton & Co., Inc. and used with their permission.

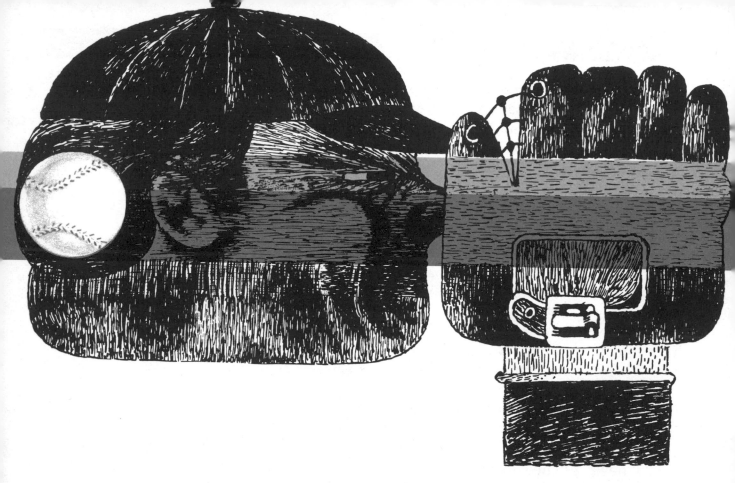

DISCUSS IT. Discuss answers to the following questions about the paragraphs:

1. How old was Babe Ruth when the incident occurred?
2. Why was this an experience that he remembered all his life?
3. What were his feelings during the experience?

Think about several experiences you have had that stand out in your memory. Jot them down on a piece of paper. Decide which experience you would like to write about. Then try to remember all the details you can about that experience. Take notes on the persons involved in the experience, your thoughts and feelings, and other related information.

WRITE IT. Arrange your notes into a logical sequence. Think of an interesting beginning and ending. Write a three- or four-paragraph composition about your experiences.

How many paragraphs are in the experience told by Babe Ruth? How can you tell? How do you know when to begin a new paragraph?

> Begin a new paragraph when there is a change in speaker or a change in topic.

EDIT IT. Reread your composition. Be sure that you have used at least three paragraphs. Check to see that you have indented the first word of each paragraph.

TELL IT. Read your experience to your classmates. Listen carefully as they tell what they like best about your composition.

What is a *biography*? an *autobiography*? You can unlock the meaning of these words by using their parts as clues. *Bio-* means "life," *-graph* means "something written," and *auto-* means "self."

> A *biography* is an account of a person's life written by someone else. An *auto-biography* is an account of a person's life written by the person himself.

TELL IT. Why do you think the paragraphs from Babe Ruth's experience were taken from an autobiography? Could the experience that you wrote about become a part of your autobiography? Why?

241

Fiction Writing

Made-up writing about real or imaginary persons or events is called *fiction*.

Why are biography and autobiography considered factual writing? What is the difference between factual writing and fiction?

WRITE IT. Make up a fictional autobiography of your life ten years from now. Use 300 to 500 words to tell what your main interests are, what you do with your time, and what your family life is like. Remember that everyone else will also be ten years older.

TELL IT. Read your autobiography to your classmates. Answer their questions about your interests and future plans. Listen carefully as the members of the class tell what they liked best about your autobiography.

Imaginative Writing

All writing, whether factual or fiction, can be imaginative if you put your mind to work. Which of the two letters below is more imaginative?

Colonial Gardens, Apt. 307
4117 N. W. 51st Terrace
Rockford, Illinois 61109
August 10, 19——

Dear Rita,

Thanks for inviting me to spend the weekend with you. I liked the sailing on Saturday afternoon and the picnic and campfire that evening. The fishing on Sunday was great. I had never caught a fish before.

It was one of the nicest weekends I have had all year. I am glad that you invited me.

Your friend,
Sally

Colonial Gardens, Apt. 307
4117 N. W. 51st Terrace
Rockford, Illinois 61109
August 10, 19——

Dear Rita,

The sun, spray, and billowing sails made me happy. The dancing flames of the campfire and the taste of delicious food gave me a sense of well-being. The leaping and arching of a large trout provided me with a tremendous thrill.

To a family who can give a visitor happiness, a sense of well-being, and a thrill, I extend my most sincere thanks. Your hospitality last weekend will stand out as the high point of my summer vacation.

Your friend,
Sally

243

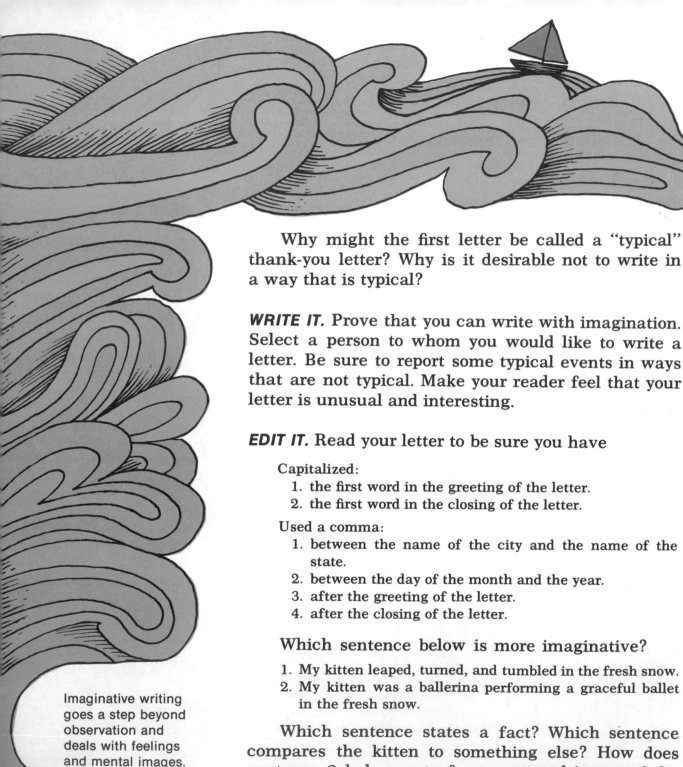

Why might the first letter be called a "typical" thank-you letter? Why is it desirable not to write in a way that is typical?

WRITE IT. Prove that you can write with imagination. Select a person to whom you would like to write a letter. Be sure to report some typical events in ways that are not typical. Make your reader feel that your letter is unusual and interesting.

EDIT IT. Read your letter to be sure you have

Capitalized:
1. the first word in the greeting of the letter.
2. the first word in the closing of the letter.

Used a comma:
1. between the name of the city and the name of the state.
2. between the day of the month and the year.
3. after the greeting of the letter.
4. after the closing of the letter.

Which sentence below is more imaginative?

1. My kitten leaped, turned, and tumbled in the fresh snow.
2. My kitten was a ballerina performing a graceful ballet in the fresh snow.

Which sentence states a fact? Which sentence compares the kitten to something else? How does sentence 2 help you to form a mental image of the scene?

Imaginative writing goes a step beyond observation and deals with feelings and mental images.

244

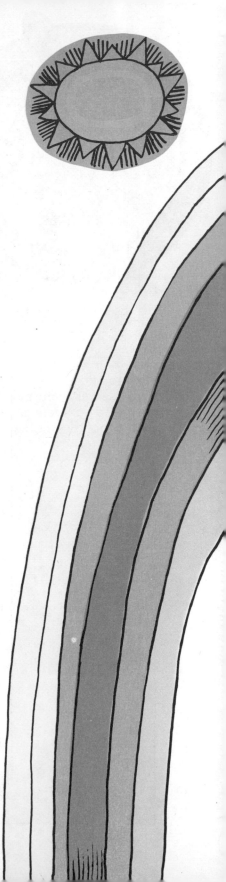

TELL IT. Tell which sentence in each pair below is a statement of fact and which is an imaginative sentence:

1. A. The little girl had bright eyes.
    B. The little girl smiled at me with her eyes.

2. A. The violent waves foamed from their efforts to batter the seawall.
    B. The large foamy waves crashed into the seawall.

3. A. The trees bent over as the strong wind whistled through their branches.
    B. The angry wind bent the trees until their branches howled in pain.

4. A. The jet was a shooting star burning a path across the sky.
    B. The jet flew across the sky, leaving a vapor trail behind it.

5. A. A giggle of girls passed me in the hall.
    B. A group of girls giggled as they passed me in the hall.

WRITE IT. Rewrite each of the following statements of fact so that it becomes an imaginative sentence:

1. A boat sailed on the lake.
2. Lights from the city reflected on the water.
3. Tree branches were covered with ice.
4. A rainbow appeared in the sky.
5. Three jets flew in formation.
6. A coyote howled.
7. The fullback ran for a touchdown.
8. Children played on the lawn.
9. A helicopter hovered above the ship.
10. Snowflakes fell.

POETRY

Poetry in which letters and words are used as pictures is called *concrete* or *visual* poetry.

At the beginning of this unit, you learned that photographers and writers use similar techniques to present information in an interesting manner.

Recently some poets have used pictures in writing poetry. Letters and words are used to form the pictures. To find the meaning of the poetry, you must see the poem as a picture and fill in the meaning with your own ideas.

Some examples of concrete poetry follow.

```
cricket ·
 cricke · ·
  crick · · ·
   cric · · · ·
    cri · · · · ·
     cr · · · · · ·
      c · · · · · ·
         · · · · · · · s
          · · · · · · ts
           · · · · · ets
            · · · kets
             · · ckets
              · ickets
               · rickets
                crickets
```

"Cricket" by Aram Saro⟨y⟩ from Jean-François Bo⟨ry⟩ *Once Again.* Copyright © 19⟨ ⟩ by Jean-François Bory. ⟨Re⟩printed by permission of N⟨ew⟩ Directions Publishing Co⟨rpo⟩ration.

What effect does the separation of the letters create in this poem? How does it help you to hear the cricket song?

How does the separation of small pieces of paper with letters on them provide you with the idea of an island?

"An Island Poem" by Vladimir Burda and "Mirror Horizon" by Ronald Johnson from Jean-François Bory, *Once Again*. Copyright © 1968 by Jean-François Bory. Reprinted by permission of New Directions Publishing Corporation.

Explain how the arrangement of the words in this poem relates to the title of the poem.

The letters in this poem show both pattern and direction. Notice how they behave like real circus acrobats springing together in diagonals and towers.

"Acrobats" by Ian Hamilton Finlay, copyright © 1967, 1973 by Ian Hamilton Finlay. Reprinted from *An Anthology of Concrete Poetry* by permission of Something Else Press, Inc.

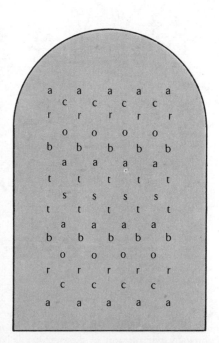

Notice how the poem demonstrates the scientific principle in the title by the arrangement of words in the poem.

like   attracts   like
like   attracts   like
like   attracts   like
like   attracts   like
like   attracts   like
like attracts like
like attracts like
likeattractslike
likeattractlike
likattracklike
likettrackike
likteralike
likelikts

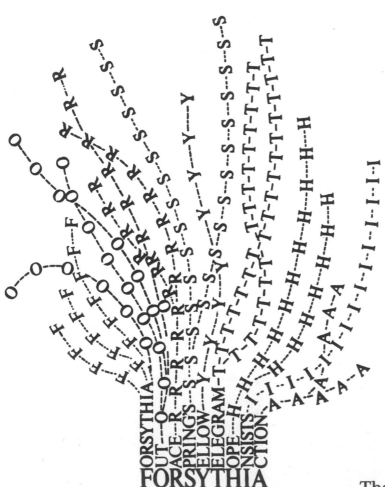

The design of this poem is made from the letters of the name *Forsythia* and their equivalents in the Morse code. Notice how the poem itself resembles a bowl of forsythia branches.

UNRHYMED POETRY

You have seen that poetry can be written in many different ways. It can be fact or fiction, rhymed or unrhymed, long or short. It can tell exactly what you want it to tell.

Notice the ideas expressed by Richard Margolis in the four unrhymed poems that follow:

Too Bad

It's too bad about substitute teachers:
they don't know our names.

The Nightmare

I dreamt I was a man
but not a man
a dwarf.
Without feet I floated down my street
and the people looked down at me.
My mouth was full of their knees.

A Trash Can's All Right for Basketball

A trash can's all right for basketball
but not if it's empty.
Every time you sink one
you have to lean way over
to get the ball.
It's hard on the ribs.
If you don't want to lean,
keep your city clean.

This Morning's News

Yesterday was so hot
kids opened 4300 hydrants
all over the city
and oceans of cold water
ran down the sewers,
drying up and turning off
all the expensive air-conditioners
in the big offices downtown,
and the man sweated in his button-down shirt.
Isn't that a shame?

DISCUSS IT. Discuss how Mr. Margolis has taken common events and written them in an uncommon way. Talk about school events about which you could write a poem. A member of your class or the teacher will list the events on the chalkboard.

WRITE IT. Make up a short unrhymed poem in which you describe a common event in an uncommon way.

TELL IT. Read your poem to the class. Choose the poems you like best and tell why you like them.

Notice the form of the following poems:

Behind me the moon
brushes a shadow of pines
lightly on the floor.
Kikaku

"This Morning's News" from the book *Looking for a Place* by Richard J. Margolis. Copyright © 1969 by Richard J. Margolis. Reprinted by permission of J. B. Lippincott Company.

Selection by Kikaku from *Cricket Songs: Japanese Haiku*, translated and © 1964 by Harry Behn. Reprinted by permission of Harcourt Brace Jovanovich, Inc. and Curtis Brown Ltd.

When my canary
flew away, that was the end
of spring in my house.
        Shiki

The tight string broke and
the loose kite fell fluttering,
losing its spirit.
        Kubonta

Since my house burned down,
I now own a better view
of the rising moon.
        Masahide

Read the poems aloud, softly tapping your finger on the desk each time you read a syllable. How many syllables are in line 1? line 2? line 3? What reference to nature is made in each poem?

This type of poem was first written in Japan more than 700 years ago and is called *haiku*.

WRITE IT. Select a topic about nature. Think of an idea you wish to express about the topic. Decide how this idea can be divided into three parts with the appropriate number of syllables. Experiment with various images and word arrangements. Write the arrangement that expresses your idea most clearly. If you have trouble getting started, the following first lines may help:

Above me, the sun
Look, the butterfly
Spring flowers blooming
Shadows on the snow
A cricket's chirping

When the forest burned
Ripples on the lake
Early morning mist
Leaves fluttering down
Birds in formation

Haiku has the following characteristics:
1. It has three lines containing seventeen syllables. Line 1 has five syllables, line 2 has seven syllables, and line 3 has five syllables.
2. The season and references to nature are included.
3. The poem contrasts ideas and uses imagery.

Selections by Shiki, Kubonta, and Masahide from *Cricket Songs: Japanese Haiku,* translated and © 1964 by Harry Behn. Reprinted by permission of Harcourt Brace Jovanovich, Inc. and Curtis Brown Ltd.

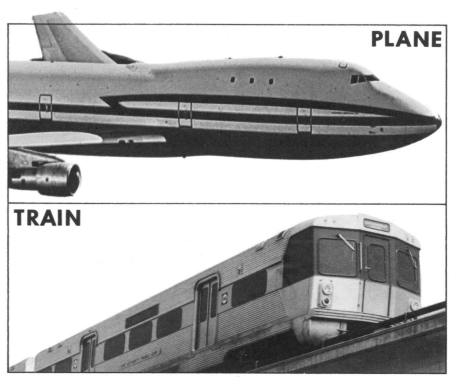

PLANE

TRAIN

C. READ Delaware River Port Authority

USING RHYME

You have already learned that poems come in all sizes, shapes, and subjects. Some poems rhyme. Two of the commonest types of rhyming poems are described below. The word *rhyme* has two acceptable spellings. Notice that the poem below uses the less common spelling.

Write Me a Verse

I've asked Professor Swigly Brown
To talk about two kinds of Rime,
If you will kindly settle down.
You won't? Well, then, some other time. . . .

PROFESSOR BROWN: The simplest of all verse to write is
the couplet. There is no argument
about this: it *is* the simplest. I have
said so.

"Write Me a Verse" from *Take Sky* by David McCord, by permission of Little, Brown and Co. Copyright 1961, 1962 by David McCord.

252

Couplet

1

A couplet is two lines—two lines in rime.
The first comes easy, the second may take time.

2

Most couplets will have lines of equal length;
This gives them double dignity and strength.

3

Please count the syllables in 2 and say
How many. Ten each line? Correct! And they

4

In turn comprise the five-foot standard line:
Pentameter. The foot's *iambic.* Fine

5

Enough! On human feet, of course, our shoes
Do match; likewise the laces. If you choose

6

A briefer line,
Like this of mine,

7

Or say
O.K.

8

Why, *these* are couplets, somewhat crude but true
To form. Try one yourself. See how you do.

LOOK
COOK

	1	2	3	4	5	6
7	8	9	10	11	12	13
14	15	16	17	18	19	20
21	22	23	24	25	26	27
28	29	30				

9

Meanwhile, I'll give *you* one. Hand me that pen.
A four-foot line——eight syllables, not ten:

10

I cán / not síng / the óld / songs nów;

I név / er cóuld / sing an / y hów.

11

Couplets, you see, should make their stand alone.
I've used some differently, but that's my own

12

responsibility.

PROFESSOR BROWN: We come now to the second easi-
est form of verse: the quatrain.
Since the quatrain in length equals
two couplets, it ought to be just
twice as easy to write. It isn't . . .
it isn't.

Quatrain

1

When there is more to say——or more than planned——
A couplet's very easy to expand.
Expansive couplets, then, if out of hand,
May nicely run to four lines. Understand?

254

2

Four lines——quatrain; long lines or short,
But *good* lines, with a good report
Of one another as they progress.
Note one / an oth / er for change / of stress

3

Or emphasis: the sudden sharpening pace.
A quatrain says its say with perfect grace.
"I strove with none, for none was worth my strife"——
First line of four* to haunt you all your life.

4

I'll not attempt a long example——
I mean with lines of many feet;
But still you ought to have a sample
Or two to prove the form *is* neat.

5

Here goes:
Suppose
Suppose
Suppose

6

The ship sails for Spain,
For Spain the ship sails;
You can't go by train,
For a train runs on rails.

* Inquire of Walter Savage Landor in *Bartlett's Familiar Quotations.*

STREET HEAT

7

Let's sail a ship for far-off Spain;
We really can't get there by train.
But still a big ship has no sails;
Why not a train that has no rails?

8

Note rimes in 1——the rime control is *planned*.
In 2, *two* pairs of rimes; in 6 we find
abab (*Spain, sails, train, rails*). Last kind
Is this (abba): *planned, find, kind, and*

9

Forget that ship that has no sails.
Let's jet by plane across to Spain
Above the sea they call the Main.
(Say something here that rimes with *sails*.)

David McCord

TELL IT. Be prepared to explain to the class answers that are found in the poem regarding the following questions:

1. How do poets make couplets rhyme?
2. Find the words *iambic* and *pentameter* in your dictionary. How are these words related to verse 4 of "Couplet"?
3. What is a quatrain?
4. What are the four different rhymes for a quatrain that are described in verse 8?
5. Which of the rhyme schemes below matches each of the verses represented by the number of the quatrain?

Rhyme scheme	Verse
abab	1
abba	3
aabb	6
aaaa	9

256

PEARHAIR

WRITE IT. Think of an idea about which you would like to write a quatrain. Write the idea on your paper. Then think of the various ways that you can express the idea in four lines. Experiment with rhyming words to see which of the quatrain rhyme schemes you should use. Write your poem.

EDIT IT. The end of a line of poetry is not necessarily the end of a sentence. Be sure that you have used the appropriate punctuation mark at the end of each sentence. Begin each new sentence with a capital letter. Each line of poetry usually begins with a capital letter. Use a capital letter to begin each line of your poem.

TELL IT. Read your poem to the class. Listen carefully to the poems of your classmates. Identify the type of rhyme used in each poem. Tell which poems you liked best and why.

257

Even poems, such as the one below, have been written about punctuation marks:

The Colon

The colon by some is thought odd,
And no wonder:
Two periods make it,
One over,
One under.

The colon resembles the eyes of a beast:
A tiger,
A fox,
Or a tomcat at least——
Two eyes ever looking, two eyes open wide,
That belong to a creature that lies on its side.

Unable to point or to say, "Over there,"
All the colon can do,
And it does it,
Is stare.
So here's a suggestion: go on, if you please,
To where it is looking, to see what it sees.

What does a colon look like? Find the colon in each of the sentences below:

1. The concert begins at 8:00 p.m.
2. The little boy took the following items from his pocket: a piece of string, a magnet, three paper clips, and a rock.

Use a colon in writing time and in introducing a list.

FOLLOW THROUGH. Make up five sentences in which you use a colon to write time and five sentences in which you use a colon to introduce a list.

The Way Your Language Changes

In many languages the order of words in a sentence is not important to meaning. In Latin *puer* means "boy," *puella* means "girl," and *amo* means "love." Certain endings are added to the words to

"The Colon" from *On Your Marks!* by Richard Armour. Copyright © 1969 by Richard Armour and Herbert Lubalin. Used with permission of McGraw-Hill Book Company.

show their function in the sentence. Notice the order of the words in these sentences:

Amat puer puellam. Puer amat puellam.

Amat puellam puer. Puellam amat puer.

Puer puellam amat. Puellam puer amat.

Each sentence says "The boy loves the girl." The endings of the words show that *boy* is in the first part of the sentence and *girl* is in the second part.

Although English has some inflectional endings, it is not basically an inflectional language. The inflectional endings do not determine the functions of the words in a sentence. The order of words in a sentence determines the meaning of the sentence. The meanings of the sentences below are quite different:

Jonah ate a large fish.

A large fish ate Jonah.

Writers of English must use words effectively to make their writings precise and powerful. Which sentence below expresses the meaning more clearly?

1. The old man with a cane was leading a dog.
2. The old man was leading a dog with a cane.

TELL IT. What word does the word group *with a cane* modify? Why should a word group be as near as possible to the word it modifies?

FOLLOW THROUGH. Rewrite the following sentences so that their meanings are more precise:

1. The boy ran across the street wearing a baseball cap.
2. An old man drove a sports car with a beard.
3. A cowboy was riding a horse in a leather vest.
4. We rented an apartment from our friend with three bedrooms.
5. My cousin was treated by a doctor with hives.
6. The sailor dropped an anchor with a tattoo.
7. A small child sat in the park with tearful eyes.
8. That quarterback threw a pass wearing white shoes.
9. The man climbed a mountain wearing hiker's shoes.
10. A girl was knitting a sweater with a ponytail.

259

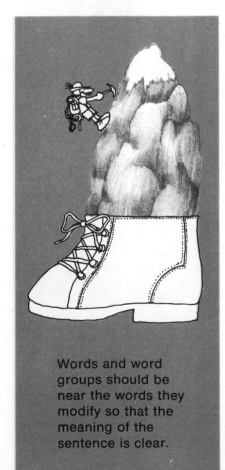

Languages in which word endings or inflections determine the function of words in sentences are called *inflectional languages*.

The interrelationship of words in an English sentence is called *syntax*.

Words and word groups should be near the words they modify so that the meaning of the sentence is clear.

Using Your Language

Other forms of *wear* are *wore* and *worn*. Other forms of *swim* are *swam* and *swum*. *Burst* is used when telling about things that are happening or have happened.

Notice the words in bold letters in the paragraph below:

The side of the canvas raft had **worn** through. The raft **burst** when it hit the rock. Dad **swam** out from the shore to rescue me.

What form of *wear* is used in the paragraph? What are the other forms? What are the forms of *swim*? Why is it easy to use the appropriate form of *burst*?

FOLLOW THROUGH. Use the appropriate form of *swim* or *wear* in each sentence below:

1. Yesterday we ☐ in the lake.
2. Have you ever ☐ a crash helmet?
3. My sister has never ☐ a floor-length dress.
4. Hal ☐ a mile in the swimming contest.
5. We ☐ every day at camp.
6. I have ☐ a hole in my shoe.
7. We ☐ in the Gulf of Mexico.
8. Lois ☐ on her back.
9. Harry has ☐ his ring for five years.
10. The campers ☐ every morning last summer.

FOLLOW THROUGH. Make up five sentences in which you use *burst* appropriately.

FOLLOW THROUGH. Now write these sentences appropriately:

1. The fan blowed the vase over.
2. Syl drawed a picture of her room.
3. The car had rode over the glass.
4. Ice freezed on the windowpane.
5. The doctor had spoke to the child.
6. Mae's bike was stole.
7. I had tore my sweater.
8. The little boy had fell off the chair.
9. Our class had chose a new leader.
10. His plane had flew 500 miles.

CHECK UP ON YOURSELF

Writing Story Titles (page 236)

Write the following titles correctly on your paper:

1. an adventure in my tree house
2. the purple cat
3. my dance recital
4. an exciting canoe trip
5. the pie-eating contest

Writing Parts of Letters (page 243)

Write these parts of friendly letters correctly on your paper:

1. 3717 n e mann street
2. columbus ohio 43205
3. march 31 19—
4. dear mrs patterson
5. your friend

Writing Imaginative Sentences (pages 243–245)

Rewrite each of the following statements of fact so that it becomes an imaginative sentence:

1. The bird sang.
2. My bicycle was twisted.
3. The halfback scored a touchdown.
4. A large tree stood in the forest.
5. Our campfire blazed.

Forms of Poetry (pages 246–257)

Answer each of the following questions about forms of poetry:

1. How many syllables are in each line of haiku?
2. What is the main subject of haiku?
3. What is a couplet?
4. What is a quatrain?
5. What are four rhyme schemes of a quatrain?

LOOKING BACK AND CHECKING UP

Classifying Listening Activities (pages 8--14)

Match each common listening activity below with one of the following types of listening:

(a) Attentive listening   (c) Analytic listening
(b) Marginal listening   (d) Appreciative listening

1. Listening for propaganda techniques in a political speech
2. Listening to directions on how to find a friend's house
3. Listening to records while you study
4. Listening to a poet recite original poetry

Using Commas (page 71)

Copy the sentences below and set off transitional words and word groups with a comma or commas:

1. First let me welcome you to our meeting.
2. On the porch however was a wide swing.
3. Finally he was removed from the game.
4. The man's brother therefore was arrested.
5. As a result we were all sent home from camp.

Forming Plurals (pages 140–141)

Write the plural form of each word below:

1. match   3. story   5. wife   7. tax   9. ox
2. half   4. toy   6. tooth   8. child   10. hero

Cause-and-Effect Sentences (page 173)

Tell which word helps to identify each sentence below as a cause-and-effect sentence:

1. Because it was cold, I put on my hat.
2. If we don't leave now, we will be late.
3. Either you stop now, or you will ruin the painting.
4. Since he was already hungry, he ate a sandwich.
5. If you go today, then you can't go tomorrow.

262

1. Find photographs in which subjects are presented in an interesting way. Explain to the class the technique used by the photographer to achieve the effect.

2. Read a biography of an interesting person you admire. Prepare a five-minute oral presentation that will make your classmates aware of the highlights of this person's life.

3. Prepare a haiku notebook. Use the kind of paper called *onionskin*. Apply a border of washable black ink along the bottom of the paper. Blow through a soda straw, causing the ink to form interesting branchlike patterns. Type or print a haiku on each decorated sheet of paper. Bind the poems in a folder on which the word *Haiku* is printed with oriental-looking letters. You may want to present the notebook as a gift to someone.

4. Prepare a written or an oral report on other poetic verse forms, such as triplets, limericks, sonnets, and blank verse. Compose original poems to demonstrate each form.

5. Record your favorite poems on tape, and make them available for members of the class.

6. Construct a bulletin-board display demonstrating various rhyme schemes of poetry.

7. Select a poet whose poems you enjoy. Prepare a short oral report in which you present a brief biographical sketch of the poet and read several samples of his work.

8. Select a favorite poem and draw a picture to illustrate it.

9. Make a display of concrete poetry. Leave space on the display for members of your class to display the concrete poetry they write.

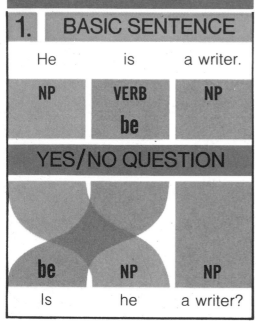

1. BASIC SENTENCE

He	is	a writer.
NP	VERB **be**	NP

YES/NO QUESTION

be	NP	NP
Is	he	a writer?

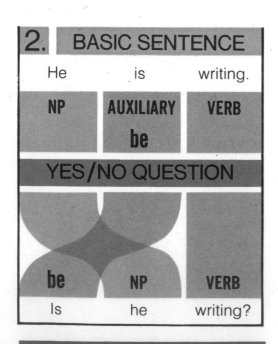

2. BASIC SENTENCE

He	is	writing.
NP	AUXILIARY **be**	VERB

YES/NO QUESTION

be	NP	VERB
Is	he	writing?

TRANSFORMATIONS

Question Transforms

Yes/No Questions

Basic sentences can be transformed also into questions.

While answering the questions that follow, refer to the Language Strip and the diagram that is related to the sentence *He is a writer.*

1. What does the **VP** in the basic sentence contain—a verb or a form of *be?*
2. To produce the question *Is he a writer?* where is the form of *be* put?

> When a basic sentence contains a form of *be,* the form of *be* is put before the subject **NP** to produce a question.

Now refer to the Language Strip and the diagram that is related to the sentence *He is writing.* Answer the questions below:

1. In the **VP** in the basic sentence, what kind of word comes before the verb?
2. To produce the question *Is he writing?* where is the auxiliary put?

> When a basic sentence contains an auxiliary, the auxiliary is put before the subject **NP** to produce a question.

Study the diagrams and answer these questions:

1. Is there a form of *be* or an auxiliary in either basic sentence?
2. What auxiliary has been added to each **VP?**
3. What is the tense form in each basic sentence?
4. What form of *do* is added to the **VP?**
5. What form of the verb follows the auxiliary *do?*
6. To produce the questions, where is the auxiliary *do* put?

> When the **VP** in a basic sentence does not contain a form of *be* or an auxiliary, a form of the auxiliary *do* is added to the **VP.** The tense form of *do* is the same as the tense form of the verb in the basic sentence. The auxiliary is then put before the subject **NP** to produce a question.

With either of which two single words can all the questions on this page and page 264 be answered? What are these questions called?

> Question transforms made by putting a form of *be* or an auxiliary before the subject **NP** of the basic sentence are called **yes/no questions.**

FOLLOW THROUGH. Transform each of the following basic sentences into a yes/no question:

1. Eleanor is writing a report.
2. It tells about Bernadette.
3. She read *The Young Bernadette.*
4. The book is in our library.
5. Eleanor used encyclopedias too.

265

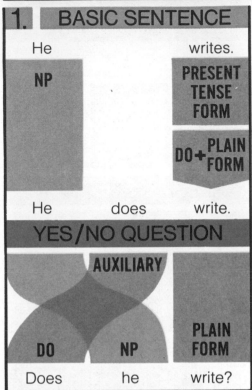

1. BASIC SENTENCE

He — writes.

NP — PRESENT TENSE FORM

DO + PLAIN FORM

He — does — write.

YES/NO QUESTION

AUXILIARY

DO — NP — PLAIN FORM

Does — he — write?

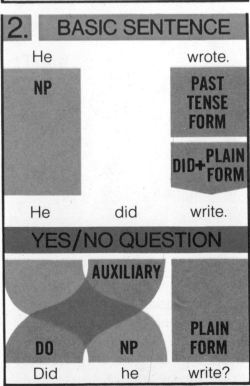

2. BASIC SENTENCE

He — wrote.

NP — PAST TENSE FORM

DID + PLAIN FORM

He — did — write.

YES/NO QUESTION

AUXILIARY

DO — NP — PLAIN FORM

Did — he — write?

BASIC SENTENCE

The book	is	somewhere.

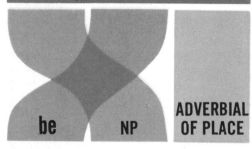

NP	be	ADVERBIAL OF PLACE

YES/NO QUESTION

be	NP	ADVERBIAL OF PLACE

WH- QUESTION

Is the book somewhere?

WHERE?

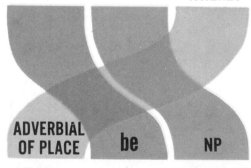

ADVERBIAL OF PLACE	be	NP

Where is the book?

Step 1. Transform the basic sentence into a yes/no question.

Step 2. Replace the adverbial of place with the word *where.*

Step 3. Put the word *where* at the beginning.

Wh- Questions

Can all questions be answered either yes or no?

> Where is the book?
> When are you leaving?
> How does Mary work?

The question transforms above are called **wh- questions** because two of the three begin with a *wh-* word: *where, when.* A question that begins with *how* is also a *wh-* question. On this page and the next two pages, you will discover the three steps for producing *wh-* questions.

Look at the diagram in the Language Strip.

1. What kind of adverbial follows the form of *be?* (Note that the *some* form is used because the answer to the question is not known.)
2. Into what kind of question is the basic sentence first transformed?
3. In the yes/no question, what word replaces the adverbial of place?
4. In the *wh-* question, where is the word *where* put?

A question that begins with *where* is transformed from a basic sentence in which the **VP** contains an adverbial of place.

FOLLOW THROUGH. Transform each of these sentences into a *where* question:

1. That story is in a book.
2. Susan found it there.
3. You will take it home.
4. I hid the book in a desk.
5. The desk is at home.

266

6. It is near a window.
7. Billy went out.
8. The wind blew his hat away.
9. The hat flew against a tree.
10. It fell on the ground.

Look at the diagram in the Language Strip and answer these questions:

1. What kind of adverbial appears in the **VP?**
2. Into what kind of question is the basic sentence first transformed?
3. In the yes/no question, what word replaces the adverbial of time?
4. In the *wh-* question, where is the word *when* put?

A question that begins with *when* is transformed from a basic sentence in which the **VP** contains an adverbial of time.

FOLLOW THROUGH. Transform each of these sentences into a *when* question:

1. Mary Ludwig was a heroine during the War of Independence.
2. She married John Hays in 1769.
3. The war broke out soon.
4. Her husband joined the army then.
5. Mary followed him later.
6. She kept busy during the day.
7. John wrote to her at night.
8. The letter arrived by midday.
9. It was sent on time.
10. The troops rose early.
11. They marched after breakfast.
12. They became tired soon.

BASIC SENTENCE

You	are	leaving	sometime.
NP	AUXILIARY	VERB	ADVERBIAL OF TIME

YES/NO QUESTION

AUXILIARY	NP	VERB	ADVERBIAL OF TIME

WH- QUESTION

Are	you	leaving	sometime?

WHEN?

ADVERBIAL OF TIME	AUXILIARY	NP	VERB
When	are	you	leaving?

Step 1. Transform the basic sentence into a yes/no question.

Step 2. In the yes/no question, replace the adverbial of time with the word *when.*

Step 3. Put the word *when* at the beginning of the question.

BASIC SENTENCE

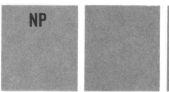

Mary · worked · somehow.

NP		PAST TENSE FORM	ADVERBIAL OF MANNER

YES/NO QUESTION

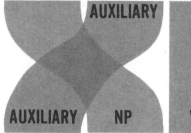

AUXILIARY

AUXILIARY	NP	VERB	ADVERBIAL OF MANNER

WH- QUESTION

Did · Mary · work · somehow?

HOW?

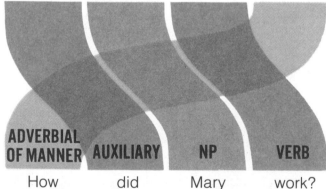

ADVERBIAL OF MANNER	AUXILIARY	NP	VERB
How	did	Mary	work?

Step 1. Transform the basic sentence into a yes/no question.

Step 2. In the yes/no question, replace the adverbial of manner with the word *how.*

Step 3. Put the word *how* at the beginning of the sentence.

Look at the diagram and answer these questions:

1. What kind of adverbial appears in the **VP?**
2. Into what kind of question is the basic sentence first transformed?
3. In the yes/no question, what word replaces the adverbial of manner?
4. In the *wh-* question, where is the word *how* put?

A question that begins with *how* is transformed from a basic sentence in which the **VP** contains an adverbial of manner.

WRITING HINT: Some *how* questions will add interest to your writing.

FOLLOW THROUGH. Transform each of these basic sentences into a *how* question:

1. Mary won her nickname from a pitcher.
2. She had carried water hurriedly to the men.
3. The soldiers drank thirstily.
4. They called her loudly from their posts.
5. Mary served them from a pitcher.
6. She spoke in a whisper to each man.
7. The water poured like a flood.
8. The general ruled his men with an iron hand.
9. The men fought bravely during the battle.
10. The bugle sounded in tune.

CHECK UP ON YOURSELF

A. Transform each of the following basic sentences into a yes/no question:

1. Elizabeth Yates has written many books.
2. One book is *Amos Fortune, Free Man.*
3. That book won a medal.
4. Another book is about writing.
5. Its title is *Someday You'll Write.*

B. Transform each of these sentences into a *wh-* question:

1. You can become a writer through work.
2. Reading can help you in one way.
3. Your inner ear will respond to words at times.
4. Those words appear in stories.
5. A dictionary should be in reach.
6. Your vocabulary grows by reading.
7. You should try words in combinations.
8. Words may be new in context.
9. You should experiment with them daily.
10. You will be a writer someday.

C. Copy the adverbial from each sentence in B. Write whether it is an adverbial of place, an adverbial of time, or an adverbial of manner.

UNIT 9

THE LANGUAGE of WORK

the words of work

Which of the following groups of words do you associate with each occupation shown above?

disease	rhythm
fever	chord
inoculation	jazz
medicine	harmony
tumor	bass clef
negative	loan
developing solution	interest
film	deposit
enlarger	savings
focus	check

270

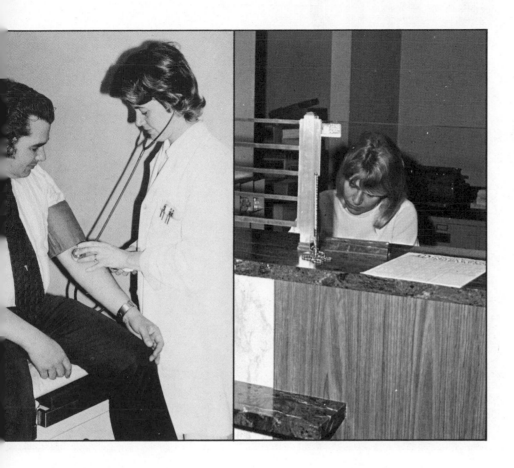

DISCUSS IT. Answer these questions about the occupational words:

1. What does the word *note* mean when it is related to music?
2. What does the word *note* mean when it is related to banking?
3. Which words in the groups on page 270 have a special meaning when considered with an occupation?
5. What is the occupational meaning? What is another meaning?

Words that have special meanings when used in particular situations are called *special vocabulary words.*

271

IMPRESSIONS

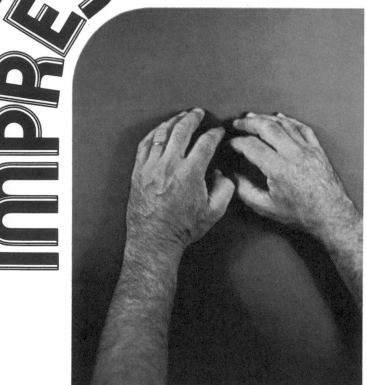

What can you imagine about the people these hands belong to? Are they young or old? Where might they live? Are they rich or poor? What kinds of work do you think these hands have done? Are the hands strong or weak? Have the persons' lives been easy or hard? Why do you think so? Which pair of hands do you find most interesting? Why? How do you think these hands would feel to the touch: smooth or

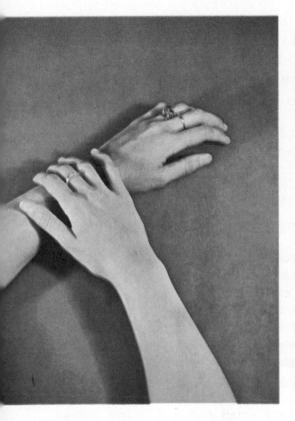
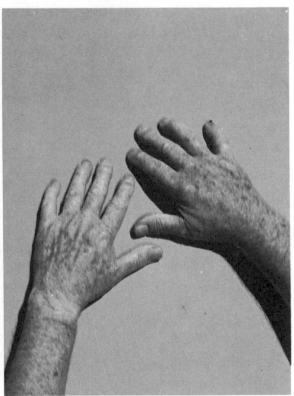

rough? tender or harsh? firm or gentle? What makes you think so?

Would you like to meet any of these persons? Why do you think you would or wouldn't like them? What things have you already found out or imagined about them from studying their hands? What surprises do you think you might have once you met them?

FINDING OUT ABOUT WORK

What types of jobs have characters performed in stories you have read? How can reading help you to learn about various types of jobs?

Two jobs in which there is a shortage of workers are law enforcement and undersea exploration. Selections you will read provide information about each of these occupations. Before you read the selections, there are some words that you should learn.

FOLLOW THROUGH. Use the following words in place of the words in bold letters in the sentences below:

aquanauts	scuba	minute	gleaned	substantial
concealed	revived	ransom	particles	a near-fatal

1. Aquanauts are **self-contained underwater breathing apparatus** divers.
2. It was **an almost disastrous** accident.
3. The kidnappers demanded a large **amount of money paid for the freedom of a captive.**
4. The police officer carried a **hidden** weapon.
5. **Divers who explore the ocean** have lived for long periods of time in laboratories beneath the ocean.
6. The diver was **brought back to consciousness.**
7. The reward given to the police officer was **considerably large.**
8. There were many **very small** fish swimming around *Sealab.*
9. Many **small fragments** of soil clung to his trousers.
10. The detective **gathered little by little** many facts about the crime.

THE CRIMINALIST'S "MUSEUM"

A case illustrating the value of a soil file occurred some years back in St. Louis. A three-year-old boy named Bernard Gould was kidnapped. The Gould family, following instructions phoned them by the kidnappers, paid a substantial ransom. The following day the little boy was found wandering in downtown St. Louis, unharmed but very dirty.

Beyond identifying them as two men, the child was unable to give any description of his kidnappers. Nor was he able to tell where he had been concealed, except that it was "not a nice house" and that he had gone on a long automobile trip to get there.

The boy's clothing was turned over to the St. Louis Crime Lab for examination. A criminalist took each piece separately, spread it on clean wrapping paper, and went over it inch by inch with a magnifying glass. Dozens of minute particles, ranging from bits of hair to specks of dirt, were gleaned in this way. Then the clothing was gone over with a special filtered vacuum cleaner and further particles were recovered. Finally the shoes were examined. Several bits of granite containing quartz were found on the soles, together with samples of mud and road tar.

The bits of mud and quartz granite were matched to samples in a soil file. The mud was of a type found only along the banks of the Meramec River, about twenty miles from St. Louis. Quartz-granite sand of that particular composition was found only at a specific beach area where there were privately owned cottages.

Knowing now where to look, St. Louis police and sheriff's deputies sped to that area. Of several private roads leading to the beach, only one had been recently tarred. At the end of it were four beach cottages. The first cottage was occupied by an elderly couple and their grandchildren. The second was boarded-up and vacant. The third was occupied by two bachelor brothers named Arthur and Joseph Peebles. When Arthur Peebles saw the police officers, he turned pale and started to run, only to be brought down with a flying tackle by one of the deputies. Joseph quickly surrendered without a fight. Most of the ransom money was found hidden in the cottage, and both brothers received long prison terms for kidnapping.

Richard Deming

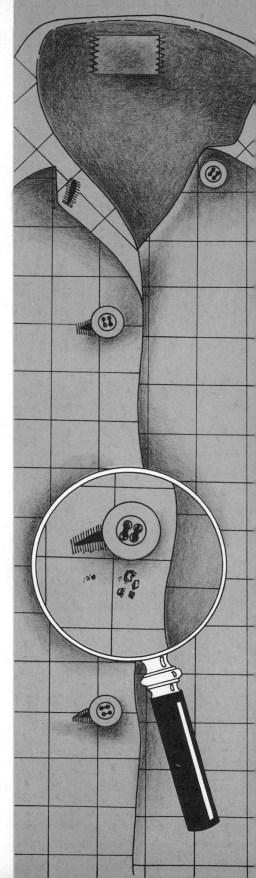

Photos courtesy of U.S. Navy.

A DOOR MADE OF WATER

What was it like to live for ten days beneath the sea? Of course, the aquanauts were not completely cut off from the world above them. *Sealab* was connected to a surface ship by hoses and cables. Air was pumped down to the underwater home through the hoses. Some of the cables supplied electric power. Others were for two-way telephone and TV hookups between the surface ship and the aquanauts.

During the first few days underwater, the aquanauts tired easily. They slept after every meal. They spent only two or three hours during the day doing real work—measuring undersea water currents or exploring the ocean floor.

Much of the time inside *Sealab* they spent watching the fish. Attracted by the lights, fish crowded around *Sealab*'s portholes. Some became tame enough to be fed by hand. The aquanauts came to recognize some of them and grew fond of them. "Killing one of those fish would be just like killing a little dog that lived next to you," said Robert Barth, one of the aquanauts.

As time went on, the aquanauts became more lively—and more careless. They began to feel as if they *belonged* in the sea. One dreamed that he was swimming in the sea like a fish, without an air supply or any protection at all.

Then came a close call. Aquanaut Sanders Manning swam out from *Sealab* to take some underwater motion pictures of *Star I*, a one-man submarine being tested by the Navy. *Star I* was on the bottom, not far from *Sealab*.

"A Door Made of Water" reprinted by permission of Julian Messner, A Division of Simon & Schuster, Inc., from *Man Explores the Sea* by Malcolm E. Weiss. Copyright © 1969 by Malcolm E. Weiss.

Manning had just started to take his pictures when he began feeling dizzy. He knew something serious was wrong. An air valve in his scuba gear had stuck. He had to get back to *Sealab* quickly. He got within a few feet of the door—and passed out.

Aquanaut Lester Anderson was inside *Sealab* at the time, but he could not see Manning. The underwater laboratory had only two portholes on either side, and Manning's body was in a "blind" spot between them.

Then, by good luck, the unconscious Manning drifted up against *Sealab*'s wall. CLUNK! Inside, Anderson jumped as if he had heard a shot and rushed for *Sealab*'s watery door. He caught sight of Manning floating helplessly, and hauled him up to safety—just in time. Manning was revived and *Sealab*'s work went on. Because of the near-fatal accident, the next *Sealab* would have *eleven* portholes along its sides.

Malcolm E. Weiss

DISCUSS IT. Check how well you read by answering the following questions:

1. What are some of the jobs performed by law enforcement officers? by aquanauts?
2. What kind of training do you think a crime lab technician or an aquanaut would require?
3. Which job do you think would be the more dangerous? Why?
4. How do both jobs help other people?
5. What type of person do you think would enjoy working in a crime lab? a sea lab? Why?

WRITE IT. Write a one- to three-paragraph statement explaining why you would or would not like to be an aquanaut or a law enforcement officer. Be sure to support your statements with facts.

Using Your Language

Notice the words in bold letters in the sentences below:

1. Aquanauts **sit** at portholes and watch fish.
2. *Sealab* was **set** on an underwater shelf.
3. The lab technician **lays** his tools on the counter.
4. After working all night, he will **lie** on the couch in his laboratory.

Sit means "to take a seat."
Lie means "to stretch out."
Set and *lay* mean "to put" or "to place."

DISCUSS IT. What is the meaning of the word *sit* in sentence 1? What is the meaning of the word *set* in sentence 2? How are the words *lie* and *lay* like *sit* and *set*?

FOLLOW THROUGH. Use *sit* or *set* in place of the box in each of the following sentences:

1. Truck drivers ⬚ most of the day.
2. Stock boys ⬚ merchandise on shelves.
3. You must ⬚ still in the dentist's chair.
4. The machinist ⬚ a wrench on the floor.
5. Crane operators often ⬚ high in the air.

FOLLOW THROUGH. Use *lie* or *lay* in place of the box in each sentence below:

1. Mechanics often ⬚ under cars.
2. The carpenter ⬚ his tools on the workbench.
3. The patients often ⬚ on the examining table.
4. Please ⬚ the bricks in a straight line.
5. The welder will have to ⬚ on the wing of the jet.

The Way Your Language Changes

Which of the following sentences deals with a real object or thing? Which deals with a quality or an idea?

Words that deal with objects or things are *concrete words*.
Words that deal with qualities or ideas are *abstract words*.

1. My uncle is a plumber.
2. My uncle is honest.
3. Her slack suit is red.
4. Her slack suit is stylish.

278

The development of language moved from concrete to abstract. The first language was picture language. What words are represented by the pictures in the message below?

DISCUSS IT. Discuss answers to the following questions:

1. What is the message told by the picture language?
2. Why do you think the first words in language represented the names of objects?
3. What are the advantages of picture language?
4. Why cannot words like *courage*, *beauty*, and *truth* be shown in picture language?
5. What are the disadvantages of picture language?

Only concrete words can be represented by picture language.

It was not until writing was developed that abstract ideas could be written. Now we have words representing several different levels of abstraction. Some of these levels of abstraction are as follows:

Levels of Abstraction

Trans-portation

The word *transportation* has a high level of abstraction. It includes every means of moving from one place to another from dogsled to spaceship. It is an extremely general word that does not deal with specific qualities.

Land Transportation

Land transportation is less abstract. It stands for qualities that a trail bike shares with trains, bicycles, and buses.

Motor Vehicle

Motor vehicle stands for even more specific qualities. It relates a trail bike to all forms of transportation having a motor.

Bicycle

Bicycle stands for those specific qualities that a trail bike has in common with other two-wheeled vehicles.

Trail Bike

Trail bike is the name we give to the object itself. It merely represents the object.

Here is the actual trail bike that we see—not the word used to represent a trail bike, but the concrete object itself.

FOLLOW THROUGH. Arrange the words in each group below into levels of abstraction. Put the most concrete on the bottom and the most abstract on the top.

1. Spot, dog, animal, living thing
2. recreation, football game, athletics, contact sport
3. record, Bread Album, music, sounds
4. living thing, human, boy, Paul
5. book, literature, communication, *A Matter of Miracles*

Why is it hard to communicate with statements like these?

> "Today's teen-agers are undermining the American way of life."
> "No, they're not. They are concerned citizens."

What is meant by "American way of life" and "concerned citizens"? Why might communication be better if the following statements were made?

> "I am offended by the long hair and sloppy dress of young people today."
> "Why should fashion styles of another generation offend you?"

TELL IT. Which pair of statements is more abstract? Which pair of statements is more concrete? Why is it more difficult to communicate on an abstract level?

WRITE IT. Rewrite each of the abstract statements below to make it a more concrete statement:

1. Our candidate stands for law and order.
2. Poor people are lazy.
3. Today's youth are not patriotic.
4. You can't trust anyone over thirty.
5. Modern art is ugly.

communicate

Applying for Work

If you wanted to get a part-time job, how would you go about it? One way—the interview—involves the use of your oral skills.

The Interview

Notice the questioning and answering techniques in the following interview:

INTERVIEWER: Good afternoon. I'm Jim Courtney. Please come into my office and take a seat.

APPLICANT: Good afternoon, Mr. Courtney. My name is Bryan Thompson. I read your advertisement for a part-time plumber's helper in the classified section of last night's newspaper. I would like to apply for that job.

INTERVIEWER: The position has not yet been filled. Tell me about your training.

APPLICANT: I am in the vocational training program of Sloan High School, where I am specializing in plumbing. I like working as a plumber and hope to make it my life's work. My father is a plumber, and I have learned things from him. He and Mr. Macy, my teacher, tell me that I am fast and accurate. They both felt that I should apply for this job. Also, Mr. Macy gave me this letter of recommendation.

INTERVIEWER: This letter is high in praise. Mr. Macy certainly likes the work you do.

Several other young men have applied for this job, since the hourly wage is very good. I must interview them before I can hire anyone. By Wednesday I'll be finished with the interviews, and I'll make my decision. Call me after 3 o'clock on Wednesday afternoon, and I'll let you know. If you are selected, you can fill out the necessary forms later that day.

APPLICANT: Thank you. From what I hear about your company, I know I would like to work for you. I'll call you after 3 o'clock on Wednesday.

INTERVIEWER: Thank you for coming in, Mr. Thompson. I'll look forward to your call.

DISCUSS IT. Form into groups of four or five and discuss answers to the following questions:

1. How do you think both persons were dressed? What kind of language did they use?
2. What were the applicant's qualifications for the job? How did he express his qualifications and his interest without being immodest?
3. How did the interviewer try to interest the applicant even more in the job?
4. What acts of courtesy took place on the part of both the interviewer and the applicant during the interview?
5. How long would such an interview last? Who should end the interview? What arrangements were made for letting the applicant know whether he got the job?

WRITE IT. Remain in the same groups and make a list of guidelines for a good interview. Ask a member of the group to record the guidelines and then read them to the class. See whether the class can select a single set of guidelines from those read.

ACT IT. Plan a role-playing situation in which one of your classmates takes the role of a person applying for a job. Another classmate takes the role of the interviewer. Act out the job interview.

EVALUATE IT. Discuss how well the interview was handled based upon the guidelines selected by the class.

The Letter of Application

The other technique for getting a job involves your writing skills. A letter of application is considered a business letter.

DISCUSS IT. Answer the following questions about the letter of application:

1. What are some advantages of a letter of application compared with an oral interview?
2. What are some disadvantages of the letter of application as compared with an oral interview?
3. What information should be included in a letter of application?
4. What should be the length and form of a letter of application?
5. What are five guidelines that could be used in writing a letter of application?

Notice how the letter of application on page 285 differs from the social letter on page 243.

DISCUSS IT. As you compare the business letter with the social letter, answer the following questions:

1. What is the extra part that is found in the business letter?
2. What items are found in this part?
3. In what order do the various items in the date and the address appear in the heading? How is the heading punctuated?
4. How are the items in the inside address punctuated?
5. What is the punctuation mark following the name in the greeting?
6. What punctuation mark follows the greeting in a social letter?
7. How does the content of a business letter differ from that of a social letter?
8. How do the purposes of a business letter differ from those of a social letter?
9. Why should a business letter be more formal than a social letter?
10. How might the signature of a business letter be different from that of a social letter?

Apt. 341, Lakeside Manor
125 Hemlock Drive
Auburn Park, Illinois 60608
November 15, 19—

Mr. Anthony Tanski
Personnel Director
Hill's Department Store
9702 Lakefront Boulevard
Chicago, Illinois 60616

Dear Mr. Tanski:
I should like to apply for a job as a
part-time developer in your photography department. My hobby is photography, and I have
had several years' experience in that line. I
could begin immediately to work evenings and
Saturdays.
If you would like a sample of my work,
I would be happy to come to your store for
a showing and an interview.

Sincerely,

Debby Taylor

(Ms. Debby Taylor)

FOLLOW THROUGH. Arrange the following word groups
of an inside address in proper order. Be sure to capitalize and punctuate correctly, as shown in the letter
above.

1. buyer's grocery stores, inc.
2. mr kevin mc clain
3. 8972 2nd avenue
4. assistant manager
5. detroit michigan   48233

285

FOLLOW THROUGH. Copy the following greetings from a business letter. Be sure to capitalize and punctuate correctly, as shown in the letter on page 285.

1. dear sir
2. dear dr reynolds
3. dear mr perez
4. dear mrs watson
5. dear madam

If you were going to work, what job would you enjoy having next summer? What qualifications do you have for the job? What organization might hire you to do the job? To whom should you write to apply for the job?

WRITE IT. Write a letter of application applying for a summer job. Be sure to use the right form, keep the letter short and to the point, and punctuate correctly.

EDIT IT. Reread your letter. Did you state your qualifications for the job? Was your form correct? Did you remember the guides for capitalization and punctuation?

Did you use an abbreviation for the name of the state in your address? It is permissible to abbreviate state names. The government recently published a simplified list of state name abbreviations authorized for use in mail addresses. Each abbreviation is made up of only two letters.

FOLLOW THROUGH. Look at the following list of simplified state abbreviations authorized for use in mail addresses. Which state has an abbreviation that answers each of the riddles below the list?

Capitalize the first word in the greeting and closing of a letter.

Capitalize the names and titles of persons; initials; abbreviations; names of buildings and firms, streets, cities, states, days, and months.

Use a comma after the closing of a letter, between the day of the month and the year in a date, and between the name of a town or a city and the name of a state.

Use a colon after the greeting in a business letter.

AK	CO	HI	KS	ME	MT	NJ	OK	SD	VT
AL	CT	IA	KY	MI	NB	NM	OR	TN	WA
AR	DE	ID	LA	MN	NC	NV	PA	TX	WI
AZ	FL	IL	MA	MO	ND	NY	RI	UT	WV
CA	GA	IN	MD	MS	NH	OH	SC	VA	WY

1. Which state is the father state?
2. Which state is a nickname for Albert?
3. Which state is a greeting?
4. Which state expresses surprise?
5. Which state says that things are all right?
6. Which state is an antonym for *out*?
7. Which states are musical notes?
8. Which state is self-centered?
9. Which state is the mother state?
10. Which state cares for the sick?

Filling Out an Application

When you send a job application to an employer, he makes a judgment about you based on your application.

DISCUSS IT. What type of judgment might you expect from a smeary, wrinkled application with misspelled words and incorrect punctuation? What type of judgment might you expect from a neatly typed or printed application that is correct in spelling and punctuation?

The application on page 288 is typical of those used by many places of employment throughout the country. Notice the items of information requested.

Why is the Social Security number requested? Do you have a Social Security number? If not, you should apply for one before you apply for a job. You can obtain an application from your local Social Security office.

DISCUSS IT. In what situations might height and weight be important in selecting employees for particular jobs?

287

APPLICATION FOR EMPLOYMENT

PERSONAL INFORMATION

DATE

SOCIAL SECURITY NUMBER

NAME

AGE

SEX

last   first   middle

PRESENT ADDRESS

street   city   state

PHONE NO.   DATE OF BIRTH

HEIGHT   WEIGHT   COLOR OF HAIR   COLOR OF EYES

EMPLOYMENT DESIRED

POSITION

DATE YOU CAN START

SALARY DESIRED

ARE YOU EMPLOYED NOW?

IF SO, MAY WE INQUIRE OF YOUR PRESENT EMPLOYER?

NAME OF PRESENT EMPLOYER

EDUCATION	NAME AND LOCATION OF SCHOOL	YEARS ATTEND- ED	DATE GRAD- UATED	SUBJECTS STUDIED
GRAMMAR SCHOOL				
HIGH SCHOOL				
COLLEGE				
TRADE, BUSINESS OR CORRESPONDENCE SCHOOL				

SCHOOL ACTIVITIES

REFERENCES

GIVE BELOW THE NAMES OF THREE PERSONS NOT RELATED TO YOU, WHOM YOU HAVE KNOWN AT LEAST ONE YEAR.

	NAME	ADDRESS	BUSINESS	YEARS ACQUAINTED
1				
2				
3				

Which of the following responses do you think would be best for the section entitled "Employment Desired"? Why?

1. general work   2. stock clerk   3. handyman

In applying for a job, you should apply for a specific job instead of a general one.

DISCUSS IT. Explain what is meant by the following statement: "The applicant who says he can do anything really means that he can do very little."

TELL IT. Form groups of three or four. Think of several guidelines you should use in selecting persons to use as references. Share your guidelines with other members of the class.

WRITE IT. On a sheet of paper, answer each of the items on the application for employment. For "Education," enter the schooling you think necessary for the position you desire.

EDIT IT. Check your responses to be certain that your ideas are stated clearly and that your spelling is correct. Copy your responses neatly.

DISCUSS IT. Discuss the items of information included on the application. Talk about answers to the following questions:

1. Why should a beginning employee without experience state "the prevailing rate" under "Salary Desired"?
2. What use might the employer make of the references listed?
3. Why might an employer be interested in an applicant's school activities?
4. What use might an employer make of the information regarding a present employer?
5. Why are employers interested in the applicant's educational qualifications?

289

CHECK UP ON YOURSELF

Using Your Vocabulary (page 274)

Use each of the following words in place of a box in the sentences below:

concealed   particles   fatal   revived   aquanaut
ransom   substantial   scuba   glean   minute

1. The detective will ⬚ many facts from his study.
2. Several ⬚ bits of dust were found on the dish.
3. ⬚ divers search the ocean floor for lost ships.
4. Several ⬚ of food remained in the bottom of the sack.
5. The kidnappers held the child for a large ⬚.
6. A doctor ⬚ the unconscious child.
7. My uncle earned a ⬚ sum of money in his business.
8. The criminal was arrested for carrying a ⬚ weapon.
9. An ⬚ often lives in a sea lab on the ocean floor.
10. The accident proved to be ⬚ to the driver.

Using Your Language (page 278)

Use *sit* or *set* for each blank as you write the sentences below. Then rewrite each sentence, using *lie* or *lay* in place of the box.

1. Let's ⬚ here until it is time to begin work.
2. Please ⬚ my tools on the shelf.
3. Do not ⬚ on that cold steel.
4. My boss likes to ⬚ on her new sofa.
5. Those girls ⬚ their purses on the table every day.

Levels of Abstraction (pages 279-281)

A. Arrange each group of words below in order from the most concrete to the most abstract:

1. living thing, roach, animal, insect
2. transportation, *Sea Tramp*, sailboat, watercraft
3. swimming, backstroke, water sport, athletics
4. living thing, rose, flowering plant, American Beauty
5. gingersnap, food, cookie, baked goods

B. Rewrite each of the abstract statements below to make it more concrete:

1. Our candidate believes in freedom for all citizens.
2. Modern music is nothing but noise.
3. The younger generation is going to the dogs.
4. Our local newspaper is a scandal sheet.
5. My brother is a bully.

Capitalizing and Punctuating Correctly (page 284)

Write the word groups below, capitalizing and punctuating correctly:

1. mr jerome l stevens
2. mrs h r collins lives in the brentwood apartments
3. dear sir
4. he works at the gray steel corporation at wheeling west virginia
5. sincerely yours

State Abbreviations (page 287)

Write the simplified state abbreviations for the following:

Massachusetts   Alaska   Maine   Oklahoma   Indiana
Pennsylvania   Maryland   Ohio   Louisiana   Hawaii

LOOKING BACK AND CHECKING UP

Prefixes and Suffixes (page 140)

Combine a word with each prefix and suffix below and define the word:

1. co-	4. mis-	7. dis-	10. -ment	13. -ful
2. non-	5. pre-	8. ad-	11. -ish	14. -ize
3. sub-	6. anti-	9. mis-	12. -ward	15. -hood

Identifying References (pages 139-140 and 143-145)

Match each reference with its definition.

a. dictionary
b. poetry index
c. atlas
d. quotation index
e. almanac

1. A book containing statistical and factual information
2. A listing of poems by title, first line, and author
3. A book of maps and geographic information
4. The most useful book of information about words
5. A list of quotations by topic and author

Time-Order Sentences (pages 177)

Each sentence below describes two events that happened at the same time. Substitute one word in each sentence to make the events happen at different times.

1. We planned our day while eating breakfast.
2. While he cut the grass, it began to rain.
3. The boys played cards during the lesson.
4. Dad laughed when he heard our story.
5. The campers ate during the storm.

Using Your Language (pages 187 and 260)

Use the appropriate form of the word in parentheses as you write each sentence below:

(fall) 1. He had ☐ before anybody knew it.
(fly) 2. My aunt has ☐ all over the world.
(freeze) 3. His hands ☐ soon after he lost his gloves.
(swim) 4. We ☐ all afternoon yesterday.
(wear) 5. Richard has ☐ my sweater to school all week.

MORE IDEAS FOR YOU

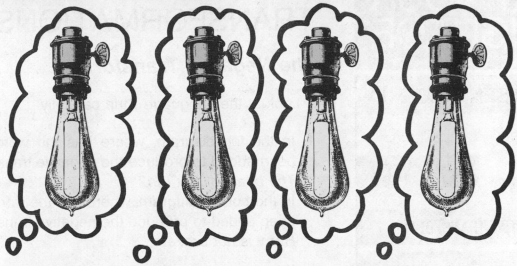

1. Select an occupation in which you might be interested and find information about it. Report your findings to the class.
2. Invite representatives of certain occupations to come to your class and explain their work.
3. In your town, locate businesses or industries that conduct tours. Work with your teacher in arranging a field trip to one or more of these places.
4. Ask your school counselor to talk with your class about interest inventories and occupational counseling.
5. Prepare a chart illustrating levels of abstraction, and display it in your classroom.
6. Make a bulletin-board display of pictures representing various types of work.
7. Work with a classmate and prepare a tape recording of a pupil applying for a job through an interview. Play the recording to the class, and lead a discussion about the interview.
8. Write business letters to several companies, requesting job information. Make a display of the occupational literature that you receive.

BASIC SENTENCE 1

The bear   will run.

AUX + VERB

NEGATIVE TRANSFORM

AUX + NOT + VERB

The bear   will not run.

BASIC SENTENCE 4

Harry   is brave.

be + Adj

NEGATIVE TRANSFORM

be + NOT + Adj

Harry   is not brave.

TRANSFORMATIONS

The Negative Transform

Look at the Language Strip carefully.

1. In the top diagram, where has the word *not* been added to produce the negative transform *The bear will not run?*
2. In the bottom diagram, where has the word *not* been added to produce the negative transform *Harry is not brave?*

One negative transform is made by adding *not* to the **VP** in a basic sentence after an auxiliary or a form of *be*.

If the **VP** does not contain an auxiliary or a form of *be,* how is the negative transform made?

BSP 2: The bear chased Harry.
   (The bear did chase Harry.)
Transform: The bear did not chase Harry.

Another negative transform is made by adding a form of *do* to the verb phrase and then adding *not*.

You have learned a name for a word like the one in bold letters below. What is it?

The bear **wasn't** chasing Harry.

In speaking and writing, the word *not* is usually part of a **contraction** in a negative transform.

FOLLOW THROUGH. Transform each sentence into a negative, using the contraction.

1. The bear was chained.
2. The bear might see Harry.
3. The keeper fed the bear.
4. Bears move fast usually.
5. They can avoid a fight.

The Request Transform

Look at the Language Strip and answer these questions about the request transform *Watch:*

1. What is the subject **NP** in the basic sentence?
2. In the **VP** in the basic sentence, what kind of auxiliary is followed by the plain form of the verb?
3. What happens to the modal?
4. What happens to the subject **NP?**

The request transform is made from a basic sentence in which the subject **NP** is *you* and the **VP** contains a modal. To make the transform, the modal is omitted and the subject **NP** is omitted.

WRITING HINT: Use request transforms in your writing to give variety.

FOLLOW THROUGH. Use the request transform as you write each of these sentences:

1. You can write about any author.
2. You must research his work.
3. You shall study his style.
4. You may report on it.
5. You will give the report orally.

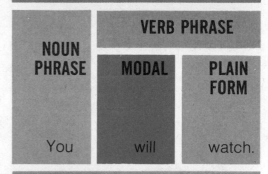

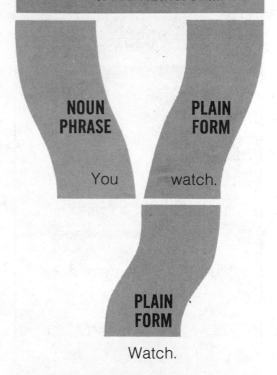

Step 1. Omit the modal.
Step 2. Omit the subject **NP.**

BSP 2 [Miss Yates] has a story.

BSP 2 [The story] portrays courage.

POSSESSIVE TRANSFORM

NP + POSSESSIVE

Miss Yates + 's

The

story portrays courage.

Miss Yates's story portrays courage.

The Possessive Transform

Study the diagram in the Language Strip.

1. What is the subject **NP** in the first basic sentence? in the second basic sentence?
2. When 's is added to *Miss Yates,* what do we call the form *Miss Yates's?*
3. What word in the **NP** of the second basic sentence does the possessive form *Miss Yates's* replace? What do we call *The?*

The possessive transform is made by replacing a determiner in one basic sentence with the possessive form of an **NP** from another basic sentence.

How do proper nouns and singular nouns form the possessive?

Miss Crandall**'s** determination   the lady**'s** hope

How do plural nouns ending in *s* form the possessive?

ladies' work

How do plural nouns not ending in *s* form the possessive?

the people**'s** attitude

WRITING HINT: The use of possessive transforms in your writing will add variety.

FOLLOW THROUGH. Use the possessive transform with each pair of sentences below:

1. One woman had courage. That courage was evident.

2. Prudence Crandall had a boarding school. The boarding school was in Connecticut.
3. The girls had parents. The parents objected to some children in the school.
4. Miss Crandall had friends. The friends intervened for her.
5. The parents had a bias. Their bias put Prudence Crandall in jail.

The Adjective Transform

What do you see in the Language Strip?

1. In the first basic sentence, what kind of word follows *be*? Which basic sentence pattern does the sentence follow?
2. To make the adjective transform, where in the second basic sentence is the adjective *young* inserted?

A basic sentence may be transformed by putting the adjective from Basic Sentence Pattern 4 before the noun in an **NP.**

WRITING HINT: The use of the adjective transform can make your writing concise.

FOLLOW THROUGH. Combine each pair of sentences by using the adjective transform.

1. The first trial ended in disagreement. The disagreement was complete.
2. The second trial brought a verdict. The verdict was startling.
3. Prudence had spirit. That spirit was great.
4. Prudence won at last. She was courageous.
5. The slaves became free. The slaves were long-suffering.
6. Prudence married a preacher. The preacher was powerful.
7. They moved to another town. The town was small.

297

BASIC SENTENCES

BSP 4: Some children were young.

BSP 2: Some children joined the school.

ADJECTIVE TRANSFORM

Some children
     were   young.

be + Adj

Some young children joined the school.

LOOKING BACK AND CHECKING UP

Subjects and Predicates (pages 20-26)

A. Use a plus sign to divide each sentence into subject **NP** and **VP** as you copy it.

1. President Lincoln delivered a speech on November 19, 1863.
2. He gave it as a dedication.
3. Reporters took down his words.
4. Edward Everett orated for two hours at Gettysburg.
5. Lincoln spoke then.
6. Everyone could hear him.
7. He gave his ten sentences in five minutes.
8. The applause was light.
9. People had sat for three hours.
10. The speech was The Gettysburg Address.
11. The speech became famous.
12. Many people know the speech by heart.

B. Which of these makes up the subject **NP** in each sentence in A: (a) a proper noun, (b) a common noun alone, (c) a determiner plus a noun, (d) a personal pronoun, or (e) an indefinite pronoun?

C. List a proper noun for each of these common nouns:

1. lake   5. woman   9. car   13. monument
2. man   6. planet   10. pet   14. street
3. city   7. holiday 11. book   15. president
4. tribe 8. document 12. store 16. mountain

D. Write the plural of each of these nouns:

1. life   5. salmon   9. mouse   13. box
2. fly   6. patch   10. burro   14. horse
3. ox   7. chief   11. shelf   15. child
4. key   8. hero   12. pony   16. lady

Words in the Verb Phrase (pages 58-62)

A. Write whether the **VP** in each sentence below contains a verb or a verb followed by an **NP**:

1. The Andersons enrolled their child in a choir.
2. People donated money for her education.
3. The girl studied hard.
4. She sang with feeling.
5. A singer placed a duet before her.
6. She sang with him.
7. The audience applauded her loudly.
8. The world recognized Marian Anderson.
9. Shirlee P. Newman wrote about her.
10. I told everyone about the story.
11. They enjoyed her biography.
12. Marian Anderson sang for Presidents.

B. For each verb followed by an **NP** in A, what kind of object appears in the **VP?** Is it (a) a common noun alone, (b) a proper noun, (c) a determiner plus a noun, (d) a personal pronoun, or (e) an indefinite pronoun?

C. Tell whether the **VP** in each sentence below is made up of a linking verb followed by an **NP** or a form of *be* followed by an **NP**:

1. People were friends.
2. One friend was Roland Hayes.
3. Her music seemed everything to her.
4. She became a contestant.
5. The winner was she.
6. Music remained her love.
7. Roland was a musician.
8. Roberto Clemente was a ballplayer.
9. He became an outfielder.
10. His name became a household word.
11. His fans were many.
12. He felt sadness for the poor.
13. They remained his concern.
14. Roberto is a hero to all people.
15. Puerto Ricans felt his loss especially.

More Words in the Verb Phrase (pages 88-93)

A. Tell whether the **VP** in each sentence below is made up of a form of *be* followed by an adjective or a linking verb followed by an adjective:

1. John F. Kennedy was courageous.
2. He was bedridden after an accident.
3. Time seemed endless.
4. He grew interested in history.
5. His *Profiles in Courage* became prize-worthy.
6. His condition remained poor.
7. Kennedy is legendary in our time.
8. His leadership was inspiring.

B. Copy the **VP** from each sentence below. Tell whether the adverbial is an adverbial of time, an adverbial of place, or an adverbial of manner.

1. John F. Kennedy wrote the book during his recuperation.
2. It received a Pulitzer Prize in 1957.
3. The public received the book enthusiastically.
4. Kennedy was a Senator by then.
5. His colleagues appointed him to the Senate Foreign Relations Committee.
6. Kennedy served with wit and courage.
7. Someone killed him brutally.

Tense in the Verb Phrase (pages 124-127)

A. Find the verb in each **VP** below and tell whether it shows present tense or past tense.

1. Speakers collect stories.
2. That speaker communicated his ideas.
3. He had many ideas.
4. Many ideas show merit.
5. You are right.

B. Use the past form of the verb as you write each sentence.

1. The man (speak) to us.
2. He (ring) the bell.
3. We (see) his notes.
4. They (be) short.
5. He (have) very few.
6. Some (blow) out of his car.
7. He (drive) here from his home.
8. We (steal) a look at his car.
9. It (be) shiny.
10. We (write) a thank-you to him.

Auxiliaries (pages 152-155)

A. Copy the **VP** from each sentence. Show what kind of auxiliary is used and which form of the verb follows it.

1. A police officer was watching three boys.
2. They had walked down the street slowly.
3. The police officer would follow them.
4. The boys did stop suddenly.
5. One had gone into a store.
6. The others were standing outside.
7. They did look suspicious.
8. They might make trouble.
9. The first boy was coming out.
10. He had bought something.

B. Use an auxiliary in each of these sentences:

1. The police officer ____ been suspicious.
2. He ____ being cautious.
3. The boys ____ be thieves.
4. They ____ have a goal.
5. They ____ running an errand.
6. One ____ bought bread.
7. They ____ going home.
8. The officer ____ relax.

Tense Forms (pages 192-195)

A. Use the present tense form of the verb as you write each sentence.

1. The dress (have) pleats.
2. Flowers (grow) in our window box.
3. These books (contain) information.
4. Frank (do) many jobs at home.
5. Ellen (make) the beds daily.
6. She (help) around the house.
7. Plants (need) water.
8. This plant (have) buds.
9. The encyclopedia (show) many animals.
10. We (like) the pictures.

B. Write each sentence, using a form of *be.*

1. The boys ⬜ in a meeting at this time.
2. My mother ⬜ in Miami last week.
3. A dune buggy ⬜ a vehicle.
4. The sandwiches ⬜ delicious yesterday.
5. I ⬜ in school now.
6. The chickens ⬜ in their coop now.
7. The astronaut ⬜ inside the spaceship at this time.
8. He ⬜ in the ocean then.
9. Passengers ⬜ in the bus at the time.
10. I ⬜ at my desk by nine usually.

Compound Transforms (pages 224-228)

A. Use a compound transform for each pair of sentences.

1. A gibbon is small. A gibbon is tailless.
2. That woman studies animals. She studies other subjects.
3. Giraffes chew cud. Cattle chew cud.
4. Some turtles live in water. Other turtles live on land.
5. Fish live in water. They breathe through gills.

B. Tell which pronoun form should be used in each **NP.**

1. That topic is easy for my friend and (I, me).
2. Cindy and (I, me) have researched it.
3. We saw you and (he, him) in the library.
4. You and (she, her) were researching another topic.
5. We'll show our reports to you and (he, him).

Question Transforms (pages 264-268)

A. Transform each of these statements into a yes/no question:

1. Anna Marie sings well.
2. She is a soprano.
3. She is preparing a program.
4. She has studied long.
5. Our class will like her.

B. Transform each sentence into a wh- question.

1. The vocal cords are in the larynx.
2. Dan will be here tomorrow.
3. The repairman will arrive by truck.
4. The knives are on the tray.
5. The runner breathed hard.

Other Transforms (pages 294-297)

A. Transform each sentence, using a negative contraction.

1. That animal can see in the dark.
2. My sister was in the Army.
3. The helicopter landed on the building.
4. This paper shows comic strips.
5. Our picture was blurry.

B. Use the request transform on each sentence.

1. You should wear a hat.
2. You can find the other shoe.
3. You should open the door.
4. You may type this letter.
5. You must follow the signs.

C. Join the sentences by using the possessive transform.

1. An elephant has a trunk. The trunk is muscular.
2. June has a dress. The dress is long.
3. The dog had a muzzle. The muzzle was tight.
4. Those men have beards. The beards are long.
5. Our parents have ideas. The ideas are interesting.

D. Combine each pair of sentences by using an adjective transform.

1. Erma has a kitten. The kitten is black.
2. Our friends were in agreement. The agreement was complete.
3. Donna told a story. The story was funny.
4. We looked up at the sky. The sky was blue.
5. Blades lift the helicopter. The blades are narrow.

Handbook

In this part of your book, you can find things you need to know for your own writing and for your editing work. You can use these pages also to see how much you have learned about your language. Use the page number at the end of each line to find more information in your textbook.

CAPITAL LETTERS

Capital letters are used for:

1. The first word of a sentence:
   The Skylab circled the earth. (10, 257)
2. The first word in the greeting of a letter:
   Dear Eleanor, (244, 286)
3. The first word in the closing of a letter:
   Sincerely yours, (244, 286)
4. The first word of a speaker in written conversation:
   "You are not," said Helen, "going to tell her!" (41)
5. The first word of a line of poetry:
   Lewis and Clark
   Said, "Come on, let's embark!" (257)
6. The first, last, and all important words in titles:
   Book—*Altogether, One at a Time!* (147)
   Magazine—*American Girl* (147)
   Newspaper—*Times Chronicle* (147)
   Poem—"Children of the Wind" (147)
   Report—"Indians of the Northwest" (147)

Song — "God Bless America" (147)

Story — "Down the Long River" (147, 236)

7. The word I (10)

8. Names of persons and pets:

    Juan Lopez, Jane Whitecloud, Spot (10, 75, 286)

9. Titles of persons:

    Ms., Mrs., Mr., Miss, Dr. (147, 286)

10. Initials:

    Myra G. Simpson, Henry B. Cole (75, 147, 286)

11. Names of towns, cities, and states:

    Jamesport, Washington, Texas (75, 286)

12. Names of mountains, lakes, rivers, countries, continents, and other geographical names:

    Mount Everest, Lake Tahoe, Rio Grande, France, Asia (10)

13. Names of streets, avenues, and roads:

    22 West Mountain Road (75, 286)

14. Some abbreviations:

    P. O., R. R., Mrs., Mr., Ms., Dr., Jr. (286)

15. Names of schools, clubs, churches and synagogues, and religious denominations:

    Henry Hudson School, Utica Art Club,

    Johnson Methodist Church, Catholics (10, 168)

16. The word God and other sacred names (168)

17. Names of days, special days, holidays, and months:

    Monday, Father's Day, Fourth of July, January (75, 286)

18. Names of languages, people of a country, and special groups of people:

    Chinese, Russians, Puritans (10)

19. Names of regions:

    We toured the East. (168)

20. Names of buildings:

    Empire State Building (75, 286)

21. Names of companies and stores:

    L. B. Singer Center (75, 286)

22. Names of railroads and ship lines:

    North Central Railroad, Central Island Line (147)

306

23. Names of documents:
    Declaration of Independence (147)
24. Trade names:
    Wowie Shirts (213)
25. The first word following an exclamation point:
    Oh! You didn't need to do that! (106)
26. The first word of a main head and a subhead in an outline, and to set off each subhead: (146)
    I. Building a house
        A. Selecting the site
        B. Preparing the plans
    II. Selecting the contractor
        A. Getting bids
        B. Signing the contract

CONTRACTION

When one or more letters are left out in joining two or more words, a *contraction* is formed. An apostrophe (') takes the place of the letter or letters that are left out.

LETTER WRITING

HEADING

28 East 9 Street
Sanford, Florida 32771
June 28, 19 —

GREETING

Dear Joella,

Last weekend Mother drove us down to see Disney World. We had a great time and saw as much as we could in two days. What traffic! It took us two hours longer than it should have to get home, but it was worth every minute of it.

When you come for a visit, Mother says she will take us there once again. You'll love it, I know.

CLOSING
SIGNATURE

Sincerely,
Edna

SOCIAL LETTER (243)

307

HEADING	19 Everett Avenue Little York, Indiana 47139 October 23, 19—
INSIDE ADDRESS	<u>Science Digest</u> 224 West 57 Street New York, N. Y. 10019

GREETING	Gentlemen:
	    I am preparing a report for school and would like to quote the first three paragraphs from your article "In Search of Seashell Treasures" as a part of it. The paragraphs appear on pages 16 and 17 of the issue for July, 1973.
	    I hope you will let me use this material. I enclose a stamped, self-addressed envelope for your reply.

CLOSING **SIGNATURE**	Yours truly, (Miss) Mary Craft

BUSINESS LETTER (285)

The return address on an envelope is the address of the writer. It shows where the letter came from and where it may be returned if it cannot be delivered.

The address on an envelope is that of the person or company you are writing to. In a business letter, it is the same as the inside address.

RETURN ADDRESS	Mary Craft 19 Everett Avenue Little York, Indiana 47139
ADDRESS	Science Digest 224 West 57 Street New York, N. Y. 10019

ENVELOPE

PUNCTUATION MARKS

APOSTROPHE

Use an apostrophe:
1. In a contraction:
   didn't   we'd   we've
2. In the possessive form of a word:
   lion's   lions' (141)

COLON

Use a colon:
1. After the greeting of a business letter:
   Gentlemen: (286)
2. After the name of a speaker in play directions:
   Mary: What is behind that curtain?
3. In writing time:
   They came at 2:30 P.M. (258)
4. To introduce a list:
   They brought these things: books, magazines, newspapers, and some dictionaries. (258)

COMMA

Use a comma:
1. After the greeting of a social letter:
   Dear Matilda, (244)
2. After the closing of a letter:
   Sincerely yours, (244, 286)
3. Between the name of a town or a city and the name of a state:
   San Diego, California (244, 286)
4. Between the day and the year in a date:
   July 4, 1776 (244, 286)
5. After a last name written before a first name:
   Howard, John J. (136)
6. To separate parts of an entry in a bibliography:
   Edmonds, Walter, *Beaver Valley.* Little, Brown and Company, Boston, 1971. (147)

7. To separate parts in the source of notes:
   Compton's Encyclopedia, Vol. 3, pp. 99-101 (147)

8. To set off the explanatory words in written conversation:
   Bill said, "Want to play baseball?" (40)
   "I'd like to," Ellen answered. (40)
   "I'll get my glove," Bill said, "and you get the baseball." (40)

9. To set off a name in direct address:
   Help me get the ball, Max. (41)
   Martha, you know where it is. (41)
   Tell me, Max, will you? (41)

10. To set off a word group used to add information about a noun:
    Helen Davis, president of our class, will hold the next meeting. (71, 147)

11. To separate words or groups of words in a series:
    Each group had a dictionary, a handbook, and a list of questions.

12. After *yes* and *no* at the beginning of a sentence:
    Yes, we will go.
    No, you cannot come along.

13. After an independent word showing mild feeling:
    Oh, I didn't think to do it. (106)
    Well, it could have been worse. (106)

14. To set off a transitional word or phrase:
    However, I didn't really forget it. (71, 147)

15. Between a name and an abbreviation like Jr.:
    Michael S. Berman, Jr. (147)

16. To indicate a pause between adjectives:
    It contained fresh, mild perfume.

17. Before the connective in a compound sentence unless the two parts are very short:
    We came down the hill, and they met us in the wheat field.

EXCLAMATION POINT

Use an exclamation point:
1. After a sentence that shows strong feeling:
    What a waste of time that was!
2. After an independent word that shows strong feeling:
    Wow! That really hurt. (106)

HYPHEN

Use a hyphen:
1. To divide words between syllables at the end of a line:
    trans-portation   sig-nify
2. In some compound words:
    father-in-law

PERIOD

Use a period:
1. After a statement:
    The trees blew in the wind. (10)
2. After abbreviations like:
    Ms., Mr., Mrs., Dr., Jr., R. R., and P. O. (147)
3. After an initial:
    Mildred S. Long (147)
4. After each numeral and letter in an outline: (146)
    I. Planning the trip
       A. Getting a map
       B. Buying the supplies
    II. Getting started
       A. Loading the supplies
       B. Checking the fuel
5. After some items in a bibliography entry:
    Edmonds, Walter, *Beaver Valley*. Little, Brown and
    Company, Boston, 1971. (147)

QUESTION MARK

Use a question mark after a question:
    Have you brought the equipment? (10)

QUOTATION MARKS

Use quotation marks:

1. To enclose the exact words of a speaker in written conversation:

   "Where," asked Eleanor, "can I find that article?" (41)

2. Around titles of chapters, short stories, and reports when written in a sentence:

   One chapter is called "Written in the Stars." (144)

UNDERLINING

Use underlining for:

1. The titles of books, movies, radio and TV programs, newspapers, and magazines:

   Do you watch <u>The Waltons</u> on TV? (136)

2. The stage directions in a play:

   Juan (<u>terrified</u>): Did you see that great big monster?

Index of Authors and Titles

INDEX

Abstract words, 278-281, 290-291
Accuracy, testing for, 214-215
Acronyms, 206, 217
Adjective transform, 297, 304
Adjectives
  after *be*, 88, 157-158, 300
  after linking verb, 89
  comparison of, 89, 143
Adverbial of manner, 91-92, 93, 158, 268, 269, 300
Adverbial of place, 90-91, 93, 158, 266-267, 269, 300
Adverbial of time, 92-93, 158, 267, 269, 300
Adverbs
  comparison of, 92-93
  in **VP,** 90-93
Almanacs, 144, 149, 292
Alphabetical order, 138, 144
Analytic listening, 12-13, 18, 56, 86, 150, 190, 262
Apostrophe, 141, 149, 296-297
Appeal to authority, 211, 213, 217
Application
  filling out an, 287-289
  letter of, 283-286
Appreciative listening, 14, 18, 56, 86, 190, 262
Atlas, 144, 149, 292
Attentive listening, 9-11, 18, 56, 86, 190, 262
Autobiography, 241
Auxiliaries, 152-155, 159, 264-265, 301

Ballads, 169, 175-180, 188
Bandwagon technique, 212, 213, 217
Basic sentence patterns
  BSP 1: **NP + (V),** 220-221, 223
  BSP 2: **NP + (V + NP),** 220-221, 223
  BSP 3: **NP + (be + NP),** 221-222, 223
  BSP 4: **NP + (be + Adj),** 221-222, 223
  BSP 5: **NP + (be + Adv$_\text{p}$),** 222, 223
  BSP 6: **NP + (LV + NP),** 222-223
  BSP 7: **NP + (LV + Adj),** 223

Bibliography, 136, 138, 144, 147, 149, 150
Biography, 169, 188, 241
Business letter, 283-287

Capital letters
  abbreviations, 285, 286, 291
  beginning a sentence, 10, 56, 117, 291
  first word in a line of poetry, 117
  first word in closing of letter, 243, 244, 261, 285, 286, 291
  first word in greeting of letter, 243, 244, 261, 285, 286, 291
  following strong independent word, 106
  geographical names, 7, 10, 56, 122, 149, 261, 285, 286, 291
  I, 10, 56
  initials, 75, 147, 149, 190, 261, 285, 286, 291
  in outlines, 146
  names of buildings and firms, 75, 285, 286, 291
  names of documents, 147
  names of languages, people of a country, and special groups, 7, 10, 56, 122
  names of newspapers and magazines, 147, 149
  names of organizations and institutions, 7, 149
  names of persons, pets, days, and months, 10, 56, 75, 149, 190, 261, 285, 286, 291
  names of railroads, ships, and ship lines, 147
  names of regions, churches, synagogues, sacred names, names of clubs, 168, 169
  proper nouns, 22-23, 27
  titles of articles, books, magazines, reports, poems, songs, stories, 136, 146, 147, 149, 190, 236, 261
  titles of persons, 147, 285, 286, 291
  trade names, 213